TERRY
DEARY'S
TERRIBLY TRUE
GHOST STORIES

■SCHOLASTIC

These stories are based on experiences that someone has claimed are factual. The Fact Files will help the reader to judge their truth. However, they have been dramatized in order to give a gripping account of the way they might have happened, and some of the characters are fictitious.

Scholastic Children's Books,
Euston House, 24 Eversholt Street
London, NW1 1DB

A division of Scholastic Ltd
London ~ New York ~ Toronto ~ Sydney ~ Auckland
Mexico City ~ New Delhi ~ Hong Kong

First published in the UK under the series title True Stories
by Scholastic Ltd, 1995
This edition published 2006

Text copyright © Terry Deary, 1995
Illustrations copyright © David Wyatt, 1995
10 digit ISBN: 0 439 95024 4
13 digit ISBN: 978 0439 9502 4

All rights reserved

Printed by Nørhaven Paperback A/S, Denmark

10 9 8 7 6 5 4 3 2 1

CONTENTS

INTRODUCTION

Do you believe in ghosts?

Well, do you?
- Is there something outside the natural life ... a *supe*rnatural life?
- Do people have spirits as well as bodies?
- Do those spirits survive the deaths of the bodies?
- And if the spirits survive, do they go on to another life? ... an *after*-life?
- Do some come back to our world?
- And, if they do come back, can some living people see them?

These are the questions that interest most people. This book will try to answer them honestly by presenting some of the most fascinating cases. The cases are retold as "stories" to entertain you ... and maybe send some shivers down your spine. But the book then gives some fascinating facts about the stories to help you make up your own mind about the mysteries of the supernatural.

Do *I* believe in ghosts?

Let me tell you my own story. Let me tell you about Mara...

Durham, England, November 1993

Mara is a great dane dog. When we adopted her she was a poor, thin creature. She'd been badly treated as a puppy and rescued from her cruel owners just in time.

For the first year in our home she was timid and afraid of humans – too timid even to bark. But slowly she learned to trust us. It was a great day when a stranger came to the door and Mara let loose a window-rattling "Woof!"

But she's never really recovered from her bad treatment and her brain is slightly damaged. Sometimes she has a small fit and wakes up shivering and lost. It takes her half an hour to remember where she is.

In the winter of 1993 she was really ill. She raced around wildly and seemed desperate to be out of the house. Someone opened the door and she disappeared along the road.

We waited for her to return. She didn't. Perhaps she had run too far while her mind was disturbed. When she recovered she must have been truly lost.

Snow was lying on the ground that night. Mara hated the cold and loved sleeping in front of the fire whenever she could. A night sleeping out in that February cold could kill her. We reported her disappearance to the police and waited.

The next day there was a phone call. Someone had seen a large, dark-grey dog on a farm five kilometres from our house. They told the police. The police told us. My daughter, Sara, and I jumped in the car and hurried to the farm.

It was five o'clock on a bitterly cold evening. The sun had set but the sky was a clear ice-blue and snow lay in a thin, crisp covering at the edge of the road. We turned off the main road and on to the farm track. The farm was two kilometres down the track, but halfway along was a small forest of fir trees that the road cut through.

Let me get the next part right, because it's important.

The farm track ran straight into the wood. I was three hundred metres away from the spot where the road entered the wood. As I looked ahead a dog trotted across the road. It was a large, dark dog. I had no doubt that it was Mara.

"There she is!" I cried.

Sara had been looking out of the side window. "Where?" she said.

"She ran across the road and vanished into the wood," I explained.

Sara shrugged. She'd seen nothing. I hurried down the frozen rutted track to the place where I'd seen her and skidded to a halt. There was no dog in sight. But the woods were thick and you could soon have lost sight of an elephant in that undergrowth.

We called her name. Nothing. Then we looked down at the snowy verges. There were the huge paw-prints of our dog.

The tracks seemed to disappear into the wood, but there was a wire fence around the edge and we couldn't follow. After half an hour of following tracks in the snow we climbed back into the car and drove on to the farm. Yes, they'd seen the dog, but that was two or three hours ago. They'd called for her but she'd run away.

We went back to the woods where I'd seen her. It was growing too dark now to see anything. We went home.

As we walked through the front door Mara trotted out to greet us, wagging her tail. At five o'clock she had wandered into the garden of a friend at the far side of the village and been given a lift home, but at ten-past five I'd seen her quite clearly trotting across the road five kilometres away ... or had I seen her "ghost"?

Could a dog be in two places at once? That's impossible. I hadn't seen her. So what had I seen?

A "double", a ghost-hunter would tell you. An "apparition".

There are two kinds of apparition – those inside your head and those outside. No one else saw Mara at the time I did, so it was probably all in my mind. I desperately *wanted* to find her there – as I drove to the farm I could almost picture my first sight of her. I simply saw *what I wanted to see*.

But to this day I would swear I *didn't* imagine it. I'm sure that I saw *something* that looked like our dog. If I didn't imagine it, then I saw a ghostly apparition.

It's an amazing fact that there are more reports of apparitions of the *living* than the *dead*! Some say a disturbed mind (as Mara's is) can throw out images of itself where a sound mind is too much in control.

So, yes, I believe in apparitions. People who have seen a ghost tend to believe in them. People who haven't seen one have to rely on reported stories and decide if they are true. That's what this book will try to help you do.

THE HALLOWE'EN GHOST
The Restless Mummy

Manchester, England, 1990

"The barn's on fire!" Rory Watson cried, clutching at the wooden five-bar gate.

His sister sighed. She knew it was a mistake to bring Rory out on Hallowe'en, but Mum had insisted, "Take Rory with you, Sarah."

"He gets so excited, Mum. He's embarrassing," Sarah had complained.

"Take him or you don't go," her mother had said firmly. "There are two turnips on the table. Start hollowing them out."

And Sarah had been right. Rory had thrown himself into the trick-or-treat visits as if he really believed he was a ghost. He'd scared the old lady in Osborne Terrace half out of her wits. She'd threatened to call the police.

Now they were on their way home. They had to pass old Birchen Farm. Sarah didn't really believe in ghosts, but the place gave her the creeps even in the daytime. Over the years a housing estate had grown up around the farm. Its fields were covered by rows of houses and roads and paths. Now the farmhouse and the barn had only a small paddock with a few grimy sheep.

"It *is*, Sarah! The barn's on *fire!*" Rory insisted.

She sighed again and walked back to where he stood. Sarah peered past the dark house and saw that there was certainly something strange about the wooden barn. Its blackened boards were warped and cracked, and through the gaps there was certainly a glow. But that glow wasn't flickering. It was steady. "Someone inside has a light on," the girl told her brother. "Let's go home."

It was as Sarah turned away that she heard the sound. At first she thought it was an aeroplane taking off from nearby Manchester Airport. It had that whining, hissing tone. She looked up into the sky. Then the sound became more human – a wail of pain or a cry of anger. The girl reached for Rory's arm but he was moving so quickly that she missed. He tumbled past her and sped down the road. Sarah stretched her long legs to catch him. Something banged painfully at her knee. It was the turnip lantern. She threw it in the gutter and sprinted home.

Brother and sister fell through the kitchen door together and it was five minutes before their mother could get the story from them clearly.

She nodded as she sat at the kitchen table. "Yes. There is a story about that farm."

"Tell us, Mum," Sarah said.

Mrs Watson looked at her son doubtfully. Sarah was right.

Rory was excitable. "There's a football match on the television, Rory. Why don't you go and watch it with your dad?"

"Okay," the boy said, picking up a can of soft drink and hurrying off to the living room.

"So, what's the story?" Sarah asked.

"Your gran told it to me. She was just a girl when the old mansion, Birchen Bower, was knocked down. She can still remember it. But the story goes back even further. It goes back to the 1740s, when a lady called Miss Hannah Beswick lived there. It seems she was a bit of a miser."

"Like Mr Scrooge in the Christmas story," Sarah put in.

"That's right. Miss Beswick was so mean she wouldn't pay someone to manage the farm; she did it all herself until she became too old. They say she made a fortune."

"What did she do with it?"

"In 1745 a Scottish army invaded England. When Miss Beswick heard they were as far south as Manchester she did what a lot of rich people did. She hid her treasure."

Sarah's eyes lit up. "Treasure? What sort of treasure?"

"Mostly silver and gold. She hid it somewhere near Birchen Bower mansion, but she worked alone and no one but she knew where it was hidden."

"So how do you know it was silver and gold? Did the Scottish soldiers find it?" her daughter asked.

"I'm coming to that," Mrs Watson said. "The Scots never came to Manchester and they were defeated. The war was soon over, but Miss Beswick decided not to disturb her treasure. There were more villains around than Scottish soldiers. She might have lived and died in peace – but something shocking happened that changed her life, something so horrible that I wouldn't tell Rory; you know he sometimes has nightmares."

Sarah nodded and looked towards the living room. The door

was closed. Her mother lowered her voice. "Miss Beswick's brother, John, fell ill. The doctor went to his house and declared him dead. He was laid in his coffin and Miss Beswick went to pay her last respects."

"What does that mean?" the girl asked.

"She went to have a last look at her brother in his coffin before they buried him."

The girl shuddered and wrapped two hands around her mug of hot chocolate. "That's horrible."

Mrs Watson shrugged. "It shows respect to the dead," she explained. "Anyway, Miss Beswick said goodbye to her brother and the undertaker moved in to put the lid on the coffin and screw it down. But just as she turned away she thought she saw the cheek twitch ever-so slightly. She called for a mirror and held it under her brother's nose. It was soon covered with a faint mist. He was breathing!"

"They were going to bury him alive!" Sarah gasped.

"They were. The doctor was called and the 'dead' man was revived. In fact they say he went on to live many more healthy years. But the effect on Miss Beswick was shattering. From then on the old woman had a terror of being buried alive. So she made a curious addition to her will."

"She asked not to be buried for a week or two after she died, I suppose," Sarah said thoughtfully. "That's what I'd do."

Her mother gave a faint smile. "Miss Beswick went one better. She asked to be buried ... never!"

"That's impossible! She'd go mouldy!" Sarah cried, pulling a disgusted face.

Mrs Watson leaned across the table. "Would she? I thought you were studying the ancient Egyptians at school this term."

"We are, but ... but ... they turned their kings into mummies!"

"Exactly!"

The girl's mouth dropped open. "Miss Beswick asked to be turned into a mummy?"

"Yes. She left money to the family doctor, Doctor White, and to all his descendants on the condition that her body was never placed below the ground. Stranger still, she insisted that her body should be brought back to Birchen Bower once every twenty-one years. And then she died."

"And Doctor White turned her into a mummy?"

"Miss Beswick died so suddenly that her great fortune of hidden treasure wasn't found. But the doctor wrapped the corpse in bandages, leaving only the face exposed, then treated it with tar to preserve it."

"Is this true?" the girl asked suddenly.

"Oh, yes. The body was put on display at Manchester Natural History Museum and lots of people saw it. It was there for over a hundred years. And five times the body was taken back to the old farm. They placed it in the barn."

"In the barn where we saw the light tonight? That's disgusting!" Sarah said.

"In 1868 the museum thought that too. They had Miss Beswick buried in a proper cemetery," her mother explained.

"I thought you said Gran told you this story. Even Gran isn't old enough to remember things from a hundred years ago," Sarah said suddenly.

Mrs Watson grinned. "No, she's not quite that old. But just because Miss Beswick was buried doesn't mean that's an end to the story. You see, she never really left Birchen Bower. The huge mansion was divided into flats. Several families lived there and most of them reported meeting old Miss Beswick's ghost at some time. First there was the rustle of her silk dress, then her figure, dressed in black, glided into the kitchen. She always disappeared at the same flagstone in the floor."

"What was so special about it?" Sarah asked.

Mrs Watson shrugged. "We'll never know. They pulled the old house down. But the barn's still there, and that's where Gran comes into the story. It seems she met a rich man once who told her the story of the mummy at Birchen Bower. He then said he'd been walking past the barn one Hallowe'en when he saw a glowing light coming from inside. He thought it was on fire, but when he went to investigate the light went out and there was nothing in the barn. He was an inquisitive man, though, and he asked the people in the area what they knew about the old barn. He pieced together the story of Miss Beswick and came up with a curious idea."

Sarah nodded. "The ghost of the old woman was wandering around the barn. But why?"

"That's what the rich man worked out. When would Miss Beswick have wandered around the barn, with a glowing lantern, when she was alive?"

The girl frowned and concentrated. "When ... when she was hiding her treasure?" Her face cleared. "She hid her treasure in the barn!"

Mrs Watson gave her daughter a playful pat on the head. "Well done, Sherlock! The man went back to the barn and started digging. He found several gold pieces and that's what made him rich. That was back in the 1920s, when Gran was just a little girl."

"So why did we see that light again tonight?" Sarah asked.

"Ah, it seems that the theft of the gold just infuriated the ghost. One of Gran's friends was walking past the barn one night and saw the ghost of Miss Beswick again. The old woman was wearing her black dress with a white collar. The figure was making terrible wailing sounds and shaking her fist as if she was upset."

"That would be the wailing I heard!" Sarah said.

"Perhaps, perhaps. Or maybe it was just a jet aircraft from the airport. You don't want to get too scared; you probably just made a mistake."

"But the light?" Sarah said.

"Maybe someone was working in the barn."

The girl nodded and finished her cup of hot chocolate. She stretched. "I think I'll go to bed."

"Sweet dreams," her mother smiled.

"Yes ... it was just the sound of a jet. And the story's just some old ghost story. It's not as if I saw a ghost, is it?" she said.

"That's right," Mrs Watson agreed. "Just don't tell Rory the story. He's not as level-headed as you."

"I won't, Mum. Goodnight."

"Goodnight!"

Sarah was surprised when Rory insisted on walking past Birchen Farm on the way to school the next day.

"You're not scared, then?" the girl asked him carefully.

"Scared? No!" the boy said.

"You ran fast enough last night."

Rory nodded and turned a little red. "You scared me when you started screaming," he said.

"You ran before I yelled," she said.

Rory stopped and frowned. "I did?"

"Yes. As soon as you heard the sound."

Her brother looked at her with wide and wondering eyes. "Sound? I didn't hear a sound."

"The screaming of that jet. It scared me. That's what must have scared you, dummy!"

"Oh, no," the boy said seriously. "It was that woman that scared me."

It was Sarah's turn to be puzzled. "What woman?"

"The one in the black dress – a long black dress with a white collar. She gave me a real fright!"

"Because you thought she was a ghost?" Sarah asked.

"No! There's no such things as ghosts! It was because she was coming towards us, looking very angry and shaking her fist. Maybe she was fed up with kids going trick-or-treating at her door, eh, Sarah?"

"Maybe," the girl said faintly.

"Come on," Rory tugged at her sleeve. "We'll be late for school."

"There are worse things that can happen," Sarah said quietly, looking at the dark and gloomy barn.

"Such as what?"

"Such as being buried alive."

"Hah!" the boy laughed and began to run down the street. "And Mum says *I've* got a strong imagination!"

GHOSTLY THOUGHTS 1

Apparitions: *The image of a dead person is seen as the person was in life.*

Explanation? *You can see images of people long after they have died. You can see them in photographs, films and video recordings. You can hear their voices on recordings. Maybe nature has some way of "recording" the most dramatic images of someone's life and "replaying" them at a certain place, at certain times to certain people. Just like a photograph, an apparition can be seen by the living – but of course it cannot see the viewer.*

F A C T

F I L E

Hallowe'en

Did you know…?

1. Hallowe'en lanterns are a reminder of an old legend concerning an Irishman called Jack. He upset the devil and the devil threw a piece of coal from Hell at him. Jack caught it in a hollow turnip and was doomed to wander the Earth showing his light until the end of time. Jack-o'-Lantern still makes his appearance at Hallowe'en in the shape of turnip lanterns that are carved out by children.

2. Hallowe'en is known as All Souls' Night – the time of the year when the ghosts of the dead are said to roam about. It is also a time when witches and devils are said to be at their most dangerous and powerful. Imagine that the land of the living and the land of the dead are separated by a curtain. At Hallowe'en that curtain is very thin.

3. Hallowe'en celebrations are an ancient idea. The Celtic people of ancient Britain held a feast to celebrate the end of summer. The Romans said that the British priests (Druids) made human sacrifices to the gods at the celebration. They claimed the sacrifices were made by fastening prisoners in a huge wooden cage and setting fire to it. (The Romans were probably lying.)

F A C T F I L E

4. The Romans celebrated a day of the dead on 21 February, but Pope Boniface changed it to All Saints' Day and made it 13 May. A later pope, Gregory III, changed it again to 1 November. The "eve" of 1 November is, of course, 31 October, and that's when most people celebrate "All Hallows' Eve" (or Hallowe'en) now.

5. On Hallowe'en many children enjoy dressing up and pretending to be ghosts who have slipped through the "curtain" from the world of the dead. They then call at houses and threaten the owners with a haunting if they aren't given a gift – this is called "trick or treat" in the United States. But a Chinese woman who moved to Britain had never heard of Hallowe'en or the game. She really believed there was a ghost at her door and she threw a pan of boiling water over the eight-year-old boy. Only his mask and bin-liner costume saved him from serious injury. The poor woman was ordered to pay the boy £750 for the scalds he received. Some trick – some treat!

GHOSTS AT WORK
THE PHANTOM BOOTS

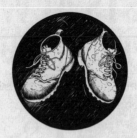

Say the word "ghost" and what do most people think of? A haunted castle or a creepy house? The spirit of a great and famous person? But there's no reason why ghosts should have to live in those draughty, miserable places. They can appear in the least likely spots at the most peculiar times.

This story was told by a coal miner, John Kitchin, and he swears it's true...

Scotland, 1973

I once knew a night-shift engineer. Sid, his name was. What his second name was I can't quite remember.

He worked up in the main control room of the pit. He used to dress like that cartoon boy, Dennis the Menace, even though he was fifty years old, and he had this big spiky haircut, straight across the top.

He was in the control room one night, looking after tub-loading, from eleven o'clock at night till seven in the morning.

It's bright up in the control room – better than the filth and dust below the ground. Still, the night shift hours can drag a bit when you're up there all on your own.

Then, in the middle of the night, around three o'clock, he gets a phone call from below the ground; I think it may have come from Number 4 transfer point, somewhere about a mile from the pit-head where two roadways meet underground.

The main conveyor pulls the coal from out the pit. It's the transfer-point lad that's on the phone.

Sid says, "What can I do for you, Tony lad?"

"You'll have to stop these belts and get some other feller on my job," the young lad says. "'Cos I'm not moving from this refuge hole!"

The refuge hole is the lad's control box, where he watches the coal run down the big conveyor belts.

Sid says, "Well, you know we can't stop the belts. What's the matter with you, Tony lad?"

He says, "There's a pair of boots that's dancing on the belt!"

Now, Sid being Sid, he says, "All right, lad, you've had your little joke. There's no way we can stop that belt."

"You've got to stop the belt and then you've got to get somebody else down here, 'cos I'm not moving from this refuge hole," he says.

So Sid says, "Do you know what that means? What stopping the belt means in terms of lost production?"

He says, "I don't care what it means, 'cos I'm not moving from this hole. And there's a great big pair of boots that's dancing on the belt, I'm telling you."

"Lad," Sid says, "I've been around for fifty years, and I think you've pulled my old leg long enough. There's no way I'm switching off that belt."

Young Tony says, "You'd better stop the belt and then you'd better get somebody down here, 'cos I'm telling you that there's a pair of boots that's dancing on the belt."

The argument goes on for about ten minutes. Finally Sid says, "You just sit down, Tony son, and think about it."

"I've thought about it long enough. I'm staying in this hole until you stop the pair of boots that's dancing on the belt."

Now Sidney thinks, a joke's a joke, but this joke's just gone far enough! The old chap starts to lose his head. "Do you know what you're going to get if you don't stop this stupid game? You're going to get the sack, young man."

The lad says, "I don't care what I get. Just stop the belt and get somebody down there."

Now, if there's a stoppage you have to put the reason, don't you? You have to write that reason in the log book. And Sid hates to write reports. So Sid says, "Right, I've had enough of you. I'm going to call the manager."

"Call who you like," the lad says. "Stop the belt and get somebody down here, 'cos I'm scared."

Sid calls the manager and he speaks on the phone to Tony. "Now then, Tony lad, we'll leave the belt running but we'll send two men down there to have a look. We'll send a man down 'A' shaft and we'll send a man down 'B' shaft. They'll be sure to get these ... boots."

"That's not good enough! You've got to stop the rotten belt!" the lad sobs.

"We've been in touch with the two deputies. They're coming now, they won't be long," the manager says.

"Are you going to stop the belt?" the lad cries, and he's screaming now.

So the belt is stopped.

That is all the coal work in the mine stopped. The pit can shift six hundred tons of coal in every hour.

The pit goes silent as a graveyard. Time passes as Deputy A and Deputy B walk slowly down the passages to the transfer point. And then, back in Sid's control room, there comes a crackle on the radio.

Deputy A cries, "Right, we've got him! Some bloke climbing on the belt."

A click and Deputy B comes in, "Yes, I can see him. Now we've got him."

Then silence once again. And then a sudden cry. "He's gone!" one of the men cries. "He must have run past you."

"There's no one gone past me," the other says.

"In that case there's just one place he can be. He must have run along that passageway between us."

"Hah!" the first one laughs. "That passageway is blind. There's no way out."

Sid nods to the manager. "They'll catch him now. He's headed down a dead-end passage. Now he's had it. Now we'll see who's playing silly jokes and trying to scare poor Tony there."

"He's for the sack," the manager says sternly.

"What, the lad?"

"No," the manager says. "This bloke that's playing games. He must have cost the pit a thousand pounds already." He taps his fingers on the table top and waits for the radio call. "Come on, come on," he mutters, staring at the radio. "How long is that passage anyway?" he asks.

"It's only short," Sid says. "They must have caught him up by now."

"Then why have they not called us back?"

"Perhaps the feller had a struggle. If they're too busy wrestling with him they can't make a radio call," Sid explains.

It seemed an age before the call came through. Deputy B is almost whispering in the microphone. "There's no one here," he says. His voice is shaking.

"There has to be," old Sid says.

"There's not!" the other deputy cuts in. "It's like he walked into a wall of coal. He never came past me."

"And he never came past me," his mate agrees. "It's dark down here but the passageway is narrow. No one could have run back past us."

"Come back up," the manager says, "and bring young Tony with you."

Half an hour later Tony is sitting in Sid's control room, drinking hot sweet tea.

"I saw the boots!" he says. His face is smudged with coal but that can't hide the grey shade to his skin.

"I might have said that you imagined it..." the manager begins.

"But we both saw it too," Deputy A says and he shakes his head. He's worked there longer than old Sid himself. He thought that he'd seen everything there was to see.

"Dancing on the belt," his mate agrees.

"You know the men who work down there," the manager says. "So tell me who it was."

"I couldn't see him very clearly, understand. Just those dusty boots that were dancing on the belt. His head was bent down so it wouldn't touch the roof. I only saw the black cloth cap."

"Cloth cap!" old Sid says. "No one wears cloth caps these days. Not for fifty years or more. They all wear helmets underground."

The man shrugs, "Aye, you're right ... but this man wore a black cloth cap."

No one cares to argue with the man.

The manager looks down at Tony. The boy has stopped his shaking now but still his pale eyes stare down at the floor. Maybe he's seeing something deep below the ground. "Only the boots," he muttered. "If I'd seen the feller I wouldn't have been so scared. But all I saw were the boots. Dancing. Dancing on the belt like they were happy."

"Maybe his head and shoulders were up in the shadows," the deputy says, quite gentle.

"That's right," his mate agreed. "We saw the whole man ... both of us."

The lad looks up quite sharp, his eyes as wild as my Uncle Paddy's terrier. "I know what I saw. And I didn't see a man. I saw a pair of boots as clear as I can see you now. I'm not going mad, you know. I'm not, you know. I saw them."

The manager just nods and mutters, "You get off home now, Tony lad. We'll see you back tomorrow night."

The boy stands up, puts the empty cup down and trudges out of the control room.

"There'll have to be a report," Sid says. "We've lost a thousand tons of coal, stopping the conveyor belts like that."

"Yes. Yes," the manager says. "You write up a report."

"Aye, but what do I say?" Sid asks sharply.

The manager turns his collar up and stares out into the early morning dark. "You'll think of something," he says.

"I'll think of something," Sid says, angry now. "But can I think of something so I won't look stupid? I can't go and write those things about a pair of old boots dancing on the belt, can I, sir? Now, can I?"

The manager steps out into the cold and doesn't give an answer.

Then Deputy A rubs a grimy hand over his grey hair. "Young Tony must have had a fright," he says.

"We'll not see that young man again," Sid says.

And Sid was right. The boy went home and never turned up at the pit again.

A few years later old Sid left the pit himself. Only then did he tell the story of the boots – the boots that danced along the belt and cost a thousand tons of coal.

A funny chap, old Sid.

Pair of braces like Dennis the Menace. Big spiky haircut, straight across the top.

Tough as a pit pony, old Sid. But he's still haunted by a pair of boots.

GHOSTLY THOUGHTS 2

Imagination: *Seeing something that isn't really there.*

Explanation? *Watching a coal conveyor is a lonely and boring job. In the middle of the night, when you're half asleep, it's not surprising that you might begin to imagine things. Tony could easily have seen lumps of coal bouncing up and down on the conveyor belt and let his frightened mind turn them into dancing boots.*

F
A
C
T

F
I
L
E

Charms Against Ghosts

For thousands of years people have feared ghosts and have made up weird spells and charms to defend against the dead. These include:

1. **Brooms** – People of Eastern Europe believed that putting a broom under your pillow would keep away evil spirits while you slept. English people preferred to lay the broom across the doorstep of the house.

2. **Candles** – The light from a candle was said to keep evil spirits away from the dying. They had to be left burning for a week after the death of the person to protect their spirit. The Irish custom was to circle the dead body with twelve candles.

3. **Cairns** – Piles of stones over a grave are called a cairn. They deter grave robbers and their weight also prevents the dead rising from their graves to haunt the living.

4. **Salt** – Carrying salt in the pocket or scattering it across the doorstep will keep ghosts at bay. Throw a pinch over your left shoulder and it will bring good luck.

5. **Iron** – Iron is a powerful defence against ghosts, witches and other evil spirits. An iron horse-shoe hung on a stable door will protect a house or stable. More gruesome, iron nails taken

F
A
C
T
O

F
I
L
E

from a coffin will stop you having nightmares if you drive them into your bedroom door. An iron bar left lying across a grave will stop a ghost rising.

6. **Silver** – Most people know the legend that only silver bullets can kill vampires. This metal is also a defence against ghosts, especially if made into the shape of a cross.

7. **Crosses** – If someone is surprised by a ghost then making the sign of the cross in the air will protect him/her against evil.

8. **Prayers** – Christians believe that saying the Lord's Prayer will protect them against ghosts. They also believe that saying the same prayer backwards is a way of raising the Devil. A common test for a witch was to ask him or her to say the Lord's Prayer. A witch (a servant of the devil) would not be able to do it, and would be punished for even one mistake. The accused witch would be very nervous; it would be easy to make a mistake while you were so frightened, so the test was hardly a fair one.

GHOSTLY CURSES
THE FLYING DUTCHMAN

ome ghosts are said to wander the Earth as a punishment for offending a god or a devil. They are cursed, and so are the people they meet. These ghosts don't only appear on land. The most famous sea ghost is probably the Flying Dutchman.

Australian coast, July 1881

George was cold. He paced up and down the deck of the warship to keep warm. He was only sixteen and the youngest sailor aboard HMS *Inconstant*. That was why they gave him the worst job. Being on night watch in the winter seas was uncomfortable … and boring.

The ship churned through the icy sea and towards the setting moon. Two or three more hours of darkness, the cadet thought. At least in the daylight he'd be able to see the Australian coast. That would be something to look at, something to break the monotony of deep purple sky and darker sea.

George stared at the ribbon of moonlight shimmering on the sea in front of him. When the ship appeared ahead of him it took a while for him to react. It was so sudden and unexpected. It seemed to have grown from melted moonlight. The wind from the Antarctic stung his eyes as he squinted into it. At the same moment a voice called down from the lookout post at the top of the mast, "Ship ahead!"

It was a sailing ship in full sail, racing over the water. It would cut across the course of HMS *Inconstant* at any moment. The laws of the sea said that the sailing ship had the right of way. George began to run towards the bridge where the first mate was in control. "Ship ahead, Sir! Off the starboard bow."

"A little late with that sighting, sir," the first mate said sourly. "I saw it before you came in."

"Sorry, sir, it just appeared."

The senior officer gave a brief nod and signalled to the engine room to slow down. He stared through the window at the glowing shape of the sailing ship and frowned.

"It's all wrong. No sailing ship ever sailed that quickly in a light breeze like this. It's all wrong," the officer said. He turned to a sailor alongside him. "Send a signal to that ship. She doesn't seem to have seen us."

"Yes, sir," the sailor answered and turned on the powerful lamp. He began tapping out an urgent signal, but there was no reply from the strange sailing ship.

Other officers of the watch gathered on the bridge to see what would happen next. The sailing ship passed across the bows of HMS *Inconstant* and out of the light of the moon. As it sailed away from the warship it seemed to fade. Within a minute the ocean was as empty and calm as ever. The first mate took a telescope and scanned the sea. He lowered it at last and shook his head.

"The Flying Dutchman," he said. Some of the older sailors nodded and one or two looked afraid. "Back to your duties," the First Mate snapped and the crew hurried to obey him.

George climbed back to the upper deck and stood next to a midshipman. "What did he mean?" the cadet asked.

"It was a ghost ship, sir," the midshipman said. "And they do say that anyone who sees her is cursed."

"I've heard about ghost ships, of course. What's the story of this Flying Dutchman?"

"Well, sir, many years ago there was a ship's captain who feared neither God nor his saints. He is said to have been a Dutchman, but I do not know, and it doesn't really matter what town he came from.

"He once set off on a voyage south. All went well until he came near land. He used to boast that no storm, however terrible, could make him turn back.

"On this voyage south he reached the Cape of Good Hope when he ran into a head-wind that would have blown the horns off an ox. Between the wind and the huge waves his ship was in deadly danger. 'Captain,' the crew pleaded, 'we are lost if you don't turn back. We shall sink if you try to go round the Cape in this wind. We are all doomed and there isn't even a priest on board to bless us before we die. We are surely bound for hell!'

"The captain laughed at the fears of his passengers and crew. Instead of listening to them he started singing. The songs were so ungodly that they could have drawn thunderbolts from heaven just by themselves.

"Then the captain called for his pipe and his tankard of beer. He smoked and drank as happily as if he were in the tavern back home.

"The others pleaded again with him to turn back. The more they pleaded the more stubborn he became.

Ghostly Curses

"The storm snapped the masts and tore the sails away. Captain van der Decken laughed and jeered at the terrified passengers.

"The storm grew more and more violent but the captain ignored it just as he ignored the people on his ship. When the men tried to force him to take shelter in a bay by grabbing the wheel, he snatched their leader and threw him overboard.

"As he did this the clouds parted and a shape appeared on the deck in front of him. The shape may have been God himself; if not, it was certainly sent by Him. The crew and the passengers were speechless with terror. The captain went on smoking his pipe. He didn't even take his cap off in the presence of the Almighty.

"The shape spoke. 'Captain, you are a stubborn man.'

"'And you are a villain! Who wants a nice, smooth voyage? Not I! I want nothing from you, so clear off unless you want me to blow your brains out.'

"The shape shrugged its shoulders and didn't answer.

"The captain grabbed a pistol, pulled back the hammer and pressed the trigger. But the bullet didn't reach the shape; it turned around and went through van der Decken's hand. At this his temper exploded and he jumped up to strike the shape in the face. But as he raised his arm it fell limp and paralysed by his side. He cursed and called the shape all the evil names under the sun.

"At this the shape spoke again. 'From this moment on you are cursed. You are sentenced to sail forever without rest, without anchorage, without reaching a port of any kind. You shall never taste beer or tobacco again. Your drink shall be bitter water and your meat shall be red-hot iron. Only a cabin boy will remain of all your crew. Horns will grow from his forehead and he will have a tiger's face and skin rougher than a dogfish.'

41

"Captain van der Decker realized his stupidity and groaned. The shape went on, 'You will always be on duty and you will never be able to sleep, no matter how much you long for it. The moment you close your eyes a sword will pierce your body. And, since you like tormenting sailors, you shall torment them till the end of time.'

"The captain smiled at the thought. The shape said to him. 'You shall become the evil spirit of the sea. You will travel all oceans without stopping or resting. Your ship will bring bad luck to all who see it.'

"'I'll drink to that!' the captain laughed.

"'And on the Day of Judgement, the devil shall claim your soul."

"'I don't give a fig for the devil!' he replied.

"The shape vanished and the captain found himself alone with the cabin boy, who had already been changed into the evil creature that the shape had described. The rest of the crew had vanished.

"From that day to this the Flying Dutchman has sailed the seven seas and takes pleasure in tricking unlucky sailors. He sets ships on wrong routes, leads them into rocks and wrecks them. He turns their wine sour and all their food to beans.

"The Flying Dutchman can change the appearance of his ship whenever he wants and, through the years, he has collected a new crew. All of them are the worst bullies and pirates ever to sail the seas. Every one of them is cursed and doomed like the Flying Dutchman himself."

"Thanks," the young cadet said. "It was an interesting story. But you don't believe that stuff about a curse, do you?"

"We'll see, sir," the midshipman said. "We'll see."

HMS *Inconstant* sailed on over the smooth sea and at daybreak George went down to his cabin. He opened his diary and began to write:

At 4 a.m. the Flying Dutchman crossed our bows. She gave off a strange phosphorescent light like a phantom ship all aglow; in the middle of the glow her masts, spars and sails stood out in silhouette as she came up on the port bow where an officer of the watch also saw her as did a midshipman who was sent forward. But when he arrived at the bows there was no trace or sign whatever of any ship, near or on the horizon, the night being clear and the sea calm.

As the cadet finished writing there was a tap on his cabin door. "Breakfast, Your Highness."

Prince George yawned, stretched and rose to his feet. The young sailor later became King George V, but his meeting with the Flying Dutchman was an experience that stayed in his memory for the rest of his eventful life.

GHOSTLY THOUGHTS 3

Demons: *Evil spirits that try to interfere with human life. They can take many forms – lights, sounds or voices inside a victim's head, fairies, goblins, phantom animals, or phantom ships like the* Flying Dutchman. *They often enter a human body and possess it; that person then becomes a "witch" and performs evil deeds for the demon.*

Explanations: *Some religions believe that pure goodness is their "God", but pure evil can also exist in a spirit form as a demon. You may choose to believe that. The superstitious used to say that the only way to get rid of the demon was to destroy the body it lived in – that's why they burned witches. Nowadays we aren't so cruel or stupid.*

Sea Ghosts

The story of the Flying Dutchman *seems very unlikely, yet some researchers claim the legend is based on fact.*

The Dutch captain's name was Hendrik van der Decken and he lived in the 1660s. Van der Decken was a greedy and ruthless ship's captain who set sail from Amsterdam to make his fortune in the East Indies. Over the years, countless sailors from around the world have sworn that they've seen something strange on the ocean. Can they all be wrong?

1. **The Dutchman's curse** – Prince George's sighting was backed up by thirteen sailors on his ship and on other ships that were sailing alongside her. If seeing the Flying Dutchman was unlucky then the curse worked for Prince George's ship, HMS *Inconstant*. Later that same day the seaman who'd first seen the ghost ship fell to his death from the mast. The admiral of the fleet died shortly afterwards.

2. **The *Lady Lovibond*** – Britain has its own phantom ship. On 13 February 1748 the *Lady Lovibond* was sailing by the dangerous Goodwin Sands off the coast of Kent, England. Her captain, Simon Peel, was on honeymoon with his bride and several wedding guests. But a jealous sailor (who was also in love with the bride) killed Peel and steered the ship to disaster on the sands. On 13 February 1798, fifty years later to the day, a fishing boat spotted a ship of the *Lady Lovibond*'s

FACTO FILE

description heading for the sands. The crew heard laughter and women's voices. It sounded as though a party was being held on board. But when the ship hit the sands it broke up and vanished. The same vision was seen in 1848 and 1898. Ghost hunters were on the lookout in 1948 but saw nothing in the mist.

3. **The blazing ghost ship** – America's *Flying Dutchman* is the *Palantine*. It arrived off the coast of Rhode Island packed with Dutch colonists in 1752. A storm drove it off course and washed the captain overboard. The ship was driven on to rocks and started to break up. Local fishermen rowed out and took the passengers to safety but began stripping the ship of its valuable cargo before it sank. To cover up their crime they set the ship ablaze, but as they rowed home they were horrified to see a woman come up on deck. She'd been hiding from the looters. Her screams carried across the water until the flames swallowed her. Over the centuries a blazing ship has been seen by many witnesses off the coast of New England.

4. **The ghost under the sea**– Not only ancient sailing ships are ghostly. The German submarine *UB65* was cursed from the start. Workmen building her had fatal accidents then, on her maiden voyage, an officer was killed in an explosion. From then on the ghost of the officer was seen on board. A new captain and crew were appointed who did not believe in ghosts and for a while the ghost did not appear. But when that captain left the submarine the ghost returned. One sailor went mad with fear and jumped overboard. Still the submarine survived enemy attacks until, near the end of the First World War, it mysteriously blew up, killing the entire crew. An accident? Or a ghost's revenge for his own death?

5. **The "ghost" from the bottom of the sea** – Many "ghost" stories have a sensible explanation. In the late 1890s the schooner *A. Ernest Mills* sank in a storm off the coast of California. A few days later the "ghost" of the schooner appeared, to the horror of the local people. The schooner had been carrying a cargo of salt when she sank. When the salt dissolved the *A. Ernest Mills* bobbed up to the surface of the ocean again. Mystery solved!

6. **The ghostly rescuer** – The first man to sail alone around the world was Joshua Slocum of Nova Scotia in Canada. He set off in July 1895 but soon met terrible storms in the North Atlantic. After struggling to control his boat for three days Slocum gave up, exhausted. He went below to his cabin to wait for the boat to sink. He couldn't swim. Then, as the storm raged he felt the boat riding smoothly as if a strong hand was at the wheel. When he dragged himself back on deck he saw a man in fifteenth-century clothes steering the vessel. "Who are you?" he managed to ask. "I am the helmsman of the *Pinta*," the man replied. The *Pinta* was one of Christopher Columbus's ships that landed in America in 1492. Slocum found the strength to survive the storm. The fifteenth-century sailor was never seen again.

7. **The leading light** – Christopher Columbus himself had a ghostly experience at sea. When his crew were getting seriously worried about ever seeing land again, he saw a light in the sky. It was a "guiding star" that would lead them to the new world. No one else saw the light and no one believed Columbus. The next day they sighted land; they had reached the American continent.

F A C T F I L E

8. **The avenging ship** – Two Arctic exploration ships, the *George Henry* and the *Rescue*, were heading for the North Pole in 1860 when they met a severe storm. The crews decided the *Rescue* was about to sink so they abandoned her and sailed off on the *George Henry*. Two months later, as they sailed back to the point where they'd abandoned the *Rescue*, they saw a battered ship following them. It was the *Rescue*. She disappeared into the mist. But that night, as they were at anchor, the *Rescue* came back, heading straight towards the *George Henry*. She seemed to be driving ice blocks towards them – maybe as a revenge for the sailors abandoning her. Finally the derelict ship itself charged towards them. At the last second it seemed to swerve away, as if the ghostly driving force had some pity.

9. **The *Waratah* Disaster** – In July 1909 Claude Sawyer was sailing from Melbourne, Australia to London when he had terrifying dreams of a disaster. He saw himself standing at the rail of his ship, the *Waratah*, when a knight in blood-stained armour rose from the sea and mouthed the word "Waratah!" over and over again. Sawyer was so shaken that he left the

ship when it reached Durban in South Africa and decided to take another ship for the second part of his journey. The *Waratah* sailed without him ... and was never seen again. Or "probably" never seen again. Seventy years after the disappearance, an aircraft pilot reported seeing a passenger ship of the *Waratah*'s description lying on its side in clear water off the South African coast. A search was made but nothing was found. What had the pilot seen?

10. The *Teazer* Terror – Another ship haunting the North Atlantic was the *Young Teazer*, an American warship. In 1813 she was surrounded by warships of the British Navy. Lieutenant Johnson did not want to be captured so he blew up the *Young Teazer* ... and himself along with it. A ship of the *Young Teazer*'s description is said to sail menacingly towards ships then swerve away in flames.

THE UNEXPLAINED
THE SPIRIT STONES

ost ghostly happenings have an explanation, natural or
M *supernatural. But sometimes there seems to be no reason*
why ghostly activity should start ... or stop.

Upper Blackwood, Australia, 1955

The sun had set but the sky was still a clear blue. The autumn
nights were colder now and fuel was expensive, so the sticks that
Jean Smith was gathering at the edge of the bush would cook an
evening meal – and keep her and Gilbert warm through the night.

The huge farm they worked on was over three hundred
kilometres from the nearest city of Perth. Strangers hardly ever
came this way. That was why Jean was puzzled. She felt there
was a stranger nearby, watching her.

She looked around carefully. There was no one in sight. Apart
from the scrub bushes there was nowhere for anyone to hide. The
blank, dark windows of her wooden cabin stared out at her. They
were empty.

She shivered and bent to pick up just a few more handfuls of
wood before she went home. And as she bent she heard the
whisper of something fly past her neck. A moment later it hit the
ground with a heavy thud.

Jean didn't wait to see who was throwing stones at her. She didn't need to. She already knew there was no one there. The woman clutched her precious twigs to her chest and ran for the cottage. At her back she could feel something chasing her. There was no way she was going to turn around and look.

Wood spilled on the porch as she scrabbled at the door handle and tumbled into the cabin. Her husband looked up, wide-eyed, and saw his wife scatter the wood on the floor, slam the door and stand with her back to it. A moment later something heavy crushed into the door and almost splintered the wood.

"Spirits!" Jean hissed. "Evil spirits!"

Gilbert jumped up from his chair and wrapped a comforting arm around her shoulder. "No, Jean. We have done nothing to upset the spirits. It's more likely to be one of the shepherds having a joke."

The woman looked at him doubtfully. "There's no one out there ... at least, no one human eyes can see."

"My eyes will see him," Gilbert assured her and he moved her gently from the door and opened it.

It was darker now. The fences were black lines against the fading grey of the pastures. The air was still. Nothing moved. In the distance a dingo howled. Somewhere closer another one answered it.

Gilbert squared his shoulders and, keeping his back to the cabin walls, walked around the outside of his home. "Hello!" he called. Only the dingo answered.

Gilbert slipped back through the door and bolted it behind him. He was just about to say something to Jean when he saw something out of the corner of his eye that made him duck. Something white rose from the corner of the room and flew towards his head. It clattered off the wall and fell to the floor. "A golfball," he said. "One that the kids have been playing with.

53

But how—"

Before he could finish there was a clatter on the tin roof as something heavy landed on it. "Spirits!" Jean moaned.

The man looked at his two dogs sleeping by the cold fireplace. They hadn't moved. "Those dogs know when anyone comes within a hundred yards of here," he said. "You're right, Jean – there's no one out there."

"What can we do?"

"I'll go for help," he said. "You'll be safe enough inside. Bolt the door behind me."

He snatched the keys to his old van and hurried out. As the sound of the engine faded the dogs woke up, jumped to their feet and began barking and howling. The woman slipped the chains from their necks and they threw themselves towards the door. "Get him, boy!" she said and pulled the bolt back. But when the dogs pushed through the opening door they began howling and vanished into the night.

Thud! Something hit the roof again.

Thud! That one hit the wall.

Jean Smith snatched her husband's rifle and pushed the barrel through the opening of the door. But from inside the house an empty jam jar flew across the room and splintered against the doorpost beside her head. She shut the door quickly and sat with her back to it. Every object in the room was a possible enemy now.

It was an hour before Gilbert returned with a neighbour. There had been long spells of silence when Jean had begun to relax, but as soon as she did so she was jerked back into terror by something crashing against the wall.

"Hi, Jenny!" Alf Krakour said as he came through the door. "Gilbert says you've been having a spot of bother, eh?"

Jean nodded dumbly.

"We'll soon get to the bottom of this," he promised and, taking his gun, he walked outside with her husband.

Five minutes later the men returned. Alf had stopped grinning now. "Too dark to see anything," he said. "We'll just bolt ourselves in and wait for them to get tired."

But it was Alf, Jean and Gilbert who were tired by next morning. The bombardment went on all night. When the sun rose the attack stopped.

"What do we do now?" Jean asked wearily.

"Tell the boss," Gilbert said. "Smart man, Mr Roberts. He'll sort it out."

That night Mr Roberts joined them. "Someone having a joke," he said.

"That's what I said," Gilbert put in.

"The attacks stopped in the morning because they knew you would see them throwing stuff," the ranch owner explained. He was going to say more when something hissed past his ear and clattered against the wall. The man's weather-beaten face turned pale. He bent to pick up a stone from the floor then gave a sharp cry. "It's hot!"

"Where did it come from?" Gilbert asked.

"Must have come through the wall," Roberts said.

"But there are no holes in the wall. How did it get here?" Jean asked. The men had no answer.

"I'll find you a new cabin," the ranch-owner promised.

Gilbert Smith shook his head. "It will make no difference," he said quietly.

He walked to the window and looked out. "There's something out there," he said. "Look."

Hanging in the dark air was an unearthly light. An oval blue light. Suddenly the light moved with an eerie whistling sound and the cabin shook. Jean Smith clamped her hands over her ears but she couldn't shut the sounds out.

Slowly the sounds faded. Jean and Gilbert moved closer together. "We must learn to live with this," she said.

"Then I'll find some specialist help," their employer promised. "There's some sort of Ghost Society over in Perth. I'll contact them. See what they say." Roberts took his hat and looked carefully around the door before stepping out.

The ghost hunters from the Perth Psychic Society tried to explain to the Smiths that this sort of spirit activity was common throughout the world ... but they couldn't stop it. "It tends to stop by itself," they said.

Jean Smith shook her head slowly. Sleepless nights and fear-filled days had shrunk her. "When? When will it stop?" she asked.

The ghost hunters shrugged. "Who knows?" they said and went away.

The woman bent wearily to gather sticks. It was autumn again. A year had passed since that first stone had been hurled at her. The sun had set but the sky was still a clear blue. The nights were colder now and fuel was expensive, so the sticks she was gathering at the edge of the bush would cook an evening meal – and keep her and Gilbert warm through the night.

She stopped and looked up. There was something wrong,

something missing. For the first time in a year she smiled. She knew she *wasn't* being watched. She knew that It had gone away. Whatever It was had decided to leave them in peace at last.

Jean clutched the sticks and hurried back to the house. She opened the door. Gilbert looked up from his chair at the side of the fireplace. "I know," he said.

"Why?" Jean asked.

Gilbert stood up and walked across to her. He wrapped a hand around her thin shoulders. "Like the people from Perth said, 'Who knows?'"

GHOSTLY THOUGHTS 4

Poltergeist: *A mischievous spirit that causes a lot of disturbance for a household by throwing objects around and making banging or rapping sounds.*

Explanation? *Perhaps everyone can move things simply by the power of the mind but most of us do not know how to do it. In some people that power may be released and it goes "wild" for a time. The victim of the poltergeist is actually causing the disturbances, but doesn't know it and can't control it.*

Haunted Australia

Many reporters visited the Smiths during their year of disturbances. they found no evidence to back the story. On the other hand, no reporter was willing to spend the night there, and most of the strange things happened at night. As many as 150 stones were said to fall on the roof on some nights.

Most of the world's ghostly experiences have been reported in Europe and particularly in the British Isles. But Australia has its own record of supernatural happenings apart from the Smith case...

1. The Min-Min Light – Western Queensland

Strange things were seen in the sky in the Smith case but such lights have been reported elsewhere in Australia for hundreds of years. In Western Queensland an oval fluorescent light is seen standing or rolling across the sky. It became known as the Min-Min Light because it has been reported so often in the area of the Min-Min Hotel in Warenda Station. Queensland police have seen it for themselves. On investigation they found the light...

- was not caused by camp fires.
- was unlikely to have been caused by a mirage effect.
- was not car headlights or their reflections.

No one has ever been able to explain where the light comes

from or goes to, though a farm worker reported seeing the light rising from the Min-Min graveyard around 1917. The worker was riding his horse past the graveyard and, understandably, galloped away from the place when he saw the light. To his horror the light followed him to the edge of the next town, where it mysteriously disappeared.

2. Lady's ghost – West Australia, 1953

Lady was William Courtney's greyhound. Every night the dog came to his bedroom and dropped on to the floor where it slept. One night he was half asleep when he heard the familiar sound of the dog flopping to the floor. William Courtney's hand trembled as he reached for the light switch, for that afternoon Lady had been put down by the vet following an illness. When Courtney finally found the nerve to snap on the light, the floor was empty.

3. Bluebird – Lake Eyre, 1964

Donald Campbell chose the flat salt-lake in Australia to race his car, Bluebird, to a new speed record. During the second run a tyre was damaged and nearly sent Campbell to his death. The support team changed the wheel but were afraid that Donald Campbell would have lost his nerve after such a frightening experience. When they looked through the canopy he seemed perfectly calm but was staring at the screen. He went ahead with another run and broke the record. His mechanic later asked him what he'd been looking at during the wheel change. Campbell admitted he'd been looking at an image of his dead father that appeared in the screen. The image had said, "Don't worry, my boy, it will be all right." The vision had given him the courage to go on.

...o some poor souls linger on Earth? Are they tied to this world ...because they have some unfinished business here? Let me tell ...u the story of Anne Walker. Then make up your mind.

Durham, England, 1632

...e market town of Chester-le-Street stands by the River Wear. A ...ter mill once stood down by the river. James Graham, the ...iller, lived by the mill in 1632.

The miller worked hard and he worked long hours. It was ...dnight as he put the last corn in the hopper one chill winter's ...ght, and a damp mist rose from the river.

He came down the creaking wooden stairs and he stopped. There was someone down there on the flour-dusted floor, yet ...knew that the door of the mill had been locked.

"Who's that?" he called, peering down into the gloom. The ...gure made no reply. He turned up the wick of his lantern and ...ok a step down.

He could make out the shape of a long-haired woman. And as ...drew close he could see that her hair was dripping. But where ...e droplets hit the floor they made no mark in the thin layer of ...ur.

F A C T O F I L E

4. **The haunted house – Newcastle, New South Wales, 1970**
Michael Cooke thought he had found the perfect house for himself and his wife and baby. But they left in fear after something...

- made the baby sit up as if jerked by invisible hands.
- rumpled bedclothes on a tidy, made-up bed.
- moved toys around/
- shook a door knob loudly.

But the final straw came when the ghost put in an appearance. As Michael Cooke described it, "Last night I saw a horrible white face looking out of one of the windows as I walked past. The eyes were white with green in the middle. I was so scared the tears just ran out of my eyes. That was the end. I was thinking of buying the house but I'll never live there again." Other tenants had reported similar problems.

THE GHOST'S REVE
The Miller of Chester-le-S

"Who are you?" he asked and the lantern trembled in his hand.

The woman raised her head. Her pale face was stained with red. It wasn't water running down her hair, but blood. The miller stared and made out four or five deep wounds that scarred her head.

No one could have such wounds and live. "Sweet Jesus, save me!" begged the miller.

Then the woman raised her bloodied head and looked him in the eyes. "No, do not be afraid," she sighed. "I am the spirit of the murdered young Anne Walker. Sit down, sir, for you look too shocked to stand."

The miller sank down on the lowest step and placed the lantern on the old mill floor. "In God's name, tell me what you want!" he gasped.

"I want revenge," the woman said. "I cannot leave this world while my cruel murderers walk free. I need the help of you, James Graham."

"I'll do my best," the miller said.

"Then listen to my tale," the spirit said. "I lived near here in Chester-le-Street. My uncle, Joseph Walker, is a farmer. Joseph took me to his house. I worked there as his maid. But Joseph took my innocence and … I found I was with child."

The miller started to forget his fear. He shook his head in horror at her tale.

"My uncle said I'd have to go away. He said I'd have to leave to hide my shame. He promised I'd be well looked after and then could return to keep his house."

"He broke his promise?" Graham asked.

"I left the house about this time of night the last new moon – two weeks ago. He sent his friend to guide me in the dark – a miner called Mark Sharp. Sharp is a tall and fearsome man. Hair black as the coal he digs and shoulders wide as a doorway. I should have been afraid of him, yet I was more afraid of travelling down that moonless road alone. We set off on the road to Durham. My guide did not have much to say. His strides were long and I stumbled as I tried to keep pace with him. I begged him to stop when we had gone five miles, and then he told me that he knew a quicker way. It meant we'd walk across the loneliest part of the moor. But I was tired, so tired, that I agreed. The road was quiet at that time of night. The moor was quieter. Only the sounds of owls and something scuttling through the rough grass. A loose sheep scared me half to death. I asked him how much farther. He told me he could see a light. He pointed to the distant hill. As I leaned forward Mark Sharp stepped behind me. He took his pick and struck me on the head. He gave me these wounds that you see on my head."

Her apparition shuddered and the blood dripped to the floor. "The law will not convict those two unless we find your body," Miller Graham said.

She nodded and her hair fell forward. Quietly she told the miller where her body lay. "He threw my body in a coal pit, then he hid the pickaxe in a bank nearby. He tried to wash the blood from off his shoes and stockings, but he could not get them clean, so he hid them by the pick."

The ghost began to walk towards James Graham. He scrambled to his feet and backed towards the door. "No one will believe me!" Miller Graham cried.

"But you must *try*. And try *again* until they do!" Anne Walker's ghost protested, "Or I shall haunt you till your dying day and then beyond the grave!"

The man tore at the bolts and stumbled down the moon-washed path. He dared to look behind and saw he was not followed. He hurried home and shivered in his bed.

Next day he went to work. He felt the ghost was just a dream and laughed at his own foolishness.

He did not work so late that night but left the mill before night fell. After supper he went to bed. The night was peaceful and he sank into a dreamless sleep.

When the moon came up, the spirit of the dead girl rose again. This time she was no gentle, pleading ghost. She was a threatening, fierce ghoul. She tore the sheets from the miller's bed and screamed that she wanted justice.

"Yes, Miss Walker, yes," he groaned. "Give me just one more chance. I will obey." The miller did not dare ignore her threat this time. Next morning he went to the magistrate and told his tale.

"And you say this was not a nightmare, Miller?" asked the magistrate. "And you say you had not been drinking barley wine?"

James Graham looked afraid and pitiful. He shook his head. The magistrate believed the honest man. "We'll do our best," he promised.

A search was made. At Framwellgate a disused pit was found. In the pit lay the body of Anne Walker. There were five wounds in the head. The bloody pick and shoes and stockings lay nearby, as the spirit had said.

The cruel uncle and his friend Mark Sharp were brought to trial. The men denied the charges.

At the trial Walker stood up in the dock and told some cringing lies. Yet, on the farmer's back, the judge could see a shadowy form ... a phantom of the murdered child.

Farmer Joseph Walker and his evil friend were both found guilty and were hanged for their cruel crime.

So, those of you who say that there are no such things as ghosts, how can you explain Anne Walker's tale?

The body would have lain there still if her spirit had not guided Miller Graham to the spot. The ghost had her revenge and she could rest in peace. So could Miller Graham.

Ghostly thoughts 5

Lies: *People lie about ghostly experiences for many reasons.*

Explanation? *Here is another explanation of the Anne Walker story that does not depend on ghosts...*

Anne Walker lived happily with her uncle, farmer Joseph Walker. She met the local miller, James Graham, when she took corn from the farm to his mill.

James Graham fell in love with Anne Walker. She felt nothing for him. He visited her at the farm. After a quarrel he killed her with the pickaxe that was lying in the barn.

Miller Graham took the body five miles along the road and dropped it down a mine shaft. No one knew about his relationship with Anne Walker, so he was safe.

But he could not sleep at night. He felt guilty about the murder and was terrified of being questioned. Magistrates were looking into her disappearance.

The only way the miller could be safe would be if someone else was tried and hanged for the murder. He couldn't say, "I know where the body is because I put it there," and he couldn't leave the body undiscovered. He'd spend the rest of his life worrying. He had to come up with some other story. A story that would get the body discovered and point the blame at someone else. A story about a visit from a vengeful ghost, perhaps?

The shadow that the judge saw could be an invention added by storytellers who repeated it years later.

True ghost story? Or a cunning lie?

Both are possible. You must make up your own mind.

F
A
C
T

F
I
L
E

Avenging Ghosts

The belief that a ghost might wander around this Earth until it avenges its death is quite common. Sometimes the ghost appears to a relative, describes its death and reveals the guilty person. In some amazing cases (like the one at Chester-le-Street) no one realized the victim had died until the ghost informed them.

In many cases a ghost seems to have returned to Earth for vengeance...

1. **The Greenbriar ghost** – Zona Shue died in West Virginia in 1897. Her husband, Edward, was in a terrible state and kept clutching at the body as the doctor was trying to examine it. In the end the doctor gave up and concluded that Zona had died of "an everlasting faint". Even when she was in her coffin Edward would let no one near her. He covered her neck with a scarf ("her favourite scarf!" he sobbed), but Zona's mother took a pillow from the coffin and tried to wash it. She found a red stain that would not come out. Then Zona's ghost appeared to her in a dream. Four nights in a row the ghost told how Edward had lost his temper and broken her neck – the ghost turned her head in a complete circle to show how loose it was! Zona's mother took the story to the police, they examined the body and found it did indeed have a broken neck, just as the ghost had said. Edward was tried and found guilty. Zona's ghost could rest in peace, knowing justice had been done.

2. **The rapping ghost** – Louise Trafford was killed in 1949 but the police had no clues to the killer. Then a medium called the detective in charge of the case and said she had evidence … from the ghost of the dead woman. The message was in the form of knocking sounds. The police didn't understand the code – it wasn't Morse code – but Louise had spent a term in prison where prisoners would send messages to each other by rapping on pipes. When one of Louise's cell-mates heard a recording of the rappings she told the police exactly what they meant. The message from beyond the grave named the killer and told the police where to find vital clues to convict him. He was arrested, tried and executed three months later.

3. **The Inverawe ghost** – Duncan Campbell was the lord of Inverawe in Scotland. One night in 1748 he gave a stranger shelter. He didn't know that the stranger had just murdered his cousin, Donald. But Donald's ghost appeared and told the lord of Inverawe that the murderer was in the house: "Blood has been shed. Do not shield the murderer." The lord of Inverawe ignored the ghost's message four times that night. Finally the ghost said, "Farewell until we meet again at Ticonderoga." Ten years passed. No one had ever heard of Ticonderoga. Lord Duncan joined the British Army and was sent to fight the French in north-east America. At Fort Carillon he learned that the native Americans called the place Ticonderoga. He knew he was going to die and told his friends. In a vicious battle many men died and Lord Duncan received a slight wound from a musket. He felt he had escaped, but ten days later the wound had turned septic. He died and the ghost's revenge was complete.

F
A
C
T

F
I
L
E

4. **The Fox family ghost** – A family called Fox lived near New York. There was farmer James Fox, his wife and two daughters, Maggie and Katie. In 1848 their house was disturbed by strange banging noises in the night. The girls discovered they could communicate with a disturbed spirit through rapping – one rap for "yes", two for "no". Eventually they learned that the rappings came from the spirit of a man called Charles Rosma. Rosma told how he was murdered and buried in the cellar. When neighbours helped the Fox family to dig in the cellar they found human hair and bones. The spirit said he was murdered by a Mr Bell, but that the killer would never be brought to justice. Mr Bell, who had lived in the house five years before the Fox family, was very angry and denied it. The case caused such a sensation in the press that the Fox girls became famous and appeared all over America. The Spiritualist movement started in America and many people copied the performances of the Fox girls. After forty years of fame Katie admitted it was all a trick, but the Spiritualists refused to believe her!

GHOSTLY DREAMS
GEORGE'S DREAM

George and Hart were brothers who lived in Cornwall, England. They were not just brothers but very close friends too.

George became a sailor and they were separated for the first time in their lives. In February 1840 George's ship reached the island of St Helena. While he was there he had a horrific dream. This is his story...

Cornwall, England, 1840

I dreamed that my brother, Hart, was at Trebodwina market and that I was with him. I was quite close by his side during the whole of his buying and selling. I could see and hear everything that went on around me. But I felt it wasn't my body that was travelling round with him; it was my shadow or my spirit. Hart didn't seem to know that I was there.

Hart spoke to people and they replied. I could hear it all. But when I tried to speak no one heard me and no one replied.

I felt that this was a sign of some hidden danger that was going to befall him but I knew I wouldn't be able to stop the danger because I had no way of warning him. All I could do was stand by helplessly and watch.

My brother Hart had a very successful day at the market and

made a large sum of money. I should have felt happy for him but all I felt was fear. As the sun set he began to make his way homeward on his horse. My shadow followed him and my terror grew as he reached the village of Polkerrow.

Polkerrow is no longer a village. It is just a collection of deserted cottages round the cross-roads. No one lives there now. It was quiet and the setting sun was casting long shadows over the road. I was frantic. I wanted to warn Hart in some way that he must go no further.

Then I noticed two long shadows moving across the path. Two men appeared from one of the deserted cottages. It seemed they had been waiting there. I knew them well – they were the Hightwood brothers. They were villainous poachers who lived in a lonely wood near St Eglos. I also knew that it was Hart they were waiting for.

The men said, "Good evening, master," very politely. "Good evening," Hart replied. "I had been meaning to call on you," he said. It seemed he didn't sense the danger. My shadow was screaming out, "Ride on! Ride on now before it is too late." But Hart did not hear any warning.

"I have some animals I want taking to market next week," Hart said.

"So why not pay us now, Mr Northey?" the older Hightwood said.

That was the first time Hart began to sense they meant no good.

"I cannot pay for work that has not yet been done," he said.

"Ah, but you can, Mr Northey," the younger Hightwood said. He was standing by my brother's saddle. The older man walked to the horse's head and took hold of the horse's reins. "We need the money now," he said.

"Come to my house and I'll see if I can loan you some," Hart said. The horse could feel my brother's nervousness and started prancing in the dust.

The older man was holding the horse's head firmly. He said, "Mr Northey, we know you have just come from Trebodwina market. And we also know you have plenty of money in your pockets. We are desperate men and you aren't leaving this place until we've got that money. So hand it over."

Hart did not reply. He lashed at the man with his whip and spurred the horse on. The man fell back but held on to the reins.

The younger poacher immediately drew a pistol and fired. He was standing close to my brother's side. He could not miss. I watched as Hart dropped lifeless from the saddle. The poachers tied the horse to a tree in the orchard. Then they stole the money from Hart's pockets and dragged his body up the stream. They hid him under the overhanging bushes.

The poachers returned to the road and covered up the marks on the road. They hid the pistol in the thatched roof of a disused cottage by the roadside and returned home to their own house in the woods.

My ship left St Helena and sailed for Plymouth. All the way home I was sure that my brother had been murdered in the way I'd seen in my dream. When I reached home two months later my father was waiting at the quayside. "I know what you have come to tell me," I said. "It's Hart, isn't it?"

"Yes," my father said.

"He was robbed and murdered two months ago."

My father nodded. "You were always close to Hart," he said. "It is no surprise that you sensed his death."

And he told me the details of the crime. They were exactly as I had seen in my dream.

"The whole county was shocked by the brutal murder," my father said. "The authorities were determined to bring the murderers to justice. Two poachers called Hightwood have been arrested. Their cottage has been searched and blood-stained clothes found. 'From skinning rabbits,' the brothers claimed. But there was no pistol. The younger Hightwood said he had owned a gun years ago, but had lost it," he went on.

"The Hightwoods were taken to the magistrates' court. There wasn't much evidence against them. That murder weapon is still missing. But the men acted in a guilty manner. They were sent for trial anyway," my father explained.

77

"In that case I think I can help avenge my brother's murder For I can tell you where the gun is hidden. The gun is in the thatch of the cottage by the roadside." I said.

That was George's story. He could have been lying about dreaming the murder – after all, the men had already been arrested and their story was known to everyone. But when the roof was searched the gun was found, exactly as in the dream.

"How did you know?" George was asked.

"Because I saw it in a dream," he answered.

"And when did you have this dream?"

"I had the dream on the very night my brother was murdered, though I was two thousand miles away."

Faced with the weapon, the Hightwoods confessed to the murder. They hoped that the confession would save their lives and they'd be sent to prison. It didn't work.

A month later they were hanged for their crime.

GHOSTLY THOUGHTS 6

Doubles: *The image of a living person is seen by a friend or relative when they are many miles away. This is usually at a time of trouble for the "double", maybe when they are on the point of death.*

Explanation? *Perhaps everyone is a mind-reader. As well as seeing, touching, smelling or hearing other people maybe we can also sense their thoughts when those thoughts are very emotional. Our sight and hearing only allow us to sense people so far and no further, but thoughts can travel hundreds or even thousands of miles.*

Ghostly Visions

In the story of the Northey brothers the "ghost" was the living relative. His spirit seems to have left his body and travelled thousands of miles to be at the scene of the crime.

Another type of ghostly vision is when the ghost of the dead person visits a relative (or friend or loved one) at the time of their death. These ghost stories are called "point of death" visions. Many thousands have been recorded over the years...

1. **The last goodbye** – Rod Nielson lived in San Diego in California. He was very close to his father, Henry. Old Henry loved his granddaughter Katie but seemed sad when he heard that Rod's wife was having another grandchild. He hinted that he wouldn't be around to see his new grandson. He was quite, quite sure that the unborn baby would be a boy. In the summer of 1972 Rod was in his office when he clearly heard his father say, "Well, I guess that's it, son. Give Katie a kiss from me. Goodbye." Rod turned and saw an image of his father in a checked shirt and old trousers. In Henry's hand was a garden trowel and a bunch of marigolds. No one else in the office saw a thing. Rod hurried to his father's house. Henry was lying dead on the lawn wearing the same clothes as in the vision. In one hand he held a garden trowel, in the other a bunch of marigolds. But that's not the end of the story. For when the baby was born it was a boy. Rod turned to young Katie and said, "Pity Granddad couldn't be here to see it." Katie shook

F
A
C
T

F
I
L
E

her head, "But Daddy," she said, "Granddad *is* here, standing next to Mummy. Can't you see him?"

2. **The Tugboat disaster** – Not all ghosts appear at the "moment of death". Mrs Paquet of Chicago walked into her pantry and saw a clear image of her brother. He appeared to trip over a rope and vanish over a low railing. She knew that he was working on a tugboat in Chicago Harbour at the time. Mrs Paquet dropped her cup of tea and cried, "My God! Ed is drowned!" She eventually received news that this had in fact happened, but it had happened six hours before her vision.

3. **The woman in white** – One of the most chilling ghosts must be the one that foretells your own death. In 1837 John Allen saw something that told him he was about to die. He was miserable for the next six months but he would never say why. Then, one day while he was at work, his daughter Polly saw a woman dressed in white walking down the hill towards her. No one else saw the woman and Polly's sister laughed at her. "People don't wear white dresses on a working day," she said. Later that day they learned that their father had drowned while he was working on the river. He died at the time Polly had seen the woman. She had not seen the dying person at the moment of his death, as in most stories, but had she seen the ghost her father had met just months before?

F A C T

F I L E

4. **The ghostly car** – At 11.30 p.m. on 4 May 1980, Joseph Hannah's father heard Joseph's car pull into the driveway at their home. He knew the sound of that car engine and the sounds his son made parking his car. He fell asleep, content that his son was home safely. At 11.30 p.m. on 4 May 1980 Joseph Hannah's girlfriend saw him driving down the main street of her town. He waved and smiled at her, then drove on. She was a little surprised because she had watched him set off home at 11 p.m. At 11.30 p.m. on 4 May 1980 Joseph Hannah's babysitter heard footsteps pacing in the baby's room. Three people thought they'd seen or heard Joseph at 11.30 that night, but none of them had. He had died at 11.10 that evening when his car was wrecked by a landslide.

5. **The white room** – Some vision stories have a happy ending. In the 1850s a little girl was walking along a country lane not far from her home. Slowly the lane faded from sight and all she could see was a bedroom in her house known as the White Room. Her mother was lying still on the floor. Instead of going home the girl went straight to the doctor and persuaded him to go home with her. They found her mother, in the White Room, suffering from a heart attack. The doctor saved her life. It seems as if the mother's spirit had carried a "panic" message to her daughter.

GHOSTLY RETURNS
THE LIVES AND DEATHS OF JANE

Have you ever visited a place and felt that you've been there before, even though you know you haven't? Many people have that feeling. One explanation is that you really have been there before ... in another life. Perhaps we have all lived many lives before, but we've forgotten them. However, if we are hypnotized we might just remember our past lives...

Cardiff, Wales, 1974

"I shall count slowly backwards from ten. When I reach zero you will be asleep. Do you understand?"

The woman nodded. Her feet were up on the couch but she wasn't relaxed. Her bright eyes were fixed on the old man. "Yes, doctor," she said. Her voice was thin with a musical Welsh accent.

He looked at her. "No, Jane, not yet. You're still a little too excited. You've been hypnotized many times before. You know you have to relax."

She closed her eyes and took a deep breath. After a minute she said, "I'm ready."

The man's voice was smooth and soothing as he began to count slowly. "Ten ... your eyelids are heavy ... nine ... you can feel them closing ... eight ... you are going to sleep ... seven ... all you can hear is my voice ... six ... your body is so heavy it is sinking through the couch ... five ... your breathing is slower ... four ... you will be asleep when I say 'zero' ... three ... but you will still hear my voice ... two ... you are slipping ... one ... zero."

Jane's eyes were closed, her mouth slightly open and her body limp. The man spoke briskly. "Now, Jane, we have done this before. I'm going to ask you to go back in time. Back to the days before you were born. Back to when you lived another life in another body. Do you remember?"

"Yes-s," she replied with a tired slur to her voice.

"But this time will be different, won't it?"

"Yes."

"In the past I have told you which date I wanted you to return to. We went back to Roman Britain, didn't we?"

"Yes ... I was called Livonia," the woman said dreamily.

"And in Tudor England you were the maid of honour to a princess," the man went on. His eyes behind the spectacles were sharp as a bird's.

"This time I want *you* to choose. Of all the lives you've lived before, is there one that stands out in your memory?"

The woman's limp face tensed in a frown. Her soft breathing became harsh and her limp hands were clenched into fists. The white-haired man leaned forward. "Let it happen, Jane ... relax."

As he watched the woman changed. Her face became alive and her eyes flew open. The slack chin grew tight and she lifted it proudly.

The man asked, "Who are you?"

"Rebecca," the woman replied quickly. Her voice was firm and there was no trace of the Welsh accent Jane had.

"Where do you live, Rebecca?"

85

"York," she said.

"The year?"

"In Christian years it is 1189."

"Tell me about your life," he urged softly.

The Rebecca character spoke quickly as if she were irritated by the questions, or too busy to stop and answer them. "It's such a hard life for us."

"You're poor?"

Her lips pursed in anger. "Of course not. My husband is a wealthy merchant. It's hard because we're Jewish."

"I see," the old man nodded and sat back a little.

"They hate us," she said and an angry spot of red coloured each cheek. "The Christians can't lend money ... it's against the law ... but we Jews can. They come to us to borrow and they hate us because they owe us. They make us wear yellow badges on our clothes. They hate us. The Christians blame us for everything. Two hundred of them died in a plague last summer, but no Jews died. They say that is our fault too. They want to kill us!"

"Why do you say that?"

"There were riots in London and Lincoln and Chester. They killed Jews then. York will be next. I fear for my children. My little Rachel is only eleven. What will happen to her?"

The woman twisted her hands in worry and her face was creased with suffering.

The man leaned forward and spoke slowly. "Rebecca, time has moved on. When we last spoke you were worried about being attacked. What has happened?"

Now the woman's face was pale. Her eyes were staring. "Hush! Keep your voice down. They will hear us."

"Sorry," the man said quietly. "Where are you?"

"We are in the Christian church near Coppergate, hiding in a cellar. If they find us they will murder us."

"What happened?"

"We woke to the smell of burning ... they'd come in the night and set fire to Benjamin's house next door. They killed his wife and children and carried off all his treasure. So we put all our money in bags and fled to the castle for safety."

"Did you reach it?"

"They followed us. Through the dark streets they chased us. They were carrying torches and screaming they wanted us burned. My husband, Joseph, took a knife and split a sack of money. The silver spilled out on the road. The mob stopped to pick it up. We reached the castle and we stood inside with all the other Jews of York."

"The mob couldn't get you in the castle," the hypnotist said.

"Oh, but they could. They began battering at the door. Some parents began to kill their own children rather than let the mob get their hands on them."

"But you didn't kill Rachel?"

"No. Oh, no. We used the last of our money to bribe a guard. He let us out of a secret door before the mob broke down the gates. Now we're hiding in this church. They tell us King John has ordered the murder of all Jews in England! It's not just the people who are chasing us now, it's the soldiers too. Joseph has gone for food. He's been such a long time. Now Rachel is crying – hush, Rachel, they'll hear us! Listen! Horses. I can hear horses."

"Perhaps it's Joseph returning with food," the white-haired man said.

"Joseph didn't have a horse. No ... I can hear their footsteps now. They're coming for us. They're shouting, 'Kill the Jews, kill the Jews!' They're searching the church now. God protect us! Hush, Rachel, don't cry. Only the priest knows we're down here. A priest will not betray us ... but listen ...I can hear the sound of the stone floor being lifted. He's told them where we are ... they're coming ... no, not Rachel! Not my Rachel! Don't take my child ... no-o-o!" the woman wailed, a long and terrified cry.

The hypnotist was shocked. "They haven't taken her, have they? They're not going to harm you, are they?"

But the woman's tortured face was blank now. Her eyes stared, sightless. She whispered just one word. So soft that the man hardly heard it. "Dark," she sighed.

The man was trembling a little as he said, "Jane? Jane?"

The woman on the couch was limp again. Her eyes closed;

"Jane, I'm going to count to three. On the count of three you will wake up. You will be Jane Evans and the year is 1974. One ... two ... three!"

The woman opened her eyes slowly. She smiled at the man and her voice was bright with that Welsh accent. "What happened, doctor?" she said. "Why, doctor, are you all right? Was it something I said? You look like *death*!"

GHOSTLY THOUGHTS 7

Reincarnation: *Many people believe that they have lived on Earth before. Some religions say that your body dies but your soul comes back over and over again. This is called reincarnation.*

Explanation? *a) Jane read a book about the massacre then forgot she'd read it. When she was hypnotized all the details were unlocked from her memory; b) Jane's spirit really had once lived (and died) in Rebecca's body.*

F
A
C
T

F
I
L
E

Ghostly Returns

Some people have seen their past lives in dreams or under hypnosis. But are they real? There are arguments for and against.

The case for reincarnation

1. Jane Evans' story was checked by a historian. Many of the facts were correct, and they were the sort of things an ordinary housewife like Jane would not know. Where did she get the facts from if she didn't get them from the memory of a past life?

2. "Rebecca" described hiding in the cellar of a church near Coppergate in York. But historians said the church nearest Coppergate had no cellar. Then, six months after Jane Evans' tape was made, workmen found a cellar just where she'd said it was. How could she have known about the cellar when no one else in this century knew?

3. Some people claim that they learn things in one life and keep that skill in their next life. A man who was a great piano player died. His spirit then entered the body of a baby who grew up to be a brilliant piano player at the age of three years old! That baby was the famous musician, Mozart. How else did he learn so quickly?

F
A
C
T

F
I
L
E

The case against reincarnation

1. An investigator looked closely into Jane Evans's story and decided that much of her information was incorrect about York and Jews of that time. The researcher also discovered that a lot of her information came from a play that had been broadcast on BBC radio.

2. Another of Jane Evans' "characters" was Livonia, who lived in Roman Britain. Much of her story came word for word from a novel called *The Living Wood* by Louis de Wohl. It seems Jane forgot that she'd read the book but the details were there in the back of her mind. This is something called "secret memory" that everybody seems to have.

3. A lot of the remembered "characters" are famous people with interesting stories to tell. Surely the chances of being a king or a queen must be millions to one. A 1980s tour guide in Egypt once complained that, in the dozens of American tourists on that trip, he had nine Cleopatras!

GHOSTLY MESSENGERS
Diary of a Haunting

Some ghosts seem doomed to wander the Earth because they need to tell someone something before they leave. It can take years – hundreds of years – before they find the right person to listen. Not everyone can "tune in" to a ghost. It seems that some people, especially nervous people, can attract a ghost to tell its story. In the case of the haunting at Ash Manor in Sussex, the ghost had a long wait before it found the right person...

The Diary of Elizabeth Keller, aged sixteen years and three months

23 June 1934

Our last night in the old house. I do hope we'll be happy in the new one. It's called Ash Manor and it is beautiful. Father took us to see it yesterday. So peaceful. I'm sure that father and mother will be happier once we settle in.

It's been hard for them, I know. Father's been so miserable. I'm not sure quite why. The doctor says it's something called "depression". I think it's the strain of running his business. Everyone is having trouble making money these days. I think that's why the last owners of Ash Manor sold it; they needed the money. Anyway, Father says it was very cheap.

Once we move in he'll have that lovely old house to come home to at night.

I can't wait.

24 June 1934

The end of our first day. The servants have been working very hard to make the house ready for us. It's so large I have my own bedroom and writing room. That's where I'm writing this diary.

The vicar, Mr Twist, said the oldest part of Ash Manor dates back to the thirteenth century and the reign of Edward the Confessor. I know from my history lessons that Edward the Confessor was king in the eleventh century. But it would have been rude to correct the good man so I held my tongue.

Most of the house is only about a hundred years old, though. Mr Twist says the original building began to crumble and was rebuilt by a Victorian owner. But I live in the oldest part.

It's so thrilling to know I'm surrounded by six hundred (or eight hundred) years of history! Hope I'm not too excited to sleep.

25 June 1934

I'm tired. I didn't sleep too well. I know the servants still had lots of unpacking and sorting to do, but I didn't expect them to be up half of the night doing it.

I spoke to the maid quite sharply at breakfast.

"Mecalfe."

"Yes, Miss Keller?" she said.

"What time did you get to bed last night?"

"I beg your pardon?" she said, surprised.

"I heard you moving about in the servants' quarters till all hours," I complained.

She couldn't look me in the face. Her hand was shaking as she served my scrambled egg. "Sorry, Miss, but we was all asleep by midnight," she muttered.

Metcalfe was lying, of course. I could tell that father had been disturbed by them too. His face was grey with fatigue and there were purplish shadows under his eyes.

He seemed very much withdrawn. Hardly spoke. I'm sure he'll be better when he's settled in and had a good night's sleep.

Mother and I explored the gardens of Ash Manor today. They'll be beautiful when the gardeners have finished. A fine place to sit and read. We had tea on the lawn, though it needs cutting.

Father was late home from work and we have all gone to bed early. I hope I sleep better tonight.

26 June 1934

Another night with very little sleep, and everyone's nerves are getting frayed. I got out of bed at midnight to climb to the servants' quarters and complain about their tramping about in the middle of the night. But the servants were nowhere to be seen. The sounds were those of footsteps on floorboards and they seemed to be coming from the attic.

This morning I asked Almond, the butler, about the footsteps.

"No, Miss Keller, there are no floorboards in the attic," he said. "The servants heard nothing," he added quickly. But I know he's lying. They're trying to hide something. When father came down he looked worse than ever. I asked him about it.

"Nothing to bother yourself about, Elizabeth," he said.

But when I persisted, he said, "The servants seem to think the place is haunted. They've been talking to the shopkeepers in the village about some old legends. All nonsense, of course. The last people to live here had no problems – and they lived here for seven years. And the ones before for thirteen. It's all nonsense. Probably just jackdaws roosting in the attic. We'll get someone to sort them out. Now get on with your breakfast." But I wasn't hungry.

I asked Mr Twist, the vicar, about the stories and he laughed. But it wasn't a very happy laugh. He made some excuse and left very quickly.

27 June 1934

I'm so tired. I don't think I slept more than two hours. I'd fallen asleep at ten o'clock but was wakened at midnight by the most terrible fuss in the corridor outside the bedroom. Father was standing at the door to Mother's room and babbling something. I ran across and said, "What's wrong?"

"Help me get him into the library," Mother said, and we led him downstairs. Mother poured him a large glass of brandy and made him drink it while I rubbed his cold and shaking hand.

"Go back to bed, Elizabeth," Mother ordered.

"No, let her stay," Father put in. "She needs to hear this too. She's sixteen now, you know."

"I know how old my daughter is, thank you," Mother snapped. "I simply think we should not burden her with the problems of your nerves."

Father looked up angrily and I was afraid they were going to start one of their terrible rows. His breathing was short and tense but he kept his voice low. "It was not my nerves, Alice," he said. "You admit you heard it too!"

Mother gave a sharp nod. Father turned to me. "I was lying awake, reading, when I heard the most fearful bangs on my door. Three bangs. But when I opened it there was no one there. I went to your mother's room. She heard them too. I didn't imagine it. There is nothing wrong with my nerves. Nothing. Nothing!"

"Of course not, Father," I soothed him.

But none of us could get back to sleep.

28 June 1934

And now my father has seen it. This time I heard the knock on his door. I hurried from my room and saw my father standing there, clinging to the doorpost in fear. When we got him into the library this time he said, "I've seen him ... it ... I've seen the thing that's been making the noise."

"Hush!" Mother said. "You'll frighten Elizabeth."

"I need to know," I said. "Go on, Father. What was it?"

He swallowed thirstily at the brandy and let out a low sigh. "Standing in the doorway was a man. An oldish man – older than me, dressed in one of those things peasants used to wear on farms."

"A smock," my mother said.

"Aye, a smock ... A green smock. And his trousers were muddy, as if he'd just come from the fields. He had a shapeless hat on his head and a sort of scarf around his throat. I thought it was one of the gardeners. I asked him what he wanted. He didn't seem to hear me. Didn't answer. So I went to grab his shoulder, but my hand went clean through it. I fell back against the doorpost almost in a faint. When I opened my eyes again he'd gone."

"We'll see what Mr Twist has to say about this," Mother said. "The vicar will soon rid us of this ... thing."

I was surprised. Mother has always blamed my father's "nerves" for everything. "You think there is something, Mother?" I asked carefully. She looked at me and her eyes were dark-shadowed like father's. "I ... I heard the knock too."

"You went to your door?"

"I went to my door," she said.

"And you saw the ghost?"

Perhaps I shouldn't have used that word. Mother's lips went pale and tight. "I saw ... something," she admitted. "I saw it walk towards the fireplace in your father's room. I'm sure there's something hidden in that chimney."

"What else, Mother?" I asked.

"It raised its head … I saw what lay beneath that scarf around its neck."

"What was it, Mother?"

She looked at me. "Pray you never see it, child!"

2 July 1934

So much has happened I haven't had the time to keep this diary up to date. Mr Twist came with his prayers and sprinkling of holy water. "Exorcism," he called it. That seemed to annoy the ghost. It's becoming bolder. I have seen it for myself.

So have the servants and that is why Metcalfe is leaving. We are becoming desperate, so desperate that we have called in a spiritualist – someone who can talk to spirits, see who it is, find out what it wants.

I sleep in Mother's bedroom now and we pray. That seems to help. I hope this spiritualist can end our misery.

4 July 1934

Mr Twist said it is mumbo-jumbo. He doesn't believe in spiritualism. But it was so amazing. The medium was Mrs Garrett, a small Irish woman about Mother's age.

She walked in the front door and stopped. "Ah, yes," she said. "I can feel the problem."

"Poppycock!" Mr Twist muttered, but she ignored him.

"There is pain. There is suffering here," she said. She had a slight Irish accent.

Mrs Garrett wandered round the house then came to the oldest part. "Here," she said. "We will try to talk to him here."

"What should we do?" Father asked nervously.

"Sit around the table," she ordered. "Draw the curtains."

"That'll be so we can't see any tricks or jiggery-pokery," Mr Twist whispered to me.

When we were sitting in the gloom lit by just one candle, Mrs Garrett said she had a link with the world of spirits, in particular a spirit called Uvani. We should not be bothered if she seemed to change during the session.

She closed her eyes. All I could hear was Mr Twist's breathing. Even he was fascinated. At last Mrs Garret opened her eyes. When she spoke her voice was stronger and she had no Irish accent. It seems it was the spirit of Uvani speaking to us.

"There is a man who wishes to speak to you. The man who is haunting this house."

"Who is he?" mother said quickly.

"His name is Charles Edward ... and he has suffered much from imprisonment," Mrs Garrett (or Uvani) replied.

"Was he imprisoned here?" Mr Twist put in. "This house was never a prison."

Uvani seemed to be talking to Charles Edward a few moments then spoke to us. "No. The prison was near here but not in this house."

"Then why does he come here?" the vicar asked.

"Charles Edward is suffering and he felt some living soul suffering in this house. Suffering attracts suffering like a magnet."

We knew Uvani meant Father and his nervous problem. We said nothing.

"Who imprisoned him?" Mr Twist asked.

"The king – King Edward, his half-brother," Uvani replied.

"Which King Edward? The fourth or the fifth?"

Uvani nodded and simply said, "Yes."

"Hah! That's a nonsense reply," the vicar snapped. That seemed to destroy the spell. The spiritualist blinked and the spirit of Uvani left her.

Mrs Garrett will return tomorrow and then we speak to Charles Edward himself.

5 July 1934

Mrs Garrett's face changed when Charles Edward took over her body. We all gasped. For her face became the face of the man in green, and her voice was a man's voice. "A trick," Mr Twist said. I wasn't so sure. Charles Edward spoke.

"I am half-brother to the king, but my followers believe I have more right to the throne than Edward. They started a rebellion and put me at the head. I didn't really want the crown, I just wanted my land back. I was robbed of my land by the Earl of Huntingdon. Of course Edward won. He locked me up here and left me to rot in gaol."

"Which king?" Mr Twist said softly.

"Edward."

"Which Edward?"

"Edward," was all the spirit would say.

"Why do you haunt this house?" the vicar asked.

"I need help – help me to take my revenge. Revenge on the friends who betrayed me; revenge on the brother who tortured me."

"They are all dead," Mr Twist said. "Long, long dead."

"I want my revenge!" the spirit cried and it brought tears to my eyes to hear him. To me he was as real a person as Mother or Father. "I will not leave until I have had my revenge."

Father gave a great sigh and buried his face in his hands. "We'll never be free of this haunting."

6 July 1934

I do not like Mr Twist, but he spoke a lot of sense today.

"The woman is a fraud," he said. "She makes money by putting on performances like she did last night."

"We paid her well," Mother admitted.

"I know a lot of local history," the vicar went on. "Mrs Garret's story was a powerful one, but a nonsense. Did you notice how she refused to name the king? I have checked all the record books and this rebellion simply never happened."

"So what is this ghost? We didn't imagine him. We've all seen him. Another servant left today," Mother said.

"I think Mrs Garrett said one thing that made sense. She said that suffering attracts suffering. Mr Keller is clearly unhappy. It is his unhappiness that is creating the haunting. This house is haunted because Mr Keller wants it to be haunted."

I looked at Father. He didn't deny it. "But who is the green man?"

"The green man is not the long-lost brother of a long-dead king. The green man only lived in one place. He was created in the mind of your unhappy father. Once your father finds happiness the green man will disappear." The vicar turned to Father. "See a doctor, Mr Keller, then come to church and find peace." He turned to Mother and me. "And you have your parts to play. Suffering attracts suffering – but remember, happiness attracts happiness. Be happy."

We talked long into the night. We resolved to try. We will help one another. Together we can destroy this ghostly green man.

7 July 1934
Last night I slept peacefully for the first time since we moved here. The green man is gone, driven away by the one weapon he couldn't face. Happiness.

Ghostly thoughts 8

Spirits: *The "souls" of dead people who don't want to leave this world. The spirit wants to talk to a friend or relative by a) appearing as a vision (often in a dream) and giving a message; b) finding a sensitive person to carry their message – a "medium". They speak through the mouth of that medium. Sometimes these spirits are friendly and want to pass on advice or warnings to their loved ones.*

Explanation: *The living may simply dream the vision. Many "mediums" have been caught out in their cheating over the years. Remember, they are often well paid!*

Fakes

The Ash Manor case is interesting. The ghostly appearance of the green man seems to be a truly ghostly happening, but the attempt to talk to the ghost through a "medium" seems to have been a trick.

In the history of ghosts there have been a lot of tricksters making a lot of money from frauds and fakes. Some unhappy people want to talk to a loved one who is dead. A "medium" will claim to put them in touch with the dead person and pass on messages, but could simply pretend to pass on their messages and invent the replies they want to hear.

In ancient Greece you could talk to the gods through the "medium" of a priest and receive replies. Even today mediums can fill large theatres with hundreds of people who believe they are in touch with the afterlife.

Sadly there is a long history of fakes.

1. **The ghost-buster** Harry Houdini was a very skilled magician whose special trick was escaping – from handcuffs, boxes, coffins, safes and even prisons. Houdini desperately wanted to get in touch with his dead mother. He spent years looking for a genuine medium but all he found were fakes. Being a great magician himself he could work out all the tricks they used.

2. **The ghostly cabinet** – The American Davenport brothers

F
A
C
T

F
I
L
E

used a special cabinet in their performances in the 1860s. They were tied up and locked in the cabinet. On the darkened stage ghostly hands reached from the cabinet and played musical instruments. When the cabinet was opened they were found to be tied up as tightly as ever. Many people saw this as proof of a spirit world and no one ever caught them trying to cheat. A religion called Spiritualism grew up in the nineteenth century from such contacts with the dead. Many other mediums began to copy the cabinet idea. Before Ira Davenport died he confessed to Harry Houdini that it was all a clever fraud, and showed him the conjuring tricks the brothers had used.

3. **The fairy photographs** – Sir Arthur Conan Doyle was the writer of the Sherlock Holmes detective stories and a great believer in Spiritualism. He was shown photographs of fairies taken by two girls in Yorkshire. He was quite sure that the photographs proved that fairies existed and never considered that two girls aged ten and sixteen could create cunning trick photographs. Doyle and thousands of others believed the pictures were real. They weren't! The "fairies" in the pictures were paper cut-outs. The sisters finally admitted their trick sixty years later, long after Doyle's death.

4. **The solid ghost** – Mediums can produce rapping noises and make tables rise from the floor. But their most amazing skill is to make a ghost "materialize" – take a solid form and walk round the room. The medium will usually step inside a cabinet and close the curtains. In the darkened room a spot of white will appear in front of the curtains and grow into a cloud. A face will emerge from the cloud and finally the whole ghost. The ghost can walk around the room and touch the visitors,

who may find the spirit solid and warm. An author called Robert Chaney explained that the solid ghost is formed from "ectoplasm" – part of the medium's own body flows out of her mouth and forms a second body that the ghost steps into. The truth is that the solid "ghost" is just the medium in a different dress. The top dress is taken off behind the curtains; the medium is wearing a second one painted in luminous paint underneath. The "cloud" is a piece of fine white material that the medium has hidden, usually in her knickers!

Perhaps the most famous case of fraud is the Cock Lane ghost of the 1760s in London...

POLTERGEISTS
THE COCK LANE GHOST

Most ghosts are harmless. Miserable to themselves. frightening to other people – but harmless.

The only sorts of ghosts that seem dangerous are "poltergeists". A poltergeist is a spirit that often begins by making rapping noises but gradually gets more violent. Objects are thrown around a room and people may be lifted into the air.

Many poltergeists have one thing in common – they appear in a room where a teenager is living. Some scientists say the poltergeist is in fact the spirit of that teenager. Because the young person is growing up they lose control of the spirit inside them. This "out-of-control spirit" is so strong it can move objects. The trouble is that because it is "out of control" the teenager can't "switch on" the poltergeist whenever he or she wants. That means it can't be tested very easily.

If you were a teenager with poltergeist problems you'd get a lot of attention. If you enjoyed that attention then you might want the disturbances to go on. How do you do that? Sometimes you have to cheat. The trouble is, if you are caught cheating just once then no one will ever believe there was a true poltergeist spirit.

That's what happened to little Lizzie Parsons...

London, England, 1762

The room was dim. It was hot. There were too many people crowded in it to meet the famous Cock Lane Ghost.

They shuffled and sniffed, they coughed and they muttered the odd word here and there. Some sat on chairs around the bed. Some stood. No one leaned against the wooden walls. They'd heard the stories. There was something there, behind the walls. Something strange and menacing.

There was a bed against one wall, and in the bed lay a girl of about thirteen – a small girl with wide eyes over a snub nose and pale cheeks. Lizzie Parsons.

A thin man in a black coat spoke quietly. "The ghost will be here soon, ladies and gentlemen," he said. He said it for the fifth time. Someone sighed.

"It's not there, Pa," the girl said. "Too many people in the room, I think."

Some people groaned and grumbled.

"Sorry, I'll have to ask you to leave," Richard Parsons said.

There was a clattering of chairs and louder grumbles as the watchers rose and wandered out of the door. Finally there were just three men in the room with Richard Parsons and his daughter, Lizzie.

The large man with a red face turned to Richard Parsons. "So they are all lies, are they? All these stories you've been spreading about me are lies, eh?"

Parsons wrung his hands. "I've said nothing about you, Will Kent. It's the spirit. The spirit has been saying those things. You can't blame me!"

"But I do blame you, Parsons," the big man said, and his face turned a darker red. "I even read about myself in the newspaper. Read about the things you said I'd done."

Will Kent took a step forward and Parsons backed away. The big man's hand clenched into a fist. He began to raise it. Parsons whimpered and turned his head away. Suddenly there was a sharp noise.

Rap!

Will Kent looked round quickly. The two men who were with him shrugged their shoulders. "The spirit!" Parsons squeaked. "The spirit is ready to speak! Sit down, Kent; sit down Minister; sit down, Doctor." Parsons fussed them like a hen with chicks until they were seated in a half-circle round the bed.

Little Lizzie lay perfectly still in the bed, her eyes fixed on the ceiling. Her father spoke quietly but clearly. "Are you there, spirit?"

Rap!

"That means, 'yes'," Parsons explained quickly. "It's two raps for 'no'."

The visitors looked around the room. The noise seemed to have come from the wall behind them. The minister crossed himself quickly. The doctor looked puzzled. Kent looked at Parsons with hatred.

"Oh, spirit, have you a message for us?" Parsons asked.

Rap!

"Will you tell us who you are, spirit?"

Rap!

"Are you the spirit of Will Kent's wife?"

Rap!

"His first wife?"

Rap Rap!

"His second wife, Frances?"

Rap!

"We wish to know how you died, Frances. Did you die naturally?"

Rap! Rap!

"Then, were you murdered?"

Rap!

"Who murdered you, Frances? Was it your husband Will Kent here?"

RAP!

There was a louder clatter as Kent jumped to his feet and the chair crashed to the floor. "You lie, spirit! You lie! I know I didn't kill my Frances. That's the truth," he roared.

The doctor put a hand on his shoulder to calm him. Kent tore it away. He pointed a thick finger at Parsons. "This ghost must repeat the accusation in front of a magistrate. If it doesn't then you'll suffer for this, Parsons."

"It's not *my* fault," the thin man cringed. "The spirit—"

"It is *your* spirit! You are doing this to get me hanged for killing my wife. The way I see it, Parsons, you are trying to kill me. You are the murderer. And the penalty for attempted murder is death."

"But—" Parsons began to object. Kent and his two friends were already out of the door and pushing through the crowds who had huddled outside to hear the argument.

"We'll just have to prove ourselves in front of a magistrate, Lizzie," the thin man said to his daughter.

"I'll try, Pa," the girl said from her bed. "I'll try."

News of the ghost spread through the streets of London. Crowds gathered at Cock Lane the next day to get a glimpse of the spirit. In the local tavern the landlord Franzen served beer to the crowds. The beer was dearer than usual, but they got their money's worth. "A thin, pale ghost it was. Saw her with my own eyes. Wandering past the window of the house. Wailing and crying."

"When was that, landlord?" someone asked.

"That would be Christmas 1759," Franzen said.

"Then you can't have seen the ghost of Mrs Kent – she didn't die till the February of 1760," the man argued.

The landlord gave a wide, smug smile that showed the blackened stumps of rotting teeth. "Ahh ... but the first Mrs Kent died two years before that."

The crowd gathered closer round the beer barrel. "You mean he murdered *her* as well?"

The landlord narrowed his red-rimmed eyes. "Arsenic poison in her beer, same as the second Mrs Kent," he said.

"You think the spirit will speak to the magistrate?" someone asked.

"It has to," Franzen said. "It has to."

And a week later Richard Parsons was saying the same thing to little Lizzie. "It has to appear today, Lizzie. Do you understand?"

"Yes, Pa," she said, and there was a tremble of fear in her voice.

"The magistrate will be here in a minute. Are you comfortable?"

Yes, Pa."

"Good. Then I'll let them into the room. That spirit has to appear today or I'm in trouble, understand?"

"Yes, Pa," the girl murmured and gripped something under the bedclothes.

"Come in, gentlemen," Richard Parsons said. He was twisting a handkerchief in his thin hands.

The magistrate looked at him severely. "You know, Parsons, that it is a serious offence to accuse a man of murder?"

"Oh, yes, your honour. But I'm not accusing anyone. It's the spirit."

"We'll see," Will Kent said as he stepped into the room behind the magistrate.

The two men sat down while Richard Parsons turned towards the bed. "Spirit, are you there?"

This time there was no delay. There was a sharp rap. It seemed to come from the floor under the bed. Will Kent leaned forward. This wasn't the same strange sound that came from the walls before. "Are you the spirit of Frances Kent?" Parsons asked.

Rap!

Kent edged forward again. "Were you murdered, Frances?" Parsons was asking.

Rap!

Will Kent jumped to his feet and snatched the cover off the bed. Lizzie Parsons was lying there in a grubby white night-dress on even grubbier sheets. The big man picked her up easily and dragged her towards the magistrates' chair.

"Show the gentleman what you have in your hand, Lizzie," he shouted.

The terrified girl raised her hand. It held a heavy piece of wood. Kent snatched it and waved it under the magistrate's nose. "Your spirit, I think."

"Richard Parsons, you are under arrest," the magistrate said solemnly. "You are charged with conspiring to bring about the death of William Kent. You will appear before a court tomorrow to

115

answer the charges."

Parsons looked at his daughter.

"Sorry, Pa. I thought that's what you wanted," she said miserably.

All the newspapers of the day wrote about the fraud. None of them were interested in exploring the strange, true happenings before the fraud.

Parsons got two years in jail, four sessions locked in a pillory, and a lot of sympathy. Being locked in the pillory could be a cruel punishment; a man had been stoned to death in the same pillory by angry crowds. When Parsons appeared in the pillory the crowd collected money for him!

It seems some people are determined to believe in ghosts even when fakes have been uncovered. The Cock Lane Ghost was the first time a ghost story had been properly investigated in England.

Would you be able to tell the difference between a real ghost and a fraud if you had the chance? Over the years ghost hunters have drawn up a series of "rules" to try to help people make sensible decisions about ghosts...

Ghost-hunting

Good ghost-hunters will attempt to prove a ghost exists by taking some sort of recording equipment, and will go to the site of a reported haunting prepared for anything.

Ghost-hunting Equipment

Ghost-hunters will equip themselves with the following:

- Recording equipment (see ghost-hunting rules)
- Torches (plus spare bulbs and batteries)
- Candles (to test for draughts)
- Thermometer (to check if that chill running down the spine is just fear)
- Compass (to check the direction of a sighting or to sense magnetic change in the site)
- Warm and waterproof clothing
- Food and drink
- Notebook and pens/pencils (to record experiences while they're fresh in the mind)
- Talcum powder (scattered on the floor to test for footprints. Sugar has the same effect but also gives a "crunching" sound to warn of unexpected movement.)
- Thread (stretched across corridors or stairs to catch people who are trying to fake a ghostly appearance)
- Maps and plans of a place are helpful, especially if they show underground streams and mine tunnels or buried power cables

117

Ghost-hunters can prepare by taking the right equipment. But they also need to follow certain rules if they are going to increase their chances of proving ghosts exist.

Ghost-hunting Rules

1. Hunt in pairs

You may be told that a headless horseman haunts a wood. You go to the wood *expecting to see a headless horseman*. Your imagination *tells* you there is a headless horseman on that path ahead of you. You really believe you see it! A good ghost-hunter will take at least one other person. That second person should know as little as possible about the reports so that they *do not know what to expect*.

2. Take recording equipment

A ghost-hunter is looking for *proof*. The more records you have the better. These records can be

- photographs
- video or film
- tape-recorded sound
- footprints
- temperature changes

3. Be patient

Ghosts don't appear very often or very regularly. If you don't see anything in a graveyard on a particular night then you may have been there on the wrong night. Ghost-hunters often have to try over and over again; they don't give up easily.

4. Look for sensible explanations first

Most ghost reports are simple mistakes: strange knocking sounds that turn out to be central-heating pipes; pale

phantoms that are simply wisps of fog; eerie lights that are reflections of moonlight on a window. The majority of ghost reports are the result of mistakes.

5. Know the haunt

If you are going to spend a night in a castle then spend as much time as possible getting to know it in the daytime. Ghost-hunters should be able to find their way around even on the darkest nights.

6. Believe no one

Don't believe any report until you have checked it out for yourself. People who report the ghost to you could be wrong. They could even be lying. In the history of ghost reports there are a lot of fakers, frauds and liars.

7. Know the history of the place

Try to find out as much about the site of the haunting as possible. You need to find out what was there *before* the building existed. Old maps and local history books from the nearest library might help. Then you need to know as much as possible about the people who used to live in the building. Lastly, you need to talk to people who've lived in the area for a long time; what have they heard or seen?

8. Don't be frightened

That's easy to say, of course! But you have to remember that ghosts rarely harm anyone. There are reports of damage to furniture and to rooms, but not to people.

9 Don't move

If something appears then don't move until it disappears, making a note of exactly how it vanishes. Is it through a wall?

F
A
C
T

F
I
L
E

Try to move to the other side of the wall to see if it appears there. Does it go through a door? Then follow it.

10. Don't speak

Ghosts don't usually talk. It seems as if they move in a world of their own and can't see us. But talking can disturb the conditions and cause them to disappear.

EPILOGUE

Do you believe in ghosts?

When someone asks you that perhaps the best answer is to reply, "What sort of ghosts?" There have been several types described in this book. Some are more likely than others.

Did you know...
Most ghosts are not seen, but people report
- a sound
- a smell
- a feeling of heat or cold
- a feeling of terror
- mysterious movement of objects
- strange lights or shadows

Ghosts are not something you should worry about. Most "ghostly" experiences turn out to have a natural explanation. (In fact some ghost-hunters reckon that out of every one hundred reports only two turn out to be truly unexplained.)

You've read some of the millions of ghost stories that people have told about ghosts. Now do you believe in ghosts?

Only *you* can answer that.

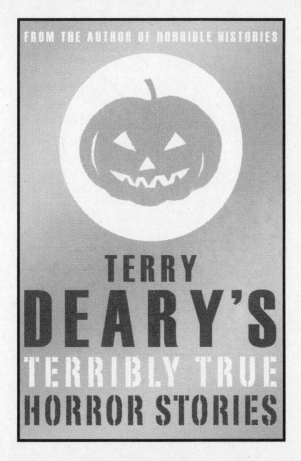

DON'T MISS THESE GRIPPING SPY STORIES

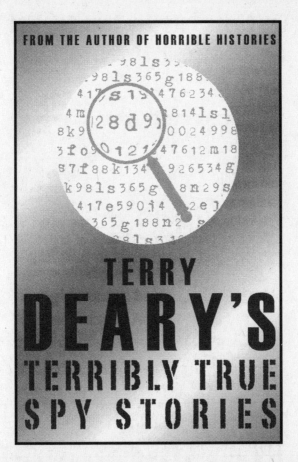

FROM THE AUTHOR OF HORRIBLE HISTORIES

TERRY
DEARY'S
TERRIBLY TRUE
SPY STORIES

They're guaranteed to bring out
the armchair agent in you!

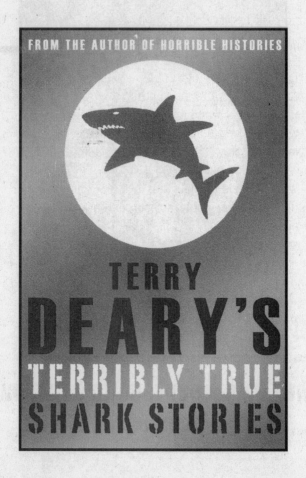

4. **The haunted house – Newcastle, New South Wales, 1970**
Michael Cooke thought he had found the perfect house for himself and his wife and baby. But they left in fear after something...

- made the baby sit up as if jerked by invisible hands.
- rumpled bedclothes on a tidy, made-up bed.
- moved toys around/
- shook a door knob loudly.

But the final straw came when the ghost put in an appearance. As Michael Cooke described it, "Last night I saw a horrible white face looking out of one of the windows as I walked past. The eyes were white with green in the middle. I was so scared the tears just ran out of my eyes. That was the end. I was thinking of buying the house but I'll never live there again." Other tenants had reported similar problems.

THE GHOST'S REVENGE
The Miller of Chester-le-Street

Do some poor souls linger on Earth? Are they tied to this world because they have some unfinished business here? Let me tell you the story of Anne Walker. Then make up your mind.

Durham, England, 1632

The market town of Chester-le-Street stands by the River Wear. A water mill once stood down by the river. James Graham, the miller, lived by the mill in 1632.

The miller worked hard and he worked long hours. It was midnight as he put the last corn in the hopper one chill winter's night, and a damp mist rose from the river.

He came down the creaking wooden stairs and he stopped.

There was someone down there on the flour-dusted floor, yet he knew that the door of the mill had been locked.

"Who's that?" he called, peering down into the gloom. The figure made no reply. He turned up the wick of his lantern and took a step down.

He could make out the shape of a long-haired woman. And as he drew close he could see that her hair was dripping. But where the droplets hit the floor they made no mark in the thin layer of flour.

Before that they say there was a big statu
e biggest in the world.' He looked round a
ning. 'In those days nobody fucked withou

er to imagine Stalin's frown brooding over th

appened to it?'
exploded it many years ago.'
rossed a bridge, but they seemed to be climb
vay from the centre of the city. Ahead of the
er, three pillars of shiny metal like the needl
ets thrusting upwards into the supine grey sk
ter, fine and delicate lines of wet beads, bega
ations along the outside of the glass.
rains in Prague,' George said.
never lived in Berlin,' Joseph told him. 'I
in London.'
ge said. 'When I was born he was not there
over to the kerb and stopped. Peering ou
at they were parked in a street where a gaggl
alternated with offices and apartments, mos
ed to be lined with scaffolding. Everywher
city it occurred to him, there was scaffolding
the building were usually long ruled block
the grand streets of an English seaside town
nothing elegant about them. Instead the
peeling and spotted, some of them with
en look, as if only the grey piping of the
holding the plaster in place.
ar was a massive doorway faced with rusty
painted black, but the gloss was crumbling
he grey patches giving it a scaly, diseased

,' George announced. 'Come.'
ut of the car and looked over at George on

enough,' he said firmly. 'I'm going to take

of a sudden, they had an established and long-standing relationship.

'There is no problem,' George said. 'You come. You are my brother. My son you are his uncle. Yes? There is no problem.'

'I don't know that,' Joseph declared firmly. 'Even if what you say is true this is still weird. I phoned my father in London, but he wasn't in, and until I speak with him all bets are off. So cut the brotherhood shit till I know what's going on here.'

George frowned, listening intently, his lips moving fractionally, as if mouthing some of the words.

'I understand,' he said slowly. 'This is not easy for you. No one has told you. But for me, too. Because you are English you think this is some mad man from the East.'

'That's not it,' Joseph cut in quickly. 'That's not how I feel. Not the way you think.'

He was about to say that he was troubled and disturbed, that he couldn't begin to describe how he felt, but it struck him at the same time that to do so would be to enter George's story, to tell him that it was real. He stopped, uncertain how to proceed. George's eyes, he noted, a tremor starting somewhere inside his guts, were the same colour as his own. A few seconds passed while they stood staring at each other.

'So,' George said slowly. 'You come?'

THREE

George's car was a shiny dark-red Jaguar. It looked brand new. The interior was lined with soft cream-coloured leather into which Joseph sank, his muscles relaxing and coming to rest by an instant reflex. Through the darkened windows a premature twilight softened the harsh geometry of the city's suburban fringe. Suddenly Joseph felt like a part of the surroundings, gliding imperceptibly through its streets, floating on a carpet whose discreet vibrations filled him with a sense of power and command. As soon as they'd got into the car the stereo had started up, playing a Stevie Wonder album that Joseph remembered buying as a teenager. George tapped his fingers on the wheel in time to the music, looking round and smiling at Joseph, but for a couple of minutes he said nothing.

In spite of his determination to maintain his distance, Joseph found himself studying George's profile, searching it for signs of a resemblance to himself or his father. He was conscious of waiting for George to speak, to explain more about who he was, how he had arrived at this time and place, but in a few minutes he was also overwhelmed by the ridiculousness of the situation. He looked round the interior of the car again. There was no way, he thought, that George could be a common or garden confidence trickster. To drive a car like this he'd need to be making some serious money.

'What do you do for a living?' Joseph asked, pitching his voice above the music.

George grinned, as if the question amused him.

'Business. I'm a businessman.'

'All right,' Joseph said. 'What kind of business?'

'Business, you know. I bu
There was something fina
said this, as if he had no inter
further, and Joseph tried an
'How old are you?'
'I was born in 1958. In B
That would make him fo
'Is that where you live?'
George glanced sideways
as if he understood the po
had no intention of giving
'Sometimes.'
His enigmatic manner I
high point of exasperation
trying to control his irritat
of wood.
'Letinsky Sady,' George
ing.
'What?'
'Letna Park.'
It didn't look much I
England parks were ma
and garden reclaimed fi
the royal parks, which
time, were designed and
comparison Letinsky lo
somehow survived from
ing up a steep slope wl
block of rusting concre
the middle of the city
which made Joseph t
abandoned among the
'When Michael Jac
'he placed a big statue
peered out trying, wi
nodded his head as i
There were kids fuc

was great.
of Stalin, t
Joseph, grir
permission.
It was eas
dark wood.
'So what
'Oh, they
They had
ing, going av
reared a tow
noses of rock
Streaks of wa
tracing decor
'All year it
'My father
1958 he was
'Yes,' Geor
He pulled
Joseph saw th
of shopfronts
of which seen
he went in the
The façades o
of plaster, like
but there was
surfaces were
a bulging rott
scaffolding wa
Next to the
metal. It was
and peeling, t
air.
'We are here
Joseph got o
the other side.
'I've gone far

a taxi back to my hotel. Maybe after I phone my father we can talk.'

George frowned. He put his keys in his pocket and walked round the front of the car towards Joseph. As he came closer Joseph made a quick sweep of the street behind him. Apart from a couple of pedestrians on the other side it was practically deserted. This was a feature he had noticed earlier. Once outside of the central district of the city, there were very few people to be seen walking around. In comparison the suburban streets in London were thronging with traffic. Suddenly the empty street seemed alive with menace. Anything could happen, Joseph thought. As George came closer he took his hand off the car and stood up straight, holding his ground.

'My father is always called Kofi, but his full name begins with the English letter "a". Akofi. He trained to be a lawyer at the School of Economics, the great institute in the centre of London. He was a freedom fighter against the British. When his country was liberated he became an important diplomat in Russia. In 1957, one month before Christmas, the authorities in Moscow demanded his deportation. They sent my mother away on the same day. That is how I was born in Berlin. When my mother heard you speak on the TV, it was the first time she'd heard his name in over forty years.' He paused. His jaws clenched tight, the lines of his face set stone hard. He took the keys out of his pocket. In the silent twilight of the street they jingled. 'We came to Prague to see you. My brother. But come, go, phone. No difference. Fuck you.'

He turned away from Joseph and quickly walked round the car, across the narrow pavement. Without looking back he stuck the key in the lock, yanked the door open and went in, slamming it shut behind him.

Left alone, standing by the car, Joseph experienced a moment of irrepressible doubt, and without pausing to think about what he was doing, he ran after George and banged on the door. It opened immediately, and Joseph had the feeling that George had simply been leaning against it, waiting for him to knock. In the moment before George opened the door Joseph had been full of angry words, but as their eyes met he was dumb. They stood like this, on either side of the open door, before Joseph spoke.

'What do you want from me?'

George took a deep breath. He shrugged.

'I don't know.' He gestured with one hand. 'So?'

'All right,' Joseph said. 'All right.'

The stairs were dingy, wide and bare, their footsteps echoing back from the muddy brown walls. In contrast the apartment was neat and gleaming with the air of being newly painted and furnished.

They had come in through a short hallway into the big living room. On Joseph's right the wall was dominated by a huge abstract painting, a curling red shape which flowed ominously off the bottom corner of the canvas. Beside it a group of framed photographs which he guessed were views of the city. On the other side of the room a big round table, already laid out for dinner, was posed next to a pair of French windows which opened on to a balcony guarded by a sinuous wrought-iron rail. The apartment building was close to the top of a hill, and beyond the windows Joseph could see a wide vista, the grey slate of roofs punctuated by the pointing fingers of the church steeples, sweeping upwards to the sky out of gracefully curved triangles. This was the frame within which he saw Radka for the first time, her back towards him, and silhouetted against the pearlescent twilight of the evening city. Remembering the moment later on, he guessed that there must have been a stray beam of late sunlight striking through the glass, because her light fair hair seemed to be shining so that her head was shrouded by a bright and golden aura. It was only when George called her name, and she turned, smiling, to greet him, that Joseph noticed little Serge standing beside her.

'This is my son, Serge,' George said proudly. He pushed the little boy towards Joseph. 'Speak. Speak to your uncle.'

The boy's forehead furrowed with anxiety. He was about six years old, Joseph guessed, with a pale freckly skin, light green eyes, and a mop of reddish-brown curls in a halo round his head. At first Joseph had been startled by his appearance, but when he looked closely he could see the African ancestry in the shape of the boy's lips, in the dark undertone of his skin, and in the tight shape of the curls edging his cheeks. On the other hand he felt a peculiar flutter of disturbance somewhere inside him. His father Kofi was a man so dark that, out in the sunshine, his skin seemed to splinter and absorb the light. The thought that this pretty, curly-haired white boy might be his grandson was strange and unsettling.

Over Serge's head George smiled broadly. In the short time it had taken them to climb the stairs his mood had lightened, and he was now cheerful and expansive, the genial host. The contrast with his outburst of rage on the street left Joseph bewildered and uncertain.

'Speak,' George told the boy. 'Speak.'

'*Ahoy*,' Serge said eventually.

'Not Czech,' George muttered, stooping down behind him. 'English.'

The boy's lips worked silently for a moment.

'Hello,' he said eventually.

Standing behind George, Radka clapped her hands loudly.

'*Bravo Liebling. Gut. Gut.*'

'Speak English,' George said quickly, looking round. He stood up. 'This is Radka.'

Joseph put out his hand to shake hers, but she came past George and grabbed his hands, pulling him towards her and kissing him on both cheeks. As she did this George watched with an ironical smile, as if he could sense Joseph's unease at being cast in the role of an affectionate brother-in-law. The odd thing, Joseph thought, was that he could already

73

sense the changes in George's mood, and even work out what he was thinking.

'You are just like him,' Radka said, still holding his hands. Her voice had a husky sound, unexpectedly low in pitch. Joseph shrugged. After all, everything that had happened in the last hour had been a shock, and somehow it seemed natural and inevitable that the touch of Radka's hands should be alive, tingling in his nerves like the aftermath of electricity.

They drank vodka sitting round the table. Serge sat opposite Joseph playing with a long thin glass filled with some kind of fruit juice. He was quiet, his eyes round and fixed on the visitor, and Joseph guessed that his English had been exhausted with the single word. Occasionally he asked his mother a question in German.

'He wants to know,' Radka said, 'if you have seen a lion in Africa. Like the Lion King.'

Her eyes laughed at Joseph. They were a light blue, and against the slight tan of her skin they gave her face an exotic reckless look, as if she was making him a dare.

'I saw one once in Africa,' Joseph said. 'But I live in London where they keep the lions in a zoo.'

Radka translated and the boy gave a sharp, 'Ah,' as she said the first bit. His eyes grew wider, glued to Joseph's face.

'My mother wanted to come,' George said suddenly. 'To see you. But her health is not good, you know.'

'She lives in Berlin?' Joseph asked politely.

There were many other questions that he wanted to ask instead, but with Serge's eyes following his every move he felt constrained about challenging George. Looking across at the boy he wondered whether this was what his brother had intended. In the next instant he realised, with a slight shock, that for nearly an hour this had been how he was thinking about George. As his brother.

The first course was a cold beetroot soup, the earthy flavour heightened by the resin taste of the wine. Joseph's head was swimming after his second glass, and he remembered that since they had arrived George had been drinking steadily. It didn't seem to affect his manner, but Joseph could feel his own senses clouding.

'She refused to leave,' George said. 'She lived in the same apartment until the Wall came down. Berlin is her home.'

'And yours?'

George smiled.

'For me change and movement is still possible.'

'Can you come to Berlin?' Radka asked. She took in Joseph's look of surprise. 'Katya was so excited to hear your voice. She wants to meet you.'

'I don't think so,' Joseph told her. 'I'm leaving here in a couple of days.'

'There is a message,' she said, as if she had anticipated his reply.

She'd hardly completed the sentence before George broke in, speaking rapidly in German. Immediately Serge slid off his seat and stood next to Radka, reaching out to hold her hand.

'It is now his bedtime,' George told Joseph.

The boy seemed surprisingly obedient, walking round the table to shake hands with Joseph and then toddling off serious-faced behind Radka.

'There is a message,' George said.

He reached into the breast pocket of his jacket and brought out a lilac-coloured envelope. On the front there were only two words, written in an elegant copperplate script. His father's name – *Kofi Coker*.

Joseph turned the envelope over in his hands.

'You'll give this to him?' George asked.

Joseph was about to say yes, then it occurred to him that in all the time he had been discussing his father with George he had never once considered the effect that this event might have on the old man. If it was true.

'He had a heart attack a couple of years ago,' he told

George. As he said this he felt a curious sense, almost of betrayal, at revealing such an intimate matter.

'He's okay now?'

'Yes,' Joseph replied, 'except I'm worried about how he'll take all this. He's an old man.'

If George understood the hint implicit in his words he ignored it. I'd take no notice too, Joseph thought, if it was my dad whom I'd never seen.

'You must understand this,' George said quickly. 'My mother and father were separated by the authorities. She still loves him. Everyone loved him. He was known to everyone. Even Nikita Khrushchev spoke with him.' He grinned at Joseph. 'Maybe he was not such a great hero as she thinks, you know, but that is what she told me. This is forty years ago. She was fighting the rules when I was born.' He snapped his fingers. 'Regulations. She could have made me never to exist – that would have been easy – or sent me away. But that would have been surrender.' He looked away from Joseph, gazing through the French windows out into the evening sky. 'This was not easy. I lived with a German family when I was a small boy, like Serge. I called the mother my *mutti*. You have two mothers, they told me. What a lucky boy. Then Katya married a German, an important policeman. He wanted to forget me, I think, but my mother insisted.' He chuckled. 'I think he hated me. No one would think I was his son, you know. But I was lucky. Only a few years, then he was killed.' He got up and paced to the window without looking at Joseph. 'My mother still speaks of Kofi, Kofi, Kofi, as if no time has passed. But I think she had believed that he was dead or lost, that she would never see or hear of him again. Then she hears you and her life begins. If she cannot touch him in some way she will die.' He paused. 'She is a woman of great passion.'

He said this last bit with a kind of gloomy pride. In the corner of the room the phone began to ring. George ignored it. The ringing stopped.

'Maybe wrong number,' George said carelessly.

'Could it be your mother?' Joseph asked. Somehow he couldn't bring himself to say her name.

'No. No. We spoke before. She is waiting for me to call.'

The ringing started again. After a while Radka came into the room and picked up the phone. She listened in silence, then held it out towards George. He got up, his face expressionless, took the phone from her, and reeling out the long cord by which it was attached to the wall, went out and shut the door behind him.

It was dark outside now, and before Radka sat down she turned on a standard lamp perched in the corner below the photographs. She had changed her clothes, switching from the sweater and jeans she'd been wearing to a long white dress in some sort of crinkly material, which seemed to wrap around and envelop her body, giving her a comfortable, relaxed air, as if she had slipped it on to illustrate the fact that this was her province in which she was at home. She smelt of flowers – something with a lemony undertone which Joseph couldn't identify. Citrus, but not lemon. Earlier on her hair had been bundled together into a bun on top of her head. Now she had let it down and it rippled in smooth flowing waves, over her shoulders and across her back. In the margin of the pool of light around the lamp, she glowed.

'This is very important to George,' she said. She gazed at him seriously, her eyes intent. 'There was always something missing in his life. Just as his mother's. Being with you is a great experience. Already he loves you.'

Joseph shrugged, too embarrassed to speak. It wasn't so much the idea of what she was saying that disturbed him. It was the fact that she was saying it.

Suddenly he could hear George shouting, a ranting, angry sound. Radka's expression didn't change.

'I put some photographs in the envelope with Katya's letter,' she said calmly. Outside the door George's voice had risen to a roar without eliciting any apparent reaction from Radka. Perhaps it was the language, Joseph thought. To English ears emphatic German speech still carried the sound of a threat. 'She wants to see him,' Radka continued.

The door flung open and George strode in.

'I have to go,' he said without preamble. 'Half an hour.' He pointed at Joseph. 'You wait? Okay?'

Joseph started to object, but before he could find the words George had turned and walked out. Radka got up quickly and went out after him, closing the door behind her. Joseph hovered for a moment, undecided about whether he should get up and follow, but then he heard their voices echoing in the hallway. It sounded like an argument, so he stayed where he was, and in a moment he heard the sound of the outer door slamming shut.

FOUR

'Where are you going?' Radka asked George.

She had followed him out on an impulse which was something to do with Joseph's presence. It wasn't unusual for George to leave the house without explanation, and in normal circumstances she wouldn't have asked. There had been a time when such questions would have seemed impolite or even suspicious, and the old habit of reticence about these matters died hard. But this was different. Seeing it through the eyes of someone who, like Joseph, knew nothing of the way they had lived, George's departure seemed abrupt and strange. In any case, she also felt a sudden surge of resentment at his assumption that he could simply leave her with someone, his brother, who they were both meeting for the first time.

George's hand was on the bolt of the door, but, halted by the tone of her voice, he stopped and looked round.

'It's business,' he told her quickly. 'I have two madmen at the garage who are about to fight each other. The customer is crazy and making a fuss, and the Roma is worse. It won't take long.'

She nodded her head, accepting the explanation. Since the time that he and Valentin had set up business in the city, she'd become accustomed to the eruption of minor emergencies.

'Can't Valentin do it?'

'I don't know where he is.'

She gestured in resignation and let him go, but instead of returning immediately into the room with Joseph, she walked along the corridor to listen at Serge's door. The sounds he made might have been imperceptible to anyone

79

else, but she could tell that he was still awake, reading or playing with one of his toys. Usually she would go in and look at him, kiss him, perhaps, and pick up the toys and books which he left scattered around the floor. On this night she didn't want to take the risk that he would wake up and detain her, so she merely listened. She had intended to go back to Joseph after a few seconds, but, instead she found herself walking on into the kitchen where she stood looking through the window. Her excuse was that she was about to make coffee, but the truth was that she wanted to be alone for a few minutes before facing her husband's brother. She felt restless and disturbed, in need of a breathing space in which to calm the turmoil inside herself.

Reflecting on how she felt, she knew that it wasn't simply to do with Joseph's visit or George's sudden departure. In fact it struck her that it was something to do with the game Serge had been playing as she gave him his bath. There was nothing extraordinary about what he had done, and although it sometimes annoyed her a little she was accustomed to seeing him stretched out in the bath tub, his arms along his sides, his mouth opening and closing. This was how he pretended to be a carp, floating in the water like the giant fish George had brought home just before Christmas and dumped in the tub. During the season there were people all over Prague taking home bundles of carp wrapped in wet paper, or stuffed in dripping parcels. Born and brought up in the city, Radka had found this custom unremarkable until she left it. So there was nothing astonishing about Serge's little game, and he was just as likely to be converted, when she lifted him out of the water, into a roaring lion. On this particular evening, however, she didn't know why, the sight had triggered a memory of her childhood in Prague, which darkened her mood.

It had been twenty years ago, when she was twelve, coming home from school; she had walked past one of the trestle tables which were laid out everywhere on the street corners. This one was on a busy junction and there was a crowd of people jostling round it. On the previous day there had been a heavy fall of snow and the mob of shoppers was like a herd of cattle, their feet stamping and their breath steaming in a cloud round their heads. Over the entire scene hung the raw smell of the fish, but Radka didn't find this unpleasant. On the contrary all the activity gave her a feeling of excitement and anticipation that was associated with the coming festival – the smells, the look of the milling crowd, the tight freezing air. Smiling, she circled round the pedestrians, almost stepping into the road, and stumbling a little as an old woman pushed past her. A few paces further on, she felt something different about her right foot, a wet feeling as if she had sunk into a puddle of melted snow. She looked down and saw the dark stain of fish blood around the toe of her boot, and looking back at where she had walked, she saw that she was leaving a trail of bloody footprints. She scraped at the ground, wiping her boots on the thick carpet of snow, but the pink indentations refused to disappear, following her remorselessly as she ran down the street.

On the landing in front of the apartment where she lived with her mother she stopped and took off the boots before going in. Then, holding them at arm's length, she rushed down the corridor towards the bathroom. The door was open a crack, and she could hear her mother's voice. She'd heard her mother talking to herself before, and eager to wash the blood off her shoes, she shoved the door open. It seemed to stick a little, then it went back, but with difficulty, as if something was in the way. Inside the room, her mother was kneeling by the tub. For a moment, it seemed as if she was playing with the carp which had been floating in the tub for a couple of days, but then Radka realised that the obstacle which had been blocking the door was the same fish wrapped in a wet towel. At the same time she saw that it was her father who was sitting in the tub. As she came in he turned his head and smiled at her. It was a curious smile, tremulous and almost timid as if her entry had frightened him. That was how she remembered him in the period before his death. When she saw him in the bath tub he had been away for two years. On the day he was arrested her mother had told her it was all a mistake, a story which she accepted with relief, but as the weeks and then months wore on she knew that he wasn't coming back. He had been imprisoned, her mother said, not because he was a bad man, but because of something he had written, and for a time Radka's dearest wish was to read his book in order to see, with her own eyes, the appalling thing that had ruined her life. At school no one mentioned her father, but she understood that everyone knew about him by her classmates' ripple of response to certain names, or by the way that some of them turned to look when teachers mentioned saboteurs or threats to the state. That summer was to be her first visit to a pioneer camp, but a week before the event she told her teacher that she would have to stay and spend the vacation with her mother. Afterwards she avoided taking part in most of her classmates' activities, inventing one plausible excuse after another. She knew that her anger was connected with her father and his absence, but after a while she stopped thinking about it, and, when her mother said that he would be coming back soon she chose not to believe it, putting that prospect out of her mind in case it turned out to be yet another deceitful hope. His return was a surprise, but it was his appearance and his manner which shocked her.

Before he had left, he was a broad, powerful man. She seemed to remember his voice booming, and he could still pick her up and hold her high above his head before hugging her against his chest. The man who came back was thin and slouching, with downcast eyes and an apologetic smile. He never recovered his old self. Instead he would shuffle out every morning, clad in neatly pressed blue overalls.

'This is paradise,' she heard her mother say in the kitchen one day as she got up to get ready for school. Her voice had a deep, angry pitch, and Radka could tell she was close to tears. 'A professor sweeping floors.'

Her father didn't answer. When he came out of the door and saw her standing there, he gave her his thin smile and walked past without touching her. He died soon after this, and in later years when the carp began to appear on the street corners Radka would often think of the bloody footprints and of her father's strange smile.

George was the only person she had ever told about the carp. This was when he proposed returning to Prague, and she had held out against it stubbornly while he ran through all the obvious and good reasons why they should. Setting up the business would be easier there, he said. The materials and skills they needed would be more readily available. There would be better chance of success for a business run by a Russian and a black man. In Berlin who knew what would happen? Maybe one night they would wake to find the place burning.

At that point she told him about the carp, and the irrational fear she had always nursed, that the blood she tracked through the snow had somehow been linked to her father's fate. George listened without comment, simply holding her hand and stroking it. Then he told her that their lives might be in danger. After that she surrendered to his will, but some part of her had never forgiven him.

George should have realised, even though she never managed to explain it properly to him, that both she and her mother had somehow been imprisoned along with her father. Before that time she had experienced no problems in seeing herself as a part of every activity at the school and among her friends. At the age of ten she had competed for the Youth Union banner. Her entry was a dramatic recital from Jirásek's rendering of 'The War of the Maidens', and the judges had been taken with the sweetness of her voice and the innocent intensity of her pose as she recounted

83

the massacre of Sharkah's Valley. At the end she threw up her arms, shrilling Jirásek's words: 'Pay attention, men, to this sign from the gods! Hear me, and do not take the warring women lightly.' The hall exploded with applause, and, as her mother always said, she would have won by a kilometre had she not been immediately followed by a nine-year-old who recited, from memory, a long section of the speech Lenin made in Petrograd during 1917. She had left with an honourable mention and the acclaim of her schoolmates, confirming her position as one of the leading spirits in her year. But her father's incarceration changed everything, and when he returned she lost even the secret hope that his presence would restore her life to normal. At first she imagined that her anger was directed at this tattered relic of her dad, who had taken from her what she had without putting anything in its place. Later on, after he died, she understood that the hot rage hidden in her chest was really about the sense that she, too, had been locked into an airless room. This was a perception which had merely grown deeper as she grew older. Berlin had been the key to her escape, the place where, in her mind, she had broken with her own past and begun remaking her future. In Prague she hardly knew anyone now. The friends with whom she had been through school and university were scattered, and her closest relatives, people she had not seen since childhood, were in Pilsen, a few hundred kilometres away. Sometimes she encountered a man or a woman whom she had known well more than a decade in the past; it made her feel more than ever like a stranger in a place which echoed with hidden loyalties and hatreds. Even stronger was the sense that during her childhood she had learnt to prepare a face to meet the faces that she met, a surface which covered in deceit all that she felt. This wasn't merely a question of politics. Her politics before Berlin had been unformed, a matter of resentment and irritation at the restrictions and stupidities about which everyone grumbled. It was more the feeling that she could not be herself, and that she didn't know what it might mean to be exactly the kind of individual she wanted to be. When she left the city she had rejected the numb emptiness she had filled with the diligence of study, sitting night after night with her books while her mother slept. In Berlin, she had thought she would become the person she was meant to be. She always knew that the city was in many ways drabber and life more controlled than the one she was leaving, but she also knew that no one would recognise her there, that the future would be a blank, like a sheet of fresh snow on which her footprints would trace a new, untrodden path.

In this sense she felt her return to Prague as a kind of defeat, a step backwards, and walking in the park with Serge, she felt the memories clouding round her, coupling her again with the self she'd left behind.

Ironically, her work there gave her more time and freedom. In Berlin she'd worked for a magazine, translating documents and articles from Czech and Russian, and assembling diaries about events and attitudes in Eastern Europe from information that she picked up on the Internet. When she left Germany she continued writing, filing her copy by e-mail, but now she made her own schedules and wrote about a broader range of subjects, whatever caught her fancy. Most of it, George told her once, was a kind of therapy in which she explored her own identity, using as raw material the passions and frustrations of people, like herself, who had grown up in the shadow of the Party and its methods. For instance, when a young man in his twenties was appointed as head of Czech broadcasting, the profile she wrote started with a fairly curt biography, then went on to argue that men and women between the ages of thirty and fifty had disappeared from public life because they were all compromised by their past complicity with the system, or incapable of coping with the challenges of a new society. George read it without comment, then he smiled at her.

'I'd agree with this,' he said, 'except that you're defining public life in the same way as the old comrades. Head of this and secretary of that. Everything's changing so quickly that in a couple of years all the people you thought had disappeared might be back.'

She shrugged. When they first met it was the kind of exchange which would have been the signal for a pleasurably heated argument. Now the prospect offered no excitement to either of them.

From time to time he asked her why she felt the urge to be so busy. She was no longer tied to a routine, and now that Katya no longer lived nearby, caring for Serge took up more of her time. Even so, she worked occasionally for a language school where she taught English to businessmen. They had enough money, George would say, and it wasn't necessary. When she didn't answer it was partly because she was convinced that he already understood, and that the question was a provocation whose purpose was to expose the distance between them. In the years since they had come together everything had changed, and now it was as if she hardly knew him.

It was tempting to imagine that this was something to do with the move, but the truth was that after Serge's birth their relationship had been different. When they'd met she was just twenty-one, and George had been beautiful and exotic, curly and dark like a Roma, with a tint of gold under his skin. The odd thing was that seeing Joseph had immediately reminded her of how George seemed at that first moment when she saw him threading his way through the crowd in the Freundschaft Hall at the university. It wasn't so much that they looked alike, although they did. It was something about the way he moved, a slight hesitation in his step, and a kind of wide-eyed boyishness which had long ago disappeared from George's features. Watching him as he walked through the door behind George she had felt for a second or two as if time had spun backwards and she was once again the young innocent making eyes at a golden stranger across the room.

Remembering, she smiled, searching the shadowy image in the glass of the window for traces of the child she had been. She had imagined that George was a foreigner, a student or teacher from somewhere like Cuba or Mozambique. She soon found out who he really was, but the thrill she'd felt in that first instant hadn't gone away. It was true enough that George was different. He was an experienced man, more than ten years older, who had lived through a stint in the army and suffered disappointments at which she could only guess. He also had a contempt for the bureaucracy of politics and administration which Radka shared, and the confidence of his sarcasms and jokes about the system made her feel lighter, almost joyful, as if her isolation was at an end. Like herself, he was an outsider who played by the rules, and kept his feelings to himself, expressing them only within the confines of their mutual privacy. For Radka, being with George was like a final release from the mould in which the first crack had appeared at the time of her father's imprisonment. In their first couple of years they seemed to have been always together, but later on, when she found out more about what George had been doing at the time, she knew that the memory was an illusion, like a magic trick in which he'd caused the truth to disappear.

Her first clue had come on the night they started demolishing the Wall, tearing with their bare hands at the chips and lumps of concrete. It was a moment she remembered like a piece of music, starting slowly then building rapidly to a crescendo. The first notes, distant and piercing, came as they paced along Stargarder Strasse, following the streams of people, sometimes a couple like themselves, sometimes a chattering group of students, or a dozen young men chanting slogans in unison. Up ahead the columns of pedestrians thickened around the bulk of the Gethsemanekirche. Clinging to George she pushed her way behind him into the entrance in the Greifenhager Strasse, and caught up in the eddying movement of the mob, they drifted further and further in, moving, without volition, among the press of bodies as the crowd broke away and headed for the Bornholmer Gate. Around her was the smell of garlic, tobacco and sweat, then strange vagrant streaks, the sweet taste of roses and wine. Walking up Bornholmer Strasse, she linked arms with Peter, whose father had become a drunken closet fascist, and then Wolfgang, who reached under her coat to hug her, his fingers digging into her breast, indifferent in his exaltation to George marching on the other side, and Renate, who clasped her hand tightly, swinging it up and down in the rhythm of their steps. The noise was unbelievable but she didn't hear it. 'The Wall must fall,' they chanted, and all up and down the line people, their spirits fired by the magnitude of the event, were spouting off impromptu bursts of rhetoric. 'Let us go see the Ku'damm,' Peter shouted over at her, 'and then we'll come right back.' Sometimes George looked round at her, laughing, and from time to time they kissed openly, squeezing each other's bodies, more united than they had ever been. She remembered all this as if it had been a drunken roaring dream, oases of clarity alternating with moments of crazed frenzy. At the Wall they shouted, kicked and tore at the crumbling fabric with their hands, tossing the fragments around them like so much rubbish. In one of the moments she remembered, Peter leapt on to a pile of bricks, a few metres from where she stood, and holding up a piece of the concrete, began making a speech, shouting at the top of his voice. 'Tonight!' he yelled. 'Tonight we sweep away all lies, all illusion.'

Turning round she saw George grinning. 'Without a few lies and illusions,' he muttered, 'none of us will survive.'

She'd laughed then, but later on it struck her that this was exactly how it had turned out.

FIVE

They were drinking more vodka. When Radka tilted the bottle the long strand of grass in it wavered like weed in a pond. Joseph tried to count the number of glasses filled with the spirit that he had drained so far, but somehow he couldn't concentrate. The ends of his fingers felt numb. Radka emptied her glass with a long fluent swallow. When she threw her head back the long muscles rippled in her velvet throat. His head spun with drink and the desire to touch her smooth pale skin.

'Perhaps I should go,' Joseph said.

'No.' Radka stretched her arm out along the back of the sofa and put her hand on his. 'Please stay. If you leave now it will be bad for George. And for me. Waiting to see you he has been like a cat on a hot tin roof.' She frowned as if conscious that there was something wrong about the expression. 'No. Cat on hot bricks. Right? You must wait.' Her eyes were fixed on his with an intensity which gave him the sense that there was something more beneath the surface of her words. Something she wanted him to know without her having to say it.

Joseph sat back against the cushions. The truth was that he wanted to stay with Radka so much that the feeling frightened him.

'Tell me about George's mother,' he said.

Radka gestured as if trying to gather the words up out of the air.

'She loves three things in life. Her memories of Kofi, George and Serge. She told me this. Without George she would have been glad to die.' She paused. 'She lives in the past, I think. I don't know if she always did this, but now

89

she speaks to Kofi as if he was there next to her. She talks about what happened during the day and what she thinks about her son, as if he was sitting on the other side of the room. She's not mad. Her brain is still good. She cooks, she cleans the apartment, her appearance is good, she watches TV and she votes. Everything. It is just that her companion is her memory of Kofi.'

Hearing his father spoken of in this way gave Joseph an unpleasant feeling, and he felt the urge to reply sharply, to utter some kind of sarcasm. These people talked about Kofi as if he belonged to them. You know nothing about him, he wanted to tell her. You have no right. At the same time he had the uneasy feeling that somehow he was the interloper. It struck him, also, that his feelings about Kofi had always been ambiguous. 'A slippery customer' was how he had often heard his mother refer to him, and he realised now that this was how he had always thought of his father. Looking back to those times thirty years later he understood that his attitude had largely been shaped by the things his mother had said. 'I threw him out,' she would say to her friends, and, 'I couldn't put up with that shit any more.' Sometimes, overhearing this, he thought that he hated her, but the worst times were when Kofi was late picking him up on Sundays, or when he didn't come at all. His mother would telephone various people, her voice either low and complaining or shrill and angry. Once she had made him telephone a woman who sounded irritable and puzzled when he started asking to speak to his father.

As Radka spoke he was remembering one of these Sundays. Ten years old, he was sitting in the single armchair in Kofi's room. It was somewhere in Kentish Town, facing an adventure playground, where they would usually wander listlessly for half an hour before going back to the room to watch television. In normal circumstances they spoke very little, largely because neither of them could think of anything to say. Kofi busied himself making tea and sandwiches, which Joseph would nibble politely, because although he never said so, he disliked the food his father gave him. Somehow it didn't taste right, and, listening to Kofi bustling about at the end of the room he was flexing his stomach, nerving himself to bite into the thick triangles of floppy white bread.

'I've been there,' Kofi said suddenly, coming up behind him and pointing at the TV. In the picture Joseph half recognised the onion-shaped domes, although he had no idea who the men were, filing across the square in front of it. 'Moscow,' his father said. 'I've stood there. Before you were born. Many years ago.'

Joseph nodded.

'Was it nice?'

Kofi laughed his great roar, a noise which, according to Joseph's mother, used to make people look round and stare in the street.

'Nice – I don't know about nice. It was unforgettable. Very cold. In winter sometimes the snow came up to here.' He pointed to his waist. 'But the people were warm. Passionate.' He paused. 'Those were great days for me. I spoke with Khrushchev.' He peered down at Joseph, trying to read his expression. 'Do you know who Khrushchev was?'

Joseph shook his head.

'He was the Russian leader. Very important man. Maybe if it wasn't for him I'd still be in Moscow.' He put the plate of sandwiches in Joseph's lap. 'Would you like to go there?'

What Joseph wanted to do was to go home, but something about the tone of Kofi's voice told him that this was somehow important to his father, so he nodded.

'Maybe. One day.'

Later on, when Joseph told his mother about this conversation she clicked her tongue with annoyance.

'It's just one of his stories,' she muttered.

Remembering all this, Joseph experienced a quick spike of anger. He wasn't sure why. He wasn't sure, either, whether he was angry with Kofi, his mother, or himself.

'He's not dead,' he said to Radka. 'You talk about him as if he were dead.'

'I'm sorry,' she said quickly, and made a little ducking movement of her head. 'This is how Katya speaks of him.'

Joseph nodded, his anger receding.

'Forgive me,' Joseph said, 'but it sounds a little strange. George said that the authorities separated them. What happened? What did they do?'

She didn't reply for a few seconds. Instead she stared at him openly, her eyes exploring every line of his face. Looking back at her, watching the tiny movements of her pupils, Joseph felt irresistibly drawn, as if she was exercising some hypnotic power over him.

'It was a long time ago,' she said. 'People didn't have to do anything to be sent away. It is hard for someone from the West to understand how it was. You must ask Kofi.'

'I'm asking you.'

She shook her head firmly.

'No. This is their story. Those two people. You should ask them.'

She stared at him with a tinge of defiance, as if declaring that nothing he could do would drag the secret out of her.

'What about you?' he asked. 'Are you allowed to talk about yourself?'

She laughed. An intimate, throaty sound.

'Of course. Ask me.'

She poured more vodka, the bottle rattling against the rim of his glass. As the liquid ran down the side of the glasses and pooled on the table she laughed again. Her senses were as pickled as his own, Joseph guessed.

'How did you meet George?'

'At a recital of African poets in Berlin in '89. I was language student.' Her grammar, Joseph noted, had deteriorated, but that was the only sign that the vodka was having an effect. 'I went there to improve my English.' She giggled. 'I don't know why George attended. He was not a student there. I had never seen him before, and he is bored by poetry. Of course he says that he loves Pushkin, but that is because he's Russian. A special Russian, he says, like Pushkin.'

Joseph guessed she was talking about Pushkin's African origins and he nodded in acknowledgement.

'Afterwards we went to demonstrate at the Wall. In the morning we went to his room and went to bed. We have been together since that time.' Her voice was suddenly sober. 'We were changing the shape of the world.' She paused. Her hand touched his, a light pressure. She grinned at him, signalling the irony. 'You should have been there. It would have made a great movie.'

A stream of images flowed through Joseph's mind, a mob of young people chanting, ecstatic with fear and rage, a row of grim-faced refugees, curling nests of barbed wire. At that moment, as these pictures passed in review, he found it hard to tell whether he had actually seen them on the TV screen or whether he had cobbled them together out of his imagination.

'Tell me about England,' she said. 'It's better than Germany?'

He struggled with the words. His brain felt numb when he tried to think about what to tell her.

'What do you mean?'

She gestured, and gave an abrupt gurgle of laughter.

'For a black man. In Berlin it's difficult. Before unification it was not so bad. Only the Vietnamese had such trouble.' She frowned. 'Maybe I didn't notice because I lived among students. After the end of the Wall everything changed anyway.' She gave him a clown smile, the corners of her mouth arching high up under her eyes. 'You have skinheads in England?'

'They were invented in England. A long time ago. Now they're out of fashion. They don't matter.'

He noted, with a flash of amusement at himself, that he felt a kind of unreasonable pride in saying this.

'But there is no problem for you,' she said. 'You are a director.'

He could tell, by the way she said this, that what she had in mind was something like a director of Hollywood features.

'I'm not that sort of director,' he told her.

A frown momentarily creased her forehead, and spurred on by her puzzlement he explained that he was the first-time director of a small TV documentary. 'It didn't even come out the way I wanted it.'

She frowned again, searching for the word she wanted. 'Censorship?'

'No, it's not like that.'

Now it was his turn to struggle for words, and, slowly, he found himself beginning to talk about his conflict with the producer, and about the way she had frustrated his intentions.

'This is censorship,' she interrupted.

Suddenly he remembered that Radka had lived through times when censorship was backed up by banning or imprisonment. In comparison, his story must make him seem spineless. George would have dealt with it differently, he thought. From the moment they met he had sensed a hard core to his brother's personality which he was certain that he himself didn't possess, and yet George had survived growing up isolated and surrounded by whites. Now he was thriving. His father's comments after the preview flashed through his mind, along with the suspicion that, like Kofi, George would have begun with a clear understanding of who his enemies were and where the lines were drawn. George would have had the guts to say no.

Radka was still frowning at him and he wondered whether she was comparing him with his brother. Perhaps she imagined that his mother had been a woman like Katya, someone who encouraged her son to think of his absent father as a hero. Would Radka understand if he told her now that he had been brought up to doubt the part of himself which he identified with Kofi?

'So,' she said suddenly. 'You are married?'

'I was. We separated.'

Her eyebrows arched and her lips pouted.

'Ah. She was like you?'

'No. She was white if that's what you mean.'

He felt a curious irritation about telling her this.

'It was difficult? To be married to a white woman?'

It wasn't a question, he realised, that anyone he knew in England would have asked him, not unless they were trying to be offensive, and in normal circumstances he would have told anyone who asked to mind their own business. The fact that their presence in a room together could excite hostility or a prurient curiosity was an irritant that he had shared with Liz.

'No. Not really,' he said. 'Other people's behaviour was sometimes difficult. For us it was normal. In the beginning we read the same books, watched the same movies.'

The night they met he'd walked into a pub out of the rain and she'd been sitting with a bunch of students. Two of them were in his seminar group and he'd sat down next to her. It was one of those boring Saturday nights, when no one could afford to go anywhere interesting and they'd all had it with the local clubs, and all that remained was to sit there and talk and get pissed. Just before closing time she had taken his hand and pressed it against her stomach.

In bed later on she told him that their sex was a poem of contrasts, and that it was this contrast between their skins which excited her so much, especially his dick, the darkest part of his body. 'Is that a terrible thing to say?' she asked immediately. He had laughed, partly because the earnest anxiety of her question seemed incongruous. The other reason was that he felt the same about the pale gleam of her flesh and the bright gold fringes of her hair. In a far corner of his mind the sight stirred a distant memory of going into his mum's room at night and seeing her body glowing like this.

'We're not writing an essay together,' he told her, 'and sex isn't about all that boy-next-door shit, and all that courtly love propaganda. It's about the pleasure and excitement we're getting from each other's bodies. Otherwise the human race would have died out long ago.'

In those days it was the one idea in which he had total confidence.

'It was like finding a best friend I didn't know I had,' he told Radka.

'In the beginning,' she repeated thoughtfully. 'The beginning is always good. Yes?'

'Is it difficult for you with George?' he asked.

Asking the question seemed to release something inside him, and in that moment he realised that he was, somehow, jealous of George. He felt a twinge of guilt at the thought, and he wondered whether Radka sensed what he'd been thinking. But she didn't reply. Instead she looked at him, her forehead crinkling as if she was considering her answer. Their eyes met, and he looked away.

'It's very bad now,' she said quietly. She was still staring at him with the same look of serious consideration. 'I'm glad you came.'

The room seemed to have gone silent. Joseph was on the verge of asking what was wrong between her and George, then he remembered that he had only known them for a matter of hours, and there was something more to his silence. It was as if he was standing in front of a dangerous cliff, where to utter one more word would be to step over the edge. His head swirled as he tried to think of something safe to say to her.

'Your family,' he ventured. 'They still live in Berlin?'

She frowned, then she shook her head irritably.

'I'm not German. I was born here in Prague.' This surprised Joseph. He had assumed she was a German. 'My mother was Hungarian. Born near Bratislava. Slovakia.'

'So you're Slovakian?'

She was laughing now at his confusion.

'No. No. No.' She shook her head, her mane of hair swirling round and settling back to spread itself lazily on her shoulders. 'My father is Czech.'

They seemed to have come closer together on the sofa, and as if for emphasis, she tapped lightly with the hand which now rested on his arm.

'Your father's here?'

For some reason he looked around as if expecting her father to walk through the door.

'He died.'

In a flash her expression was sombre. Her forehead creased and her eyes flickered away from his.

'I'm sorry,' Joseph said. He felt as if he was stumbling after her, through a maze of indirection.

'It was a long time ago.' She was silent for a few seconds. On the other side of her profile a red light in the black night sky blinked. On his arm her fingers tightened as she was about to speak. 'He was professor of languages at the university. He wrote supporting the charter in '76. After that they sent him to prison. When he came out they sent him to dig graves in the cemeteries and sweep floors. He was not so old. But after a year, more or less, he was dead.' She sighed, then she turned to face him again. 'He was too brave, I think. Like Kofi. It is not so good to be the child of such men.'

It was odd hearing his father's name in this context, especially when they talked about him as being brave or important. According to Joseph's mother his father used to have an embarrassing habit of boasting about his friendship with famous men and his involvement with affairs of state. She knew that he had been on the staff of his country's consulate, but his claims were so grandiose that she had never known what to believe. He had to understand, she told Joseph once, that black men like his father suffered a series of crippling wounds to their egos, as they grew old in Britain, and were condemned to shabby obscurity. She had meant it kindly, he knew, but the idea had filled him with contempt for these fantasies of power, and when he went to visit his father he had made a point of discouraging him from talking about his past. Hearing Kofi's name now, he was struck, for the first time, by the idea that it was his mother who had been wrong. If this vision of Kofi was correct, his mother must have seen him through the lens of her own narrow experience, and missed the plain fact that his boasts were simply true.

''89 was bad for my mother,' Radka said. 'When we were full of celebration, she was thinking of my father. How happy he would have been.'

She closed her eyes, drew her breath in sharply, and covered her face with one hand. With the other hand she squeezed Joseph's arm convulsively. Her shoulders heaved. He reached up and patted her hand awkwardly. She opened her eyes. The lashes shone with tiny wet beads. She blinked, got up abruptly and walked away, the dress falling back in swirling folds down her thighs. At the window she stood looking out.

'I'm sorry,' she said. 'This is too much vodka. Too much vodka makes me cry. I'm sorry.'

Joseph watched her from the sofa, wondering whether her tears had been precipitated by her memories of past grief or whether he had said or done something to upset her. She'd said that she was glad he'd come, but perhaps she didn't mean it. Perhaps his mere presence had set something off. Perhaps he'd walked into the middle of a row between her and George. Perhaps that was why George had disappeared. For a few seconds he felt at a total loss. He knew nothing about these people or about how they might behave. Perhaps he should have returned to his hotel after the meal. Perhaps he should never have come.

As if in answer to his thoughts there was a jangling of keys outside, and the door of the apartment creaked open, announcing George's arrival. He came swinging through the door, his manner breezy, spreading his arms out towards Joseph.

'Sorry. Sorry. Business never ends. But pain in the ass is over. For now.'

He threw himself on to the sofa in the space that Radka had just vacated, shooting out his legs in front of him. As he sat down Radka turned away from the window, came back to the table, poured a glass of vodka and gave it to George who took it with a brief nod of his head. Joseph avoided looking at her and if George noticed that she'd been crying he didn't comment.

'I think it's time I went,' Joseph said.

George looked round at him, an expression of shock on his features.

'No. This is too soon.' He slapped his hand hard down on Joseph's leg. 'You must stay with me a little longer. We have much to say.'

SIX

'Look there,' George said. 'Václav.'

They were swinging round the corner into Wenceslas Square past the massive statue of King Wenceslas. Joseph had seen it a couple of times already, but he didn't want to disappoint George, who had insisted on taking him sightseeing.

'Jan Palach sat there and burnt himself to death. Then a month later Jan Zajic also,' George said. 'I hate these monuments. All over Europe, in every city, there are monuments to some hero. But all they did was to create terror. Then they put these monsters there to remind you that such things are possible. When I was a little boy I could never bring myself to look these statues in the face. I had the belief that somehow they would recognise me as a foreigner, someone who didn't belong.' He paused. 'Pushkin understood all this. He wrote about Peter's statue, but I think of his poem every time I come here: "The Rider of Bronze". This is what frightened me. "And softly, slowly his face was turning . . ."' He stopped. 'I don't know how to do it in English.'

'In English it's called "The Bronze Horseman",' Joseph told him.

Joseph, weighed down and bewildered by the sheer strangeness of the evening's events had insisted on leaving the apartment, and when George pressed him to stay he said that he had already drunk too much. Radka had wished him good night, her face expressionless, and disappeared. Joseph asked about taxis, but George insisted on driving him home.

'In Prague all taxi drivers are thieves,' he said confidentially. 'Thieves and pimps. I take you to the hotel.'

Once in the car he drove in the opposite direction, towards the centre of the city. He was taking Joseph on a tour, he announced. It would take five minutes.

'No it won't,' Joseph objected.

'All right.' George looked round at him, grinning. 'So? It will take longer.'

In fact it had only taken about five minutes to get down past the statue of Wenceslas. It was close to midnight, but the square, Vaclavske Namesti, which was actually more like a broad avenue flanked by shops and hotels, was crowded with pedestrians. Most of them seemed to be tourists.

'This is a fact of sociology,' George said. 'Twins who grow up separated, marry the same kind of woman, have the same tastes, wear the same clothes.' Joseph thought about Radka. George looked round and grinned. 'Your wife. I think she looks like Radka.'

Joseph hadn't thought about it until that moment, but once he did he had to concede that there was a resemblance.

'No,' he said curtly. 'She didn't.'

George laughed as if he'd said something funny.

'I think so. You love Pushkin, I love Shakespeare. You love Shakespeare, I love Pushkin. I know this.'

'We're not twins,' Joseph told him.

'We're brothers,' George shouted.

'You're crazy,' Joseph said, but in spite of himself he couldn't help being infected by George's high spirits.

'I want you to meet someone,' George said. 'My cousin Valentin. He's Russian.'

Joseph laughed. Suddenly it was as if he had entered a parallel world in which every element was so surreal as to be downright comical.

'You've got no idea,' he told George, 'how weird all this is.'

George looked round, a little puzzled.

'Weird?'

101

'Strange, peculiar, exotic.' Joseph gestured towards the scene outside. 'I'm driving through a city which was behind the Iron Curtain till a few years ago, with a brother I've only known about for a few hours, and he tells me he's taking me to meet his Russian cousin. Yesterday I wouldn't have dreamt that this would happen. It's weird.'

'I think it's weird too, finding you.'

Joseph shook his head vigorously.

'That's not what I mean. None of this would have surprised me much if it had been the USA or South America. Anywhere except Eastern Europe. These are places where you expect to find black people. We're part of the culture, we helped to shape it, we're part of what it is. It seems natural somehow to be there. Out here it's as white as a bowl of milk. That's the way it's always been. You can't imagine how black people can live and grow here. That's what European means. White people.' He looked at George's profile, wondering whether he understood. 'Being here was interesting, but nothing else. Just another country, until you showed up. Now I've got relations who belong here, but there's no way I can feel that someone like me is part of all this. That's what makes it weird.'

A few seconds of silence in the car. They stopped at a traffic light and a clatter of American voices came through the window as a trio of backpackers crossed in front of them, heading for the bright lights of the McDonald's opposite. Across the street Joseph saw a group of men he recognised as having been at the showing of his film that morning. They were conversing animatedly as they walked along and he wondered whether they were talking about the film. At the same time it struck him that during the entire evening he hadn't thought about the reason why he was here in Prague. At any other time his mind would have been occupied with selling the rights or hooking up with a distributor in some new part of the world.

'America,' George muttered. 'I don't like Americans.'

'Have you met any Americans?' Joseph asked him.

George caught the sarcastic note in his voice and gave him a quick glance.

'I've met plenty,' he said. 'My work used to be renting cars at the airport. Because I spoke English.' He paused. 'At school my passion was English. I had an idea that when I met my father we would speak in English.' He sounded amused, but there was an undertone to his voice which made Joseph suspect that there was nothing amusing about the memory. 'Most of the customers were Americans. Some were okay, but mostly they treated you like shit on their shoe. The blacks are bad, too. They call you brother but then the way they act is the same as the whites. They can't believe that there are black men who don't speak the same kind of English. Like them.' He grimaced, his face arranging itself into a caricature, jaw dropping open, eyes rolling. 'Hey man,' he drawled. 'How come you talk like a German?'

It wasn't a very good impersonation, but Joseph smiled in recognition.

'They've said the same kinds of things to me.'

George laughed.

'Imagine the face on one of those guys meeting two brothers, one sounds like a German, the other sounds like an Englishman!'

Joseph laughed with him, warmed suddenly by the sense that he liked the man.

'In England it's different?' George asked suddenly.

The answer was on the tip of Joseph's tongue.

'It feels different,' he said. He pointed. 'Look around you. You're the first black person I've seen here. In England it would be impossible to pass through the centre of a large city without seeing hundreds of black people or Asians.'

In normal circumstances, he would hesitate before describing his nationality, but from the moment he got on the plane he'd been more and more conscious that he thought of himself as English. Climbing into the clouds above Heathrow he had craned his neck, as he usually did, trying to pick out the district of London where he lived. At the customs barrier the Czech inspector had subjected his European passport to a long scrutiny, glancing repeatedly at him and running his fingers over the photograph. Can't you see, Joseph had thought, almost angry, that I'm English?

'Maybe it was like this in England fifty years ago,' he continued, 'but now it's different.' George didn't reply. Looking at his profile, trying to guess what he was feeling, Joseph found himself noting signs of resemblance. How alike we are, he thought, and how little I know about him.

They came to the end of the square, and George turned left to bump over a stretch of paving. A few blocks further on he pulled around another corner and stopped. Then he pushed open the door on his side and turned to look at Joseph.

'Come.'

Joseph hesitated.

'Where are we going?'

'To a café.' George pointed and Joseph saw a splash of light spilling out from under a covered walkway. 'We meet Valentin here. No tourists here. Only Czechs and Romas. You call them gypsies. You'll like it. Come.'

Joseph got out of the car and looked around. Unlike the square the street had the air of gloom and abandonment. The lamps, dim and far between, cast a light so feeble that it seemed to deepen the darkness which lined the street. On the other side he could see the mouths of alleyways which seemed filled with shadows. On the corner two women leant back against the wall, for an instant posing expectantly, then lapsing into indifference as they went past. The thought flashed through his mind that he might be walking into some kind of trap and in a moment George would throw off the guise of brotherhood and reveal his true colours. Then he dismissed the idea as quickly as it had arrived. He would have known if Radka had been lying, he thought. Radka had to be genuine.

The café was smoky and crowded. Along one wall ran a row of high-backed benches. An oval-shaped bar bulged from the wall opposite. They sat in a booth near the back, behind the curve of the bar. George ordered beer.

'What will he say when he hears this news?' he asked Joseph.

Joseph took his time answering. The truth was that he didn't know. It was possible, he thought, that his father wouldn't remember, or perhaps, that for him, the events which Katya remembered with such dedication had merely been a casual episode. Perhaps, he thought viciously, the old man had been doing a dozen Russian secretaries. He wouldn't put it past him.

'I don't know,' he said.

'What kind of man is he?'

Joseph shrugged.

'He's old. About seventy, I think. He and my mother separated when I was young. He used to take me to museums and the cinema. Later on I didn't see much of him. Then my mother died and I didn't see him at all for a while. He lives in a flat by himself.'

It must have been five years ago that he'd got the phone call late at night. He had just put the key in the door. Liz stood behind him, her face set and angry. He couldn't remember now what they'd been arguing about, but that was in the terminal stage when they'd been arguing all the time. He'd picked up the phone intending to tell whoever it was that he'd call them back. Then the cold female voice told him that his father had suffered a heart attack earlier in the day.

At the hospital his father lay in the bed staring at the ceiling. At first Joseph thought he was asleep, then his head turned slowly. For a few seconds it seemed that Kofi hadn't recognised him, then Joseph realised the expression on his face was one of complete indifference.

105

'I will come to London soon,' George said.

His look was speculative, as if he was waiting to be told that Joseph would somehow smooth his way.

'How soon?'

Before George could reply a man loomed up behind him, bent down and slid into the seat. He was African, smartly dressed in a red silk shirt and a check jacket. Joseph stared openly. It was two days since he had seen a black face, apart from George, and seeing the African all of a sudden in this place gave him a kind of shock. Trying to place the man, he discounted the idea that he was Nigerian or Ghanaian. Apart from the style of his clothes, there was a kind of elegance about his bearing which would have been unusual among the Africans he knew. Probably from a French-speaking country, Joseph guessed.

'*Wie geht es*, George?' the African said.

George grunted. He gestured at Joseph.

'*Bruder.*'

The African nodded seriously.

'*Wie geht es?*'

'He's English,' George told him.

Joseph saw the African look up and he sensed a movement behind his chair, but he smelt her perfume before she sat down next to him. She was young; not much more than her early twenties, Joseph thought. Thick black hair, a broad round face, heavy eyebrows, a complexion dark enough to be Indian. She was wearing a low-cut sweater, mesh holdups and a short, tight black skirt. When she sat down the skirt rode up to display the smooth brown skin above her stockings. She saw Joseph looking and grinned cheerfully at him.

'I speak English,' she said.

She put her hand on Joseph's leg, and smiled at him.

'Milena,' George told Joseph, nodding at the woman.

'How is your name?' Milena asked Joseph.

He told her, and she laughed.

'Hey Joe,' she said.

The African said something in German to George and laughed. He got up, went over to the bar and came back with four small glasses. The liquid in them had a yellowish tinge. Milena pressed closer against Joseph, her hand rubbing lightly up and down his thigh.

'*Becherkova*,' George said, lifting his glass.

'This is a drink for ladies,' the African said. He laughed again.

The drink was sweet and so strong that Joseph almost choked as he sipped at it.

'*Haben Sie meinen Leichenwagen?*' the African asked George.

Joseph caught the end of the sentence, and remembered that 'wagen' was something to do with cars.

'So you're a car dealer,' he said.

George burst out laughing.

'Almost, but no. This deal is about hearses. *Leichenwagen*. Arnaldo is buying hearses. He's a businessman from Angola.'

'You're an undertaker?' Joseph asked.

The Angolan shook his head, smiling.

'Importer. In Angola there's a big demand.'

'We convert,' George said, before Joseph could ask the question. 'This is my business with Valentin. We take vans and estate cars, make them into hearses, then we sell them. Very cheap. You can buy six from us for the cost of one new transport. Arnaldo makes a big profit.'

'Where is the Russian?' Arnaldo said in a complaining tone. 'He promised me two days ago, but I can't find him. When I go to the garage the gypsies say he's coming. But I don't see him. Tonight you tell me to come here. Okay. He's not here. Every day is costing me money, I should have gone to Holland.'

George held up his hands in a placatory gesture.

'You would have had to pay them double,' he said. He turned to Joseph. 'You see? This is the problem. This is why I had to go to the garage tonight. Arnaldo was

107

there making a big noise, but there is nothing I can do. Valentin went across the border to buy parts and we have to wait.'

The African muttered something insulting about Russians, but Joseph hardly heard him, because his attention had been distracted by what Milena was doing. Under the table her hand had been searching for his erect penis and when she found it she held on and squeezed.

'You like me?' she whispered.

Joseph put his hand down and held hers. She shifted, pulling his arm round her waist, trapping it behind her body. She put her other hand back under the table and stroked him gently.

'I want your banana,' she said. She grinned at him. Joseph was startled into laughter. 'Banana, banana,' she chanted softly into his ear.

On the other side of the table George was looking at him with something speculative in his gaze, as if trying to gauge his reaction. Meeting his eyes Joseph suddenly recalled seeing Radka for the first time as he entered George's apartment, and he began shifting along the seat, trying to pull away from Milena.

'Here is Valentin,' George said.

For some reason Joseph had expected Valentin to look like a construction worker, a tough guy with a five o'clock shadow. In contrast, the man threading his way through the tables was dressed in a smart dark suit, a light-blue shirt and a matching tie. When Joseph offered his hand Valentin clasped it in both of his.

'Joseph, Joseph, Joseph,' he intoned soulfully. He looked at George and Joseph in turn, his head switching dramatically from side to side, a curl of tow-coloured hair flopping over his forehead as he did so. '*Bruder, bruder.*' He gestured at them. 'Good. Good.'

'I've been looking for you three days,' Arnaldo said, breaking in abruptly.

Valentin scowled for an instant, his jaw tightened and his

eyes squinted. Then he grinned broadly and swung towards the African. He spread his arms.

'Mr Arnaldo,' he exclaimed. 'Good news. We deliver tomorrow.'

'You told me that four days ago,' Arnaldo answered. 'If I don't see you tomorrow it's finished and I go to Holland.'

Valentin's mouth worked as he struggled for a reply in English. Then he gave up.

'Tomorrow. Tomorrow,' he said heartily. 'You come.' He looked at the gold watch which glittered on his wrist. 'Ten o'clock. You come.' He glanced over at George and nodded. 'Now we go.'

Without pausing he turned and made for the door. In the same moment George stood up.

'Let's go,' he told Joseph.

Milena had his genitals in her grip and he reached down to prise her fingers away.

'You have dollars?' she whispered into his ear.

Joseph fumbled in his pocket. He had changed his money for US dollars at the airport, and he still had most of the twenties they'd given him. He gave one to Milena, and she took it without looking. Instead she kissed her fingers and put them to his lips.

'Come again. Come to Resslova.'

After the café the street seemed even darker and more threatening than before. Valentin was carrying a big cardboard box and they walked in single file on the narrow pavement, footsteps echoing off the thick brick walls of the buildings. Opposite where George had parked the car was a building faced by a group of statues, still cast in the heroic manner of socialist realism, an assortment of tools and implements jutting from their upraised fists, poised as if about to take flight from the first floor. Emerging from the dark sky above him, they had a lowering air of menace, as if it would only take a word for them to come alive and launch themselves at him.

Valentin sat in the front seat next to George.

'What is Resslova?' Joseph asked.

'A street. It goes to Jiraskuv Bridge. This is where you find Milena.'

'Who is she?'

'Roma. From Romania. Same thing. Her brother works for us, fixing the cars. She works for herself. On the street.' He chuckled. 'You like her?'

Talking about her made Joseph remember the feel of her hands on him. He shifted in his seat and tried commanding his erection to go away.

'Not much,' he replied.

George chuckled again as if he could read Joseph's mind.

'This is the city of Faust,' he said. 'The Faust House is near Resslova in Karlovo Namesti, Karlovo Square. They say that a student lived there. He found gold and had a good time, gambling, drink and women, but he didn't know the price until the devil came and took him away. In this city you have to be careful of your soul.'

He chuckled again, enjoying the story. Valentin had been listening, his expression blank, frowning, unable to follow the English phrases, and now he twisted round, his expression serious, and spoke in German. Joseph didn't understand a word.

'What's he saying?'

'He says he is very pleased to see you, because we're so much alike. It's like having another cousin.'

Valentin grinned broadly and reached over to pat Joseph on the shoulder. George laughed out loud.

'He says that he is sorry to take you away from the café, but he has just come back from Switzerland and he's very tired. He says that if we had stayed in that place for one more minute he would have killed that African.'

He grinned at Joseph as if to make sure that his brother recognised this was a joke.

'He went to Switzerland for car parts?'

George stopped grinning, giving it a tiny pause before he replied.

'There was other business.' He hesitated. 'There are some things you can buy here, but some parts for the engine, only Germany.'

They were crossing another bridge. To the right Joseph recognised the lights of the Charles Bridge glowing along the river, and it struck him that his hotel was on the other side of the town.

'Where are we going?' he asked. 'I thought you were taking me back.'

'Sure. We take you back. First we go to Smichov. We must see the hearses and give Milos the parts so that he can do the work.' George twisted round and winked at Joseph. 'If not Arnaldo will be angry and Valentin will kill him. Don't worry. Five minutes.'

Joseph felt a sudden spike of irritation. He hadn't asked to see the things, and he wanted nothing more than to get back to his hotel and be alone.

'You wanted to know about my business,' George said, reading his mood again. 'I show you. Don't worry. This is,' he hesitated, '*rechtmässig*.' He glanced round at Joseph, searching for the right word in English. 'Legitimate business.'

There was a note of pride in his voice, and it occurred to Joseph that George wanted to show his new-found brother how well he was doing.

'You only make hearses?' he asked.

'No, no. This is a big market. Everywhere they need specialist transport, hearses, small buses and trucks, water carriers, containers. These are very expensive to buy in from Western Europe, and no one here makes them. When we came here one year ago we bought an old factory in Smichov, and now we take cars, vans, anything that still runs and convert them for special use. We sell them very cheap.'

'You're a mechanic?'

111

It seemed a bizarre idea.

George laughed.

'No, no. I make deals. This city is full of mechanics looking for work – Romanians, Bulgarians, Poles, Russians. Labour is cheap.'

So much for his suspicion that George was some kind of gangster. At the same time it crossed Joseph's mind that his brother was actually a species of scavenger, up to his elbows in the castoffs of the Western world.

Now they were passing through a street lined with what looked like factories and workshops. It was a few minutes since Joseph had seen another vehicle, and, in the middle of a city, the shadowed vista of empty streets had an eerie, melancholy feel. He glanced at his watch. Two o'clock. Wrapped in darkness and silence the deserted buildings loomed around them, the windows glittering in the reflected light of the Jaguar's headlamps, like the secret gleaming of hooded eyes.

George turned another corner and swung in through an open metal gate. Beyond the gate was a big square box of a building. It looked like a pile of concrete blocks slung together and Joseph guessed that it couldn't be more than thirty years old. Even so the plaster which made up the façade was already crumbling, and on one corner he could see a nest of iron rods sticking out at an angle.

The Jaguar came to rest in a maze of vehicles jumbled together on the strip of tarmac which ran between the factory and the iron railings facing the street. The cars were too many for Joseph to count. As he got out he recognised a few Ladas, but the yard seemed to be filled with every make that he'd ever seen. Their condition varied, a few were brand new, others were crumpled wrecks standing on blocks, waiting, he guessed, to be cannibalised for their parts.

A flood of light was streaming from the open garage doors at the front of the building, and Joseph followed Valentin and George as they walked towards it. Inside there

112

were more cars, mostly arranged in neat rows. In the far corner a transit van was perched up on a lift, wires dangling from its exposed underbelly. Along the walls wheels and tyres were stacked precariously. Everything was still and silent, as if the scene had been frozen in the middle of a working day.

Valentin walked towards the stairs near the entrance. They led to a platform which ran along the wall, beyond which was a cubbyhole of an office. The lights were on, but there was no one to be seen through the grimy windows. Valentin, standing at the bottom of the stairs, called out, but there was no answer.

'There should be a guard here,' George said irritably, 'for security, and they should be working.'

Joseph looked around. Next to him was a short line of what looked like transit vans, but they had been resprayed in black, the side panels removed and replaced with glass. These were the hearses, he guessed.

Valentin came away from the stairs. He came past them and made a gesture, putting his hands together and resting his cheek on them.

'Sleeping,' George muttered.

They began walking along the rows of vehicles, peering in and opening doors. Joseph stayed where he was, slumped against the wall, almost too tired to take in what was happening. Five minutes, he thought. It was clear now that when his brother said five minutes he really meant a matter of hours.

Suddenly he heard Valentin shout, the urgency of his tone jerking him into wakefulness. At the other end of the room George was running, threading his way through the cars at speed. Joseph pulled himself away from the wall and followed, charting a course to the point where he could see the top of Valentin's head. When he got there he emerged into a sort of clearing where the cars had withdrawn into a rough circle surrounding a gleaming limousine, doors open, the headlamps still glowing. Valentin and George were standing in front of the car, but they were staring at a heap of blue overalls on the floor at their feet. They'd found the staff, Joseph thought, drunk again, and in his head he framed a mocking remark about cheap labour. Then he saw the puddles of blood staining the floor all round the figure. Some of it had mingled with the grease and oil which covered most of the surface, and it shone like a dark red lacquer. Then George moved, looking back at him, and he saw the head, carefully perched at the end of the bonnet, hair stiff and plastered close to the skull with blood. The skin of the man's face was dyed the same lurid strawberry colour, and for a moment, Joseph felt that he was looking at some kind of exhibit in a gallery, a representation of death. Then his head whipped round away from it and his stomach turned over. He started walking blindly away, and he felt George's hand gripping his elbow.

'Wait.'

George pushed him against one of the cars and they stood in the silence, listening. Valentin crept softly past them, the gun in his hand pointing ahead of him. The image of the head kept running through Joseph's mind. The eyes had been open, staring, the mouth snarling. A thought struck him and he turned to ask George whether this had been Milena's brother, but as he moved George's grip tightened and he put his finger to Joseph's lips.

It could only have been a few minutes, but to Joseph it seemed like an eternity before they heard Valentin calling out. George let go of his arm, and they walked towards the entrance where Valentin was standing upright, staring at the maze of cars and vans in the yard, the gun was still dangling by his side. As they approached he spoke to George in a quiet tone.

'There's no one here now,' George told Joseph, 'I take you back to your hotel. Valentin will take care of this.'

Later on Joseph felt like a fool for asking the question, but it was the first thing that popped into his head.

'Are you gangsters?'

George frowned, and when he answered his voice seemed to have grown harsher and deeper, throbbing with an undertone of anger.

'No, mister film director,' he said. 'We are not gangsters. We are just businessmen. That is all. Businessmen.'

SEVEN

Joseph was still drowsy with sleep when the telephone rang. He had spent an uneasy night, punctuated by dreams of terror, but after the night sky had begun turning grey, he had fallen into a black hole from which he emerged with reluctance, fighting the echoes of pain and anger which the buzzing of the telephone triggered in his head.

It was a woman, and for a moment he wondered whether he had missed a session that he had been scheduled to attend at the festival, then he recognised Radka's voice and he was wide awake, his thoughts snapping back to the events of the previous night.

'Can you meet me today? We have to talk.'

'I don't know,' Joseph told her, 'I'm leaving this afternoon.'

He'd had a vague idea about staying for another day and taking a tour round the city, but after what had happened at the factory in Smichov he was determined to get away as soon as possible. His nightmares had been full of visions of the severed and bloody head, and even now, in the full light of day, it was as if a bloodstained curtain had fallen across his memories of the night. This was an almost physical sensation which had been with him since he'd emerged from the open mouth of the building and stood beside Valentin, his eyes searching the menacing shadows which shrouded the jumble of hulks in the yard.

Remembering the moment, it was as if he had been lost in the shock and horror of what he'd seen.

'Come on.'

George had walked past him into the dark, and Joseph hurried to catch up. As the car drove through the gate he looked back. Valentin had closed the garage doors, extinguishing the light. In the darkness all that remained visible was the square outline of a sombre block poised against the night sky. Joseph made a conscious effort to slow down his breathing and relax, but now he was safe, speeding away from the butchery he'd seen, his hands started to tremble. His right forefinger twitched, a tiny movement imperceptible to anyone else, but he clenched his fists and concentrated, trying to bring his body under control.

'Who was that man?' he asked.

'Milena's brother.'

Joseph searched his memory of the ghastly red features for a resemblance, then realised what he was doing and tried to put it out of his mind.

'What will Valentin do?'

'He'll telephone the police and tell them.'

'Shouldn't we have stayed?'

'No,' George said. 'Better we go. Unless you wanted to stay in Prague for much longer. Better if you leave today.'

In any other circumstances Joseph would have left it at that. George was a stranger again, and it was obvious that he didn't want to talk or explain matters further.

'What do you think it was?' he asked. 'A robbery?'

George shrugged.

'Maybe.'

'Burglars don't usually cut people's heads off,' Joseph said, 'and neither of you seemed very surprised.'

George shrugged again, and his expression didn't alter, but Joseph saw his hands move on the wheel.

'Maybe it's some kind of protection racket,' Joseph ventured recklessly, 'the Russian mafia.'

This time George looked around, a quick glance, his forehead creased in an irritable frown.

'Russians don't do that. If they want to kill they shoot you and walk away.'

With that outburst George seemed to think that he had settled the matter, and they made the rest of the journey in silence. By the time he pulled up in front of the hotel, however, his mood had changed.

'I'm sorry for this problem,' he said, turning to face Joseph, putting his hand out to touch his shoulder. 'This was not a good ending to our first meeting. Next time will be better.'

Joseph clasped his hand without speaking, then scrambled out of the car, frozen by the embarrassing sense that he did not know quite how to respond. He believed now that George was his brother, but he also felt a swelling tide of resentment at being catapulted into a relationship and a situation for which he hadn't been prepared. At the same time, looking at George, he had the feeling that, without knowing it, he had been searching for him all his life. Waking up the next morning, he had realised in a moment of instant clarity that the shadow in his mind was to do with his worry about George and whatever trouble he was in.

'We can meet this morning,' Radka's voice said. 'Now, if you like.'

Joseph looked at his watch. He would need to check out by noon, but that still gave him a few hours.

'Come to Zizkov,' she said when he muttered his agreement.

'Why don't you come here?' he broke in. 'I don't know where that is.'

'No, better if you come there. No one will see us in Zizkov. Take a taxi, and tell the driver you want to go to the church of St Cyril and St Method underneath Narodni Památnik, the national monument.'

'I've been there.'

'What?'

She sounded startled.

'On Resslova.'

Now she sounded impatient.

'No, no. That is the cathedral. Zizkov is where you must go. It is a church of the same name. Tell the driver Zizkov.'

She repeated the instructions carefully, and after he told her that he understood she hung up without giving him the chance to ask what it was she wanted to talk about or why it was important that they shouldn't be seen together.

He picked up the phone and dialled Kofi's number in England. He had meant to make the call when he got back from dinner with George, but he had been too disturbed to contemplate waking the old man in the early hours. Now there was no reply, and he guessed that his father had already left the flat. It was the routine with which he had become familiar in recent years. Kofi would get up early and set out for a nearby café where he breakfasted on a cup of tea and a bacon sandwich. Then he would walk to the public library where he perused the newspapers one by one. After that he would ensconce himself in the reading room, surrounded by reference books, and sit writing careful notes. This was a preparation for the autobiographical journal which he had been writing for the last ten years, and in his bedroom there was a pile of exercise books stacked against the wall, all of them filled with his perfectly formed, rounded handwriting.

Joseph had wanted to speak to his father before leaving Prague, but now he knew that Kofi wouldn't be back till mid-afternoon when it was time for a nap, and by then he would be high in the skies, halfway to England. He banged the phone down, feeling a snap of irritation at the thought that he would be meeting Radka again without having had a chance to hear Kofi's side of the story.

In the taxi the driver, a spotty youth with thin blond hair, switched on a Motown tape and began humming along to the music. He glanced over his shoulder at Joseph.

'American?'

Joseph shook his head.

'English.'

The driver raised his eyebrows in surprise, then his lips peeled back to display a set of rabbit teeth.

'Premier football. Manchester. Mitchell Owen.'

He raised his hand in a thumbs-up gesture, and Joseph tried to think of the name of a Czech footballer, but he couldn't remember any, so he contented himself with nodding and grinning inanely before turning to look out of the window.

They had crossed the river and were going downhill along a narrow, bustling street. In comparison with the medieval stone and plate glass of the city centre, the buildings here were fairly recent brick and plaster. Beyond the façade of the street he could see the tops of high-rise towers. Zizkov, Joseph thought, reminded him of the East End in London.

Within a few minutes the taxi swung off the main road into a cul-de-sac, which ended in a pedestrian walkway facing a courtyard of cobbled stones in front of the old stone church.

At first he didn't see Radka because his eyes were fixed on the hill which towered above the church. On the top was an oblong brick building which he guessed was some sort of tomb, flanked by a giant statue of a man on a horse. Joseph had seen plenty of statues in the last few days, but there was something ominous about this one which put him in mind of what George had said about monuments. Even at a distance the man on the horse looked as if it would only take a word to get him spurring straight down the hill, his angry sword slashing. At the bottom of the slope, Joseph could feel his presence like a vibration in the air.

'Jan Zizka,' Radka said. She had approached without his noticing until she was close enough to touch. 'The Hussite general. A Czech hero. He invented the use of wagons in war. Like tanks.'

Everywhere I go in this country, Joseph wanted to tell her, there's a monument to violence. A bunch of dead losers, he thought irritably, then he stopped himself short, puzzled by the intensity of his reaction. Perhaps it was, he reflected, that the rhetoric of the monuments was an angry, mournful counterpoint to everything he saw.

She was dressed all in black. Tight black trousers, a black silk shirt and a short black jacket. She put her hand on his arm and he hesitated, uncertain how to greet her, but she leant forward to kiss his cheek.

'I'm not going up there,' he told her, nodding at the hill.

She smiled and squeezed his arm.

'Let's walk,' she said.

The houses in the corridor between the church and the hill were red brick terraces, which looked postwar but were already dilapidated.

'There are many Romas in this district,' Radka said. 'They built houses for them here.'

As if to provide an illustration, a dark-skinned couple leading a toddler by the hand came round the next corner and walked past on the opposite side of the street. Automatically, Joseph raised his hand in greeting. The man smiled and waved back at him.

'A habit I picked up from my father,' he told Radka.

In the old days, Kofi used to say, when he first came to Europe, black faces were such an unusual sight that they would greet each other in the street like long-lost brothers. He had met many good friends that way. In London, where Joseph had grown up, there were so many black faces that the custom had been redundant for a long time. Even so, seeing the dark skins and the black Indian hair of the Romas, Joseph had felt the strange leap of kinship about which his father had spoken.

'What happened last night?' Radka asked suddenly.

'Nothing much,' he answered. 'We went to a café. Didn't George tell you?'

He was playing for time. If George hadn't told her about discovering the decapitated corpse, he must have had a reason. To blurt it out now would be disloyal.

121

'George tells me only what I need to know,' she said. 'He talked about you, but I knew there was something else. He said he might go away for a while.'

'I think you should ask him about it,' Joseph told her.

They came back round to the front of the church and Radka pointed to a café in the cul-de-sac which led up to it. They sat at a table on the pavement, and Joseph ordered American coffee. He was facing away from the monument, but he could still sense it behind him, like a tiger waiting to spring.

'There was another reason I wanted to see you,' she said.

The American accent of her English was more noticeable than it had been the previous night. She was wearing the same scent, and he turned his face away from her, almost in fear that the look in his eyes would reveal his secret longing to touch her.

'When you see Kofi,' she continued, 'persuade him to come to Berlin. For Katya.'

The request gave him a shock. He had almost forgotten about Katya, and, remembering, he felt again a slow burn of resentment at the way Radka and George spoke about him, as if, somehow, he belonged to them.

'I don't know,' he told her. 'He's an old man, and maybe he won't want to do that.' Her eyes widened as if he'd said something that upset her, and he realised that his voice had sounded curt and dismissive. 'What I mean is this – put yourself in his position. He last saw Katya over forty years ago. Now she reappears with a son he's never seen or heard of. It's going to be disturbing and he'll need some time to think about it. I don't think he'll want to go rushing off to Berlin.'

In the back of his mind was the shock that the old man would experience when he heard the news. There was something else too, a niggling thought he struggled unsuccessfully to suppress. Perhaps his father would sense his own strength in George. In Kofi's company Joseph

122

usually felt pale and insubstantial, his responses strained, almost as if he was always standing at arm's length. Liz had always commented on the distance between them. 'You're so cold towards him,' she'd said once. 'That's because he's so fucking warm,' he'd replied savagely. Somehow he knew that George would be different with the old man. He'd probably hug him and drink with him and match Kofi's interminable flow of stories with his own, and he'd stand on the street shouting with laughter. If it was possible, Joseph thought, that these people would never turn up again he would forget about them and say nothing to his father. But he couldn't take that chance. If Kofi found out that Joseph had concealed all this from him it would seem like a betrayal.

Radka's gaze was speculative, weighing him up.

'I wasn't thinking about rushing,' she replied. 'Her birthday is soon. We'll be going to spend it with her. Perhaps we could all meet in Berlin then? It would make her very happy.'

I don't care, Joseph thought, she's nothing to do with me.

'I'm not sure that's the best idea,' he said. 'Even if I could persuade him. Why don't you and George come to London and bring her with you?'

'She won't come, and George won't come without her.' She paused, a little frown of puzzlement creasing her forehead. 'She thinks that he won't want to see her.'

'I thought she was always going on about him?'

Radka hesitated.

'Maybe something happened between them, some quarrel.'

'Forty years ago?'

She shrugged.

'Maybe it's because she was young and beautiful when she saw him last. Now she's afraid of what he'll think. Maybe. I don't know, but she won't come unless she knows that he wants her.'

123

'That makes it difficult,' Joseph replied. 'You're asking me to persuade him to do something that she won't do. I don't think I can. I'm sorry, but I don't think I want to.'

This was what he'd wanted to say in the first place, and he felt a kind of relief at coming out with it. She was frowning, and now she leant forward to come closer, a note of urgency sounding in her voice.

'You don't understand,' she said. 'I want you to do it for George.'

For some reason, Joseph thought about his mother. This was the sort of problem in which she would have expected Kofi to be involved and had she been alive she would have spoken of it with an undertone of wounded triumph. He was sure that she would have known nothing about Katya, and if she had she would have relegated her to the faceless army she described as 'your father's women'. The phrase reminded him suddenly that he had grown up feeling an extra edge of anger about Kofi's absence in his thoughts. Somewhere in his childish imagination, he remembered, he used to have an image of his father lolling in a room hazy with smoke and the smell of perfume, a crowd of half-naked women stroking his supine body. Such notions had faded from his mind as he grew older, but when he thought of escorting his father to meet Katya, an echo of his mother's indignation surfaced.

'Since I met you and George,' he said coldly, 'all you've talked about is Katya and how she feels and what George wants. I don't suppose it occurs to you that my father might have feelings about this too? Or me?'

She stared at him, her face set and pale, and he wondered whether she was about to lose her temper. Suddenly her eyes blinked and he saw that the lashes were wet.

'I'm sorry,' she said. Her voice quavered. A tear ran down her face. 'You are right. I was only thinking of myself. I thought you could help us.'

She got up abruptly and began walking away. Joseph sat, watching her go, dumbstruck by her reaction. Up to that moment, he realised, he'd had the feeling that it was necessary to be on his guard; that somehow, all this was a kind of swindle he had not yet begun to understand. Now it was dawning on him that he was the one who had been thinking only of himself.

By the time he reached her she was unlocking her car, a dark-blue Opel parked on the corner, and when she heard his footsteps she stood still without turning, her fingers curled round the handle of the door.

'I'm sorry,' he said quickly. 'Let's talk about this. I don't understand why it's so important.'

She was drying her eyes with quick, efficient movements, and when she spoke her voice was controlled and matter-of-fact.

'I want to get away from here. To live in England. I want Serge to live a normal life. Here it's not possible. In England it's better.'

'It's not that good in England,' Joseph told her.

She gave him a wry smile.

'I know that, but here he is the only one of his kind. Maybe there are others, but not enough to be normal. It might be different if my parents were alive, but there is no one here for him. When he was growing up George felt like a freak.' She turned her head away, gazing out into the distance. 'Nothing has changed. I don't want Serge's life to be like that. In England there is Kofi,' she hesitated, 'and you, and many other people like him. It's better.'

It was on the tip of Joseph's tongue to tell her that her expectations of himself and Kofi were unrealistic, but he choked the words back.

'What does George think about this?'

'Maybe he would go if it wasn't for Katya. He's very loyal to her.' She said this with a slightly bitter twist. 'She will not leave, and he will not leave her.'

'Give it time,' Joseph said. 'Maybe you can persuade them.'

'There's no time!' she burst out impatiently. 'This might be the last chance for George and me.'

So that's it, Joseph thought, she wants to talk about George, and I'm the lightning rod.

'What's the problem?' he asked her.

'About four years ago we almost separated. I stayed because of Serge. I thought that later on life would be difficult for him. To take him away from his father would have made things worse. It would have been like Katya.'

Behind the sympathetic mask he'd assumed, Joseph felt a twinge of disappointment at the thought that the mystery amounted to little more than the fact that George had screwed another woman.

'He loves you, I think,' he told her. 'And Serge. Very much.'

'Oh, love,' she said sadly. 'Sometimes love is not enough.' She smiled at him. 'Now you're thinking I'm crazy.' She shook her head. 'You can't imagine how different it used to be here. Everything was corrupt, even love.'

'You're right,' Joseph said. 'I can't imagine it.'

'You've heard of the Staatssicherheitsdienst?' she asked abruptly.

'The what?'

'The Stasi. The secret police.' She made a helpless gesture. 'When we met, George was working for them. Just an informer. He was giving them information about me and my friends. He told them things like I had copies of *Sputnik*. This was a banned magazine. He told them about the meetings we went to. It's all in their files.'

'How do you know this?'

'My best friend at the university was a student named Renate. She works for the government in Berlin. I wanted to read my Stasi file. I was sure that there must be one about me. Then she told me about George. This was four years ago.'

'Was it true?'

She smiled bitterly.

'Yes. This was a confession. She knew I would find out she had been fucking with George all the time. Maybe that wasn't so bad, but she was also making reports about us.' She laughed. 'It was funny. While she was informing them about us, George was informing them about her. This was how we lived.'

Joseph watched her, tongue-tied. He hadn't the slightest idea what to say. Instead he wanted to put his arms round her and comfort her, but just as he was about to reach out and take her hand, she turned away as if she'd read his thoughts and intended to reject his sympathy.

'That wasn't why I wanted to leave. I didn't blame George too much. It was hard for him to resist, and when it started he didn't know me. Before I found out, I wasn't afraid. After that I knew he wasn't the person I thought him, and now I think he resents my judgement. I understand that too. Everyone did what they were told. There were no heroes. I can't blame George for not being different, but I do.'

'All that is over,' Joseph told her. 'I don't think you have to worry about the secret police any more.'

'There are other things to worry about,' she said. 'George is in some kind of trouble he doesn't tell me about. It's something to do with Valentin and their business deals. Before we came here he said they were being threatened by gangsters. It was very bad. He got a couple of bodyguards. We were guarded everywhere we went. He was more frightened than in the days of the Stasi. Then we came here and it seemed that it was over.' She gave him a quick sidelong glance. 'Until last night.'

'Why don't you ask him about it?'

'I'm afraid he won't tell me. That would make things worse.'

'I don't know what I can do,' Joseph said.

He was out of his depth. Suddenly the bright empty square seemed full of menace, and involuntarily he looked round through the rear window of the car, as if to check whether there was anyone there, waiting.

'If we can bring Kofi and Katya together,' she said quickly, 'there is a chance that we can all get out of here. I think nothing will change while we're here. Too much has happened. Too much history. To begin again we must leave.'

It was the hope of millions, Joseph felt like telling her. All the migrants he had ever encountered nourished this desire for new beginnings. Most of the time they were disappointed. He thought about his father. At this moment he would be sitting in the library turning the pages of his exercise books, writing the obscure tale of his secret life. What would he make of Radka?

He reached out and took her hand, and she clasped at him with a quick warm pressure. Her eyes pleaded.

'I'll try,' he said. 'I really will try.'

EIGHT

DIARY OF DESIRE

The life and times of Kofi George Coker
MOSCOW 1956

What I remember best is the wind. Moscow is a flat place. In those days, coming from the airport you could probably see all the way up Leninsky Prospekt into the heart of the city if your eyes were good enough. There was nothing in the way, and nothing to stop the wind. I don't know where it came from, but it blew without stopping during those months in the autumn of 1956 when I first arrived. It blew like knives flying, like something that circled and searched, trying to suck the heart out of your chest and the flesh off your bones, and all the time the sky got darker and greyer with every day that brought the first snows closer.

In those first days, sitting around in the big downstairs room in the hostel at Noviye Cheryomushki where all the students were sent to learn the language (so they said), we talked about it. Whatever other topics of conversation we were pursuing the wind would always come up sooner or later. One of the boys, a Zanzibari named Hussein, said once that this was why all the old churches and other prominent buildings were topped by the round onion-shaped domes, because it was the only shape that would withstand the wind. If they had those needle-shaped Gothic spires you see in the rest of Europe, he said, the whole damn thing would go flying off.

Those were the very first days when we talked without suspicion or purpose. There were boys from everywhere, mostly British colonies, although there were some from French-speaking Africa too, but English was the language we spoke among ourselves, even the Somalis and Ethiopians. Russian boys lived there too, although one or two would always correct you if you called them Russian, because they were from the Soviet Republics, not from Russia itself. My roommate Valery was one of them, a Ukrainian. He was training to be an engineer, and thirty years later when I heard about Chernobyl a picture of him came back to me immediately, flashing past me over the snow-covered slope on Leninsky Gory, or huddling on his bed, the book open over his blanket-covered knees, that funny little smile on his face. He came from the marshes and forests to the north of Kiev, he had said, and knowing how clever and ambitious he was I was certain that if there had been a major engineering project like that happening in his home country he'd have been there. That night I sat up until dawn, drinking Scotch whisky and remembering those times. I always trusted Valery, and I still believe I was right, even though, towards the end, it seemed that he had betrayed my trust. But it was his country, he had to live with the consequences, and he did what he had to do.

As far as we knew then, Valery had come by the same route as most of the other boys: a scholarship to study in Russia awarded by the local party. Nowadays when I talk about shaking hands with Khrushchev or Mikoyan or even about arriving in Moscow in 1956, people look at me as if I had suddenly grown two heads. Sometimes this makes me laugh; but sometimes I can see a certain look in their eyes and I can tell from the sound of their voices that they're humouring me, as if I was a foolish old man telling crazy stories. Ignorance. They forget, or mostly they don't know about those days just before the decade of independence, when higher education was something that happened abroad at the LSE or Oxford. Russia was only two steps away. It was true that having to learn a new language was piling difficulty on top of the strangeness, but many of us already spoke two languages, English being the official language of the courts and the administration, while we spoke something else in the villages, Twi or Fanti or Swahili. We had heard all the stories about what barbarians the Russians were, but that was at the same time that we had discovered that the British and their friends were liars who described the world in terms which would keep us quiet. Most of the boys had open minds and a dream inside them about going back as engineers or scientists to build the bridges and dams and turbines which would power their independence and abolish the poverty from which they had come.

There was only one thing different about me. I already knew, or thought I did, what would become of me. I had not been recruited by a local party boss. In fact, up to that time I'd had very little to do with the Communists. My references came straight from the top, from Osageyfo. This was a coin with two sides, but at the time I believed that my future was made, which turned out to be true, but not in the way I expected.

None of it would have happened anyway if it hadn't been for that crazy old man Ras Makonnen. That was in Manchester, of course. I was sixteen, and it was my first trip with my father. I had lied about my age, but I was big, and just as capable of the work as any other stoker on the ship. After fifty years I can remember very little about the journey, except standing beside my father in the engine room, shovelling and sweating. At night on deck, watching the sparkling trail behind us, or bunked down in the clanking dark of the galley, he would tell me stories about the place to which we were going. Education, he said repeatedly, education would make me a man who could live in the new world that was coming. He was tall, bigger than I ever became. Paul Robeson, someone would always say when we went into the pub near the custom house in Cardiff, but he was even bigger than Robeson.

Liverpool was the city in which we landed that first time. It was 1945 and the big war had only just ended. I thought the city was still buzzing with the joy of it, but my father said this was how it always was. He got me a room at the mission house, then he left, taking most of my pay, leaving me enough for food. Don't go with any of these women on the street, he told me before he went. They will take all your money and get you in trouble. The warning wasn't necessary, not because I was frightened of women. In Accra I had already been with women, but they had seemed nothing like the white ladies who smiled boldly and spoke in their strange accents as we walked down Upper Parliament Street. Their red lips, their perfume and pale skins were exciting and revolting at the same time, and I had no idea how to speak to them or where to begin. My attitude had changed by the time of my second trip, but that first time I merely stayed in the mission with the minister, a man from Sierra Leone, who gave me a cup of tea, played the piano, sang, asked me about my mother and talked gently about the Gold Coast.

It was the next day that my father took me to Manchester. He said it was a reward for how well I had worked, but later on it occurred to me that he wanted me out of Liverpool that first time because he didn't want me bumping into his other family, and he was successful in this for all the time he was alive. I'd heard rumours, of course, but it wasn't until years later that I came across my three half-sisters, with their mother, a fat Irish woman with greying red hair who said she was his wife. It was a shock but no surprise, although in those early days I had no inkling that my father had another, different life. So I was all innocence that day, going to Manchester. It was my second day in England and the first time I travelled on a train. Below my feet was a wave of warm air, while outside the window the sun shone over the fields. But I was not yet accustomed to the chill that came with this sunshine, and feeling the cold air on my skin as it rushed through the window was strange and dislocating, almost as if what I was seeing was an illusion placed there to persuade me that I was still in the same world where I had grown up.

On the way my father told me about the man we would see in Manchester. Ras Makonnen, he called him, but then he said that the man was not an Ethiopian in spite of his name. It was all something to do with his politics. There were men there, according to my father, who, in one colony or the other, had been trade union leaders or Communists, and in order to escape the authorities used two or three names. Mak must have been one of them and he was no fool, because he had become a rich man in England. Even in this country, my father said, he was more powerful than many whites. In Manchester he owned restaurants, clubs and houses. No one could tell how much he owned. But you had to be careful of such men, my father said, lowering his voice, because although he had done many good things, no one knew where he came from or who his people were, and no one knew what he had done to gain these possessions.

It was clear that he meant all this as a warning, but at my age it was a story which almost made me choke with excitement, behind which was the desperate longing to learn and understand the secrets of this hero, a feeling which grew stronger and stronger during that night at Mak's restaurant.

It was in Oxford Road. We walked there from the station through the broad thoroughfare which ran from one square to the next, and past the huge stone palace which was St Peter's. As we walked among the rows of shops and stores, richer than anything I had ever seen, I could feel curiosity inside me swelling and pounding like a pulse. What kind of African, I kept asking myself, owned one of these places in a city like this?

It was called The Cosmopolitan. An old brick house, four storeys high, with long rectangular windows. The ground floor was a big square room with a bar along one wall. On the other side a staircase which led up to the next floor, and under it was a door leading to the kitchens. The floor was polished wood which squeaked a little when you walked on it, and there were about twelve tables covered in white cloths. High on the back wall, where everyone could see it, was a large picture of the Emperor Haile Selassie in uniform, his sorrowful eyes surveying the room. All around the walls and disappearing up the stairs were huge paintings, murals of men from every nation, some of them half naked, some in the dress of their nation, others in uniform. There were Chinese, Indians, Africans and white men and women, all of them marching or running, straining towards some object, the muscles and sinews of their necks and limbs standing out, their bodies tensed as if about to leap from the walls, their eyes raised towards the heavens. I had never seen anything like it, and as we entered I stood still, almost transfixed by the sights around me.

It was early in the evening and the place was only half full. Most of the customers seemed to be black Americans in uniform and white women from the town. I had an impression of khaki

133

and shiny black hair, smooth like wet tar, next to curly yellow hair and pale skins, but I didn't look at them as carefully as I wanted to, because I knew that when you saw big men out with their women it was dangerous to stare.

Makonnen was standing at the bar talking to the white woman behind it. When we came in he looked up and greeted my father by name. At the time this didn't seem strange. Later on I realised that he knew every seaman who came in by name. The funny thing was that he looked like an Ethiopian, with the thin features and delicate frame that marked out people who came from the Horn. He was wearing a black suit, though, like a minister, with a shirt so clean and white that the collar gleamed in the dim light of the room. When he spoke, also, his English was perfect, with an accent like an Englishman. To listen to him was like reading a book.

'You came at the right time, Mr Coker,' he said to my father. 'They're all here for the conference.'

I could tell that my father was puzzled, but he nodded and smiled with an expression of respectful attention, and Makonnen carried on telling him about the conference which he said would be historic. A historic landmark, he said, and I remember the word because it was the first time I'd heard it. My father nodded and frowned as if he understood what it was all about, but I knew he didn't, and that was the first sign I had of the problem that would defeat such men as Osageyfo in the end. Because he was, in that respect at least, very much like Makonnen. They would talk and talk in their perfect English, outlining plans and strategies and demonstrating how the logic of history supported their actions, and they assumed that the approval of their audiences was the same as agreement. Most of the time, I suspect, they knew that wasn't true, but it was also true that they believed winning the argument was enough. With a man like my father it was easy to win an argument, but that would never be the end of the matter. Osageyfo and the men around him, men like Padmore, never altogether understood that. Padmore, in particular, had learnt his lack of compromise from Stalin, even though he was one of his bitterest enemies.

That night in the restaurant my father gave no indication of his real opinion, which was that when it came to African affairs Makonnen and his friends were close to dangerous fanatics. Instead he fingered the leaflets and the journal about Pan African events which Mak gave him with the same grave attention.

'The boy will read them,' he said.

We were eating lamb stew and semolina when it happened – Makonnen himself had recommended the dish before we sat down. Later on I understood that there were only two kinds of food to be had there. One was for the black American servicemen who still thronged the city in 1945 – fried chicken, pork, sweet potatoes, black-eye peas. The other kind was for the African visitors or seamen off the boats – lamb stews, ground rice, yams, semolina, cous-cous, and hot peppers. Then there were vegetables like okra, which the sailors brought him direct from the African coast. In those days Makonnen's restaurants were the only places in Europe where you could get such food. The room was quiet apart from the voices of the Americans and the screeching of their women, but they were just part of the background which we heard without hearing. In those days the Americans, with their loud voices and their jitterbug, their money and their cars, impressed no one except women. Slaves in their own country, they chose every opportunity when abroad to play the big man among poor people. So we heard them without hearing until there was a mighty shouting which, we realised when we looked up, was coming from Makonnen: Bwana macouba, bwana macouba. It was a joyous bellow which I could not imagine coming from that quietly spoken gentleman, before I saw him with his mouth open and his arms apart facing the door. From the street came an answer, a deep huge laugh, over and over, and in through the door came one of the biggest men I'd ever seen, bigger than my father. Behind him was a crowd of people and all of a sudden the room was full. There were only half a dozen of them, five Africans and a white woman, but there was something about them all which seemed to fill the place with a sparkling vitality, an aura within which they seemed to glow. That is how I remember them at that time anyway, like a group of heroes glowing with life and purpose.

Makonnen embraced them one by one, talking all the time, and over the hubbub of voices I could hear the huge booming laugh of the tall man, who, as it happens, was the only one I had really looked at so far.

'That is Mr Kenyatta,' my father muttered.

Everyone in the restaurant was staring at these people, but they seemed not to mind, looking around them with friendly smiles and nodding as if they knew themselves to be the sort of people who would attract admiration wherever they went. Makonnen bustled back and forth, shoving three tables together to make a big one for his guests, pulling out the chairs and snapping his fingers for bottles from the bar.

For my part I was so gripped by the show that I had forgotten to eat, and it was the white lady who first noticed me. She was worth looking at, as I remember. When she died she was a decrepit old bag lady who they had to haul from a stinking room in Bayswater, but at that time she still looked like what she was, a bold and beautiful aristocrat who didn't give a damn. I hadn't seen many white people until then, and they all looked strange to me, but I knew I had never seen a woman, black or white, like her, sitting at her ease, arguing and interrupting these big men. I suppose I was drinking her in with my eyes because she smiled at me and nudged the man next to her.

'Take a look at him, George,' she said, in a clear voice which didn't seem too loud but which could be heard all round the room. 'That is what you have to convince if you're going to make it happen.'

Suddenly the room was quiet, and everyone was staring at me. I ducked my head in shame, too self-conscious to eat, and I heard Kenyatta's booming chuckle start up again.

'Mr Coker,' I heard Makonnen's voice call out. 'Come here. Allow me to introduce you.'

My father poked me in the arm and I got up, my eyes averted, and walked the few steps over to their table.

'This is Mr Coker,' Makonnen announced. 'He's a stoker who just got in yesterday from the coast, and this is his son Kofi. Also a stoker.'

Each of them shook hands formally with my father. Each one

136

said his name. I didn't catch them all at the time, but I remember the faces as if it was yesterday. The Bwana macouba, Kenyatta, was first, his long arm reaching out across the table from a sitting position. Then Dr Nkrumah. I seem to remember that was how he introduced himself, although nowadays when I think of him I always call him Osageyfo. Then George Padmore. He was the quiet one. His face had a cynical twist and he smiled his crooked smile as if he knew how confused I was. Then there was Peter Abrahams. He was younger than the rest by twenty years, and there was something kindly about his face which gave me a feeling that he might be my friend, especially when he looked back at me and winked. Finally, the woman who bent her head sideways so that she could look full into my face with her big light eyes. Nancy Cunard, she said.

Osageyfo was looking at me seriously, with a slight frown as if weighing me up, but there was something else about his look that I remember. It was as if he knew me and cared about me. I looked up and met his eyes, and from that moment I was desperate to please him.

'How old are you, boy?' Osageyfo asked me.

I told him I was sixteen.

'When we're running things,' he said to my father, 'boys like this will be making a life for themselves and building our country instead of crossing the sea locked up like rats in an iron cage.'

My father nodded without answering, but I felt hurt for him. He couldn't argue with anything Osageyfo said, because we knew from his looks and from the way he spoke that he was a big man of our tribe, an educated man, one who would have the power of an elder and more. On the other hand, my father had paid a substantial bribe to secure this job for me, and to hear it described in this way by such a man must have been painful.

'Give the boy a chance,' Kenyatta said jovially. 'We won't all be doctors and lawyers. At his age I had killed a lion and had three wives.'

A burst of laughter greeted this statement. I wasn't sure whether this was because it was a lie or simply a familiar boast. Osageyfo waited quietly for the interruption to end, leaning back

137

in his chair. He was like that, completely focused on whatever it was he wanted. My eyes were looking at the ground as was appropriate, but I could feel his gaze and when I looked up I saw him staring intently at me.

'In your opinion, Kofi,' he asked, 'what does our country need most at this moment?'

'He's not a voter yet,' Padmore remarked in his mocking voice. I wasn't distracted. I knew the answer to the question, having heard it often enough from my father, and I came out with it quickly before anyone else could speak.

'Education, sir.'

He smiled for the first time.

'Education is good,' he said, 'but what we really need is independence. Freedom from the imperialists and freedom to manage our own affairs.'

'Yes, sir,' I replied, and I meant it because I knew that whatever he said must be right.

'Mr Coker,' Osageyfo said, addressing my father. 'Are you here in Manchester for a couple of weeks?'

'Yes, sir,' my father mumbled.

'We need someone to do some work, run errands and help us get ready for the conference. Give me Kofi for a few days.'

'Take him, Mr Nkrumah,' my father said.

Osageyfo smiled at me again.

'I like this boy,' he said.

That was how my apprenticeship began. I didn't know then that it would take me to Moscow in the autumn of 1956, but that was the beginning of that part of my life. To remember that time, and those people and the way my life changed is both sad and happy; and sometimes I don't know which one it is that I'm feeling.

London

September 1999

NINE

At half past nine in the morning Kofi Coker was sitting in a café near Ladbroke Grove, sipping coffee and reading a newspaper article about the IMF. He had dressed with special care because he was meeting his son Joseph. He wasn't sure why he'd taken so much trouble, but perhaps it was something to do with the note of urgency in Joseph's voice when he had telephoned just before midnight. Perhaps he wanted advice, or perhaps he wanted some piece of information about his mother. It couldn't be money, Kofi thought, an involuntary smile twisting his lips, because Joseph earnt more money than his father had ever done.

That might have been one of the reasons he had arranged their meeting in the café, and why he was wearing his second best dark-blue suit. In the last year he had spent more time with Joseph than ever before, mainly because he'd been helping him to find the subjects for his film and using what influence he had to cajole them into sitting in front of the camera. Of course, he knew that most of the old fools were lying their heads off, repeating stories they'd been told as if they were their own, and enlarging their deeds into monstrous epics. At the same time Joseph had been so pleased, and their narratives seemed so convincing that Kofi had never had the heart to contradict even those accounts he knew for certain to be completely invented. At the same time, the more intimate he was with his son, the more it seemed that Joseph's manners were unnecessarily direct, and sometimes even rude. It was not his intention, Kofi knew, but sometimes the way Joseph behaved, coming from anyone else, would have seemed insulting. For instance, the last time he visited Kofi's flat, he had refused to eat even a sandwich, claiming that he was not hungry. Just before leaving he had glanced round, his eyes resting on the battered sofa and the scarred kitchen table. 'You like living here, Dad?' he had murmured in his flat English voice. Kofi had shrugged without replying. Of course I like living here, he thought, but even while the words ran through his head, he was conscious that his son pitied him for being trapped, at the end of his years, in these two small ugly rooms. As it happened he couldn't find it in himself to resent Joseph's patronising thoughtlessness because he imagined he understood where it came from. Joseph's mother had been the daughter of a doctor, and her family was prosperous. 'Comfortable' was the word they used, and as a qualified teacher, then a writer of books for children, she had always had enough money to live in comfort. When she died of cancer, a few days after her fiftieth birthday, she had left Joseph the house which her father had bought in North London between the wars. He still lived there, and he still possessed, almost untouched, a portfolio of investments she had gathered as a result of the family legacies and gifts which had come to her over the years. She would have been a little surprised to be described as a rich woman, but the fact was that the house which had been suitable for the small family of a professional man when she was born, had become a major asset by the time she died. Her income had been Kofi's means of support when they lived together, and the riches she called her 'savings' had underlined his dependence, a canker in the mind and a barrier between them. Equally, he sometimes felt, it had separated him from Joseph. His son was a stranger to need, and it often seemed to Kofi that they existed on two sides of an immense gulf in understanding about the world and its nature.

He was still reading the article when Joseph came in through the door, and he folded the paper with a feeling of disappointment at not being able to finish it immediately, but as he stood up to embrace his son he experienced a distinct feeling of pride. There was something impressive about Joseph, so tall and cleancut, which made him want people to know that the boy was his flesh and blood.

'How are you, Dad?' Joseph asked, but the glum look on his face and the stiffness of his body put Kofi on the alert immediately.

It was an oddity to which he had never become accustomed. In his days as a young man like Joseph, whenever confronting his elders he had been used to maintaining a strict control over his features. An air of respectful attention or perhaps a friendly smile was the face he would have presented to his own father on almost every occasion. By contrast, Joseph seemed to have no inhibition about displaying his anger and frustration, no matter what the circumstances were. Kofi had long ago come to terms with his son's disrespectful manners, because it was simply the style of the English, the mode in which he had been reared. On the other hand, whenever his son's behaviour embarrassed Kofi, he felt a swelling tide of resentment against his former wife. During his childhood he had never heard his own mother say a bad word about his absent father. In comparison Joseph was accustomed to hearing his father spoken of in the most abusive and insulting terms. It was no wonder, Kofi thought, that he had never been able to teach the boy how to show respect in the company of his elders. Greeting him now, for instance, Joseph could hardly be bothered to conceal the fact that he was angry or disturbed about something, and Kofi sensed that he was unlikely to trouble himself with a period of sociable conversation before broaching whatever was on his mind. Ignoring the danger signals, he ordered more coffee and asked whether Joseph had enjoyed the festival.

'That's what I wanted to talk to you about.'

'The festival? The film was a success?'

'I suppose so,' Joseph replied. 'But I didn't mean the festival. A guy came to my hotel in Prague and said he was my brother.'

'A black man?'

Kofi smiled, thinking that some stray student must have been trying to con Joseph by claiming the brotherhood of blackness.

'He showed me a picture,' Joseph said, 'of you and a woman, his mother. Katya, he said her name was.'

The sound of her name, coming out of the blue from Joseph, gave Kofi a shock, and for a few minutes he listened without hearing, as if he already knew what his son was telling him. In his mind he was trying to summon up a picture of her face. He had begun to recall immediately and without effort moments when they were together – watching her enter the classroom on his first day of tuition, or following her through the market on Tsvetnoy Bulvar where a toothless old man had stopped him and shook his hand. This was the first time it had happened to him, and when the man got in his way he had tried to step aside, until Katya lifted her eyebrows at him and said, 'He wants to welcome you.' Another time, at the beginning of a thaw, walking on the packed snow along the embankment at Kotelnichskaya, he had slipped and when he clutched at her to save himself they had both fallen on to their backs. The sky was empty, pale and grey. Then he saw her face as she rolled over and crouched above him on her hands and knees, her eyes smiling, strands of her long hair plastered on her wet cheek, while he lay kicking his legs and laughing helplessly. These images ran through his head, as it were, involuntarily, but when he tried to see her face the details eluded him. While writing his journal he had tried to remember such matters as the colour of her eyes, and now it occurred to him that his memory of everything had been selective, and riddled with guesswork. Something like a spasm crossed his face, and he rested his fingers on his cheek to stop himself twitching. A child, he thought, a child, testing his emotions, but all he felt was bewilderment at the idea that somewhere in the

144

world there was this person, a mixture of himself and Katya. The pain he felt when he thought of her had ended long ago, he didn't know when, but he retained a memory of it which was almost physical, like an ugly wrenching ache in the guts, and he felt now a shadow of that agony, looking at Joseph's expectant frown, and picturing the man, his son, whom he had never seen or touched. The image that came was of himself, forty years younger, looking through a porthole at the vanishing landscape. This had been a moment in which he seemed to feel his heart bleeding inside his chest. Thinking back on it, a wave of anger crested in his mind and he seemed to see his child, helpless and alone, adrift in a formless ocean. If he had known, he thought, he would never have accepted their disappearance. It was true that he had waited, but if he had known he would have found them somehow, even if it meant grubbing in the deepest Siberian swamp.

'What did he look like?' he asked.

His heart was racing and his voice croaked.

The question seemed to irritate Joseph. He put his hand in the pocket of his jacket and took out the envelope George had given him.

'They said he looked like me,' he said curtly, putting the envelope down in front of Kofi. 'This is the letter she sent you. See for yourself.'

Kofi fumbled at the letter, reading the writing on the front of it, then eventually picking it up and trying to open it, but his hands shook so badly that it defeated all his efforts. At last Joseph reached out and took it from him, but as he did so Kofi slumped back in his seat, his skin suddenly grey, his mouth open and gasping. His head was suddenly light, as if filled with air, but he didn't experience the momentary collapse as pain or weakness. Instead he felt as if the rage inside him had sucked the energy from his body to feed itself, leaving him nerveless and empty.

145

'Dad,' Joseph called out, 'Dad!'

He got up and hurried round the table. Before he could do more than touch his father on the shoulder, Kofi sat up and began taking deep breaths, his face buried in his cupped hands. Then he looked up at Joseph. Part of his anger, he realised, had been to do with the fact that this news had been brought to him by Joseph, whose feelings for him seemed so ambiguous and difficult.

'I'm going home now,' he said, forcing himself to sound calm. 'We can talk there.'

They walked back to Kofi's flat in silence. When they crossed the road he stumbled a little over the kerb, and Joseph took his arm. It was the first time he had ever done that, Kofi realised, trying to collect his thoughts. From the moment he recognised Katya's handwriting on the envelope it was as if his whirling brain had leapt from his head, and was now floating independently, frantic and bewildered, as his body went through its routine and automatic operations. In this eddy of confusion the feel of his son's firm grip steadied him and gave him a sense of comfort.

Back in the flat Kofi sat on the sofa staring into space, while Joseph hurried to make a cup of tea. This was another thing, Kofi thought, that he seemed to be doing for the first time.

'You okay, Dad?'

Kofi gave him a reassuring smile without speaking. At that moment he felt that there was nothing to say. The problem was that he had forgotten the details of those forty-year-old events. He remembered Katya, of course, and he remembered the waves of emotional turbulence on which he seemed to be riding as the bus trundled down Leninsky Prospekt on the way to the airport. He knew also how much he had wanted Katya as the plane lifted into the sky, and how hard it had been, for the first few months, to bear their separation. But over the years he had come to think of her in much the same way as he thought of his dead parents, as if they had somehow been relocated in another distant and unreal world in which he had once travelled. The events which linked them together seemed to him to have happened to another person in that other universe, and the memories rushing through his brain were now a spectacle in front of which he was an onlooker, moved only by a feeling of curiosity about the motives and identity of the figures parading in procession. At the same time he felt himself being racked by uncontrollable eddies of emotion which seemed to come from nowhere.

'Aren't you going to read the letter?'

They had been sitting in silence, Kofi realised, for several minutes, maybe as long as a quarter of an hour, while he was struggling to contain his thoughts. He gestured at Joseph.

'Open it.'

Joseph tore open the top of the envelope neatly and gave it to him. Inside was a single sheet of paper folded round half a dozen photographs.

'It's in English,' he said.

The remark puzzled Kofi, until he remembered that Joseph must know little or nothing about Katya.

'Of course,' he replied. His voice was still croaking. 'She spoke it well. She taught languages. I learnt Russian from her. You knew I spoke it.'

He spoke the language badly, but he had boasted of it to Joseph and tried to teach him some of the words. The boy should have remembered, but Kofi had the suspicion that, influenced by his mother's attitude, Joseph had been dubious about the truth of everything his father said. The thought seemed to stir the turbulence inside him but, struggling for control, he put the matter out of his mind and began looking at the photos one by one, laying them down beside him for Joseph to reach. They were recent photographs, almost all apparently taken on one occasion, and featuring all four members of his new family, individually and in groups. Serge smiled into the camera, flanked by Radka and George. Close up Katya was still pretty, her white hair curling round her face, her eyes wide and level, the line of her mouth looping in a lopsided smile.

Kofi found himself holding on to one of the photographs, studying it carefully, as if trying to commit it to memory. It was different from the others, black and white, and when he eventually laid it aside, Joseph snatched it up, impatient to see what had made him linger. It was older, taken by a different camera. Katya, more than thirty years younger, but recognisably the same woman, was standing in a street. She was wearing a long black coat, but it was hanging open, her light hair blowing around her face. Beside her, holding her hand, was a small boy, who, for one heart-stopping instant, seemed to be Joseph. The resemblance was remarkable, Kofi thought, and it would have been easy to imagine that the two boys had the same mother. In a moment Joseph got up and, holding the photograph in his hand, walked over to Kofi's little collection of photographs on the wall facing him. He stood there staring at another photograph of himself at the same age, which had been taken at school. From where he was sitting Kofi couldn't see it, but he knew that it would be hard to locate the difference. Their hair curled in the same way, bristling in a peak over the forehead, and they had the same crooked, almost wry smile, curving their lips.

'This guy really does look like me,' Joseph said over his shoulder.

Kofi couldn't reply. He blinked, trying to clear the tears which had filled his eyes.

'Didn't you know about any of this?'

Kofi shook his head, suddenly becoming aware that Joseph couldn't contain his curiosity any longer.

'What does she say?'

Kofi, still unable to speak, held out the letter to Joseph.

It had been typed on an electric typewriter, and it was short enough to be taken in almost at a glance.

Dear Kofi,

I don't know what to say to you after all these years. Our time together is almost like part of my childhood, but I still remember it as the most important time of my life. For myself, I have no right to ask anything from you. I can only ask you to forgive me. We did what we had to do. I don't know what else I could have done, but I can understand it if you hate me. You have a son. I named him George because of your name. He looks like you and he thinks of you. I would like to see you again to explain everything to you if that is possible. I hope that it is.

Love,

Katya

'What's it all about?' Joseph asked.

It was obvious that the letter, with its references to forgiveness, puzzled him, but Kofi found himself wishing that he would shut up, at least for a little while, and stop asking questions. He needed to calm the buzzing in his brain, so that he could think. In the instant before he took in the words of the letter he had been gripped by a fear of what she would say about those times and about why she had disappeared. Thinking over what she had written, he was trying to remember the last words that had passed between them.

'Dad,' Joseph said, trying to claim his attention, his voice urgent as if he thought Kofi might be drifting off to sleep. 'What's it all about?'

'I don't know,' Kofi told him.

'Come on, Dad.' A prickle of resentment seemed to surface as Joseph spoke. 'You never even mentioned any of this to me. All right, you didn't know about George, but the rest of it, all this about Katya. You never said.'

'I told you about Russia,' Kofi replied. He could remember that much. In afternoons when they wandered together in the park, or he stood behind Joseph in the playground, pushing the swings, he had talked about his life. 'Maybe you weren't listening.'

It was true, Joseph remembered, and it was true that he hadn't paid much attention to his father's tales.

'There isn't much to tell,' Kofi continued. 'I was a student there in 1956 and I met Katya. We were,' he hesitated, 'in love. Then they expelled me. I wasn't able to speak to her before I left. That's all.'

'Why were you expelled?'

Kofi shrugged.

'A lot of reasons, I think. I talked too much to the wrong people. A big dispute in the Students' Union.' He hesitated again. 'I never really knew.'

'If it was nothing to do with her, why is she asking you to forgive her?'

Kofi shrugged again.

'I'm not sure.' He passed his hands over his face, a gesture of uncertainty.

Joseph, it was obvious, could hardly restrain his impatience. Just like an Englishman, Kofi thought, he imagined that the truth was a network of concrete facts and he could find it out simply by asking.

'It was a long time ago,' Kofi said. Suddenly he was too tired to work out what Joseph wanted to know. To tell everything would take a long time, and in any case the motives at which Katya had hinted in her letter were still hidden from him. 'I don't even remember all of it. I don't know if I want to remember.'

'What about George?' Joseph asked him.

George. In the photograph the boy's eyes had been wide open, giving his face a curious melancholy expression, or perhaps that was merely a reflection of his own emotions.

'That's different.'

He was thinking of the time when Joseph had been

small enough to hold in the palm of his hand, his head safely resting against Kofi's biceps, the same eyes looking up.

'Did my mum know about Katya?'

Kofi grinned, suddenly amused. Joseph's mother, Caroline, liked to think of herself as a rebellious spirit, which, he supposed, was one of the reasons their relationship had flowered at the beginning. At heart she was a slave to the romantic conventions with which she had grown up; Cupid's arrow, roses in June and all the rest of it. The fact that her knight rode into her life on a black charger had merely been a minor local difficulty. If she had known the true state of his feelings about Katya, she would have been devastated, and she would have made his life a misery, even in those early days when she said that all she ever wanted was to be with him. The irony was that he had told her a great deal about Katya, but the way he'd done it transformed the story into a romantic tale in which he was the wounded hero awaiting the healing balm of a woman's love. It had been an invaluable recipe for getting her into bed quickly. Now it struck him that while he had been calculating the effect that his portrait of Russian life would have on Caroline, Katya had been nursing George, wondering, perhaps, where his father was and whether she would ever see him again.

'I don't think she understood my life before I met her,' he told Joseph.

In his mind a series of pictures flickered, and even though he had just seen the photographs of Katya as an older woman, the images passing through his head showed her as she had been forty years earlier, her hair glinting red and gold in the sun, her booted feet striding towards him. This time, however, his imagination brought her to him as a mother, carrying the baby, his son George, as she stood in a patient queue, or sat swaying on a metro train, or trudged ankle deep through the greying slush of the streets. These were a version of the thoughts, which, when he arrived back in England, he had constantly rehearsed in his mind. Do you love me? Caroline used to ask, while he lay silent, bathed in sad, sweet memories.

'Why don't you come and stay with me for a few days, Dad?'

Kofi looked up in surprise. This, too, was the first time Joseph had spoken to him in such gentle tones, and it was the first time he had issued such an invitation. He had visited the house where he had lived with the boy's mother, of course, but these had been stilted occasions which both of them were usually glad to end. The problem was his sense of Caroline's presence in the place, which her death had done little to dispel. 'I don't want you to set foot in this house again,' was one of the last things she'd said to him just before he left. 'You can count on that,' he had replied with the recklessness of anger. Afterwards he could never feel at ease about accepting her hospitality, even when it came vicariously through his son.

'I don't think so,' he told Joseph, 'not right now.' He looked up, met his son's eyes and saw a shadow of his own pain. 'Thank you for asking.'

'What will you do?'

'I'm going to rest for a while and think things over.'

He knew very well that this wasn't the answer that Joseph was seeking, but some demon of perversity urged evasion.

'Okay,' Joseph said. 'I'll go now and let you get some rest. I'll come back later.'

At the door he looked round at Kofi, who was still sitting slumped in the corner of the sofa, the letter and photographs lying scattered beside him.

'What will you do about all this?' he asked again.

Kofi didn't move or speak for a few seconds. The truth was that the idea of doing anything had not yet entered his mind. All he wanted at that moment was to sit and nurse his thoughts, somehow to reassemble the self which felt as though it was floating in fragments around him.

'I don't know,' he told Joseph, the words emerging in a reluctant mutter. 'I have to think, but right now I don't know.'

TEN

DIARY OF DESIRE

The life and times of Kofi George Coker
Moscow 1957

When I arrived in Moscow I knew practically nothing about the people and their way of life. I learnt something new every day, but when I left I knew very little more than I had at the beginning. Nowadays friends and acquaintances who know something of my former life ask me questions about the place, and most of the time I have to restrain myself from replying with sarcasm or rudeness, because they speak in the way that so many people do now, as if there was some great surprise about the fact that the standards and attitudes of our present day do not apply to the past. They ask, for example, questions like – how did the ordinary people live? Didn't you meet any ordinary people? How did they treat you? I don't know, I tell them, and I get that look of surprise, before I can summon up the patience to explain. Try to remember, I tell them, that Russia was a totalitarian state, and this was forty years ago. During my time there I don't think I had any clear idea of what an 'ordinary' person was. We students lived in a kind of bubble outlined by our colour, our strangeness and our awkwardness with the language. The officials, teachers and other colleagues who we routinely encountered all had a position in the Party and a responsibility for our indoctrination, or for keeping us isolated from anything they considered undesirable – a concept which covered a lot of ground. The people of the city, we also discovered, were discouraged from contact with foreigners like ourselves, and anyone to whom we spoke might have been an agent reporting our words and actions to another authority.

154

The exceptions were tricksters, whores, women on the lookout for adventure, subversives and economic hooligans eager to barter for the goods we could bring in, and even those would probably have been willing to act as instruments for our entrapment. In the circumstances our behaviour was intended to be circumspect and discreet. But the spirits of young men are like water, and they usually find a way to flow, even through barriers of granite. In any case, it took some time before I began to understand the limits of my existence in Moscow.

The autumn lasted just long enough for my life to settle down into a routine. Winter came on swiftly, the days becoming shorter and the light fading under the dull grey sky which pressed closer and closer to the domes with every hour that passed. During this time we explored the city. My favourite companions were Valery and Hussein. Both of them had been in Moscow for more than a year, but they seemed to take pleasure in showing me around. Hussein was a slim, elegant man, with smooth Indian hair and a beaky Arabic profile, an economist who had studied at Harvard and the LSE, and was now writing a thesis about Khrushchev's Virgin Lands programme. This was already two years after Khrushchev had upstaged Malenkov with his dramatic proposal to expand the country's grain growing capacity into an enormous belt of undeveloped territory stretching through the south west, Kazakhstan and Western Siberia. It was all part of a master plan, Hussein said, in which we were a curlicue, a decoration in an elaborate baroque structure. Of course, Khrushchev wanted us in the country because he hoped for more than that. He believed, Hussein said, that the Africans and Asians who came here would turn out to be the cornerstones of a widespread challenge, worms eating away at the rotten heart of the Western empires. Centuries ago, he told me, Western Europe had outstripped its eastern neighbours by looting the riches of Africa and Asia, while creating new markets in the American continent. 'The Russians think there is a way to do the same now, but they really can't afford it,' Hussein said. He laughed. 'The thing is that no one has yet told Khrushchev the price.'

He reminded me of Padmore, witty, cynical and with no

155

inhibitions about showing his contempt for most of the students. His family was mostly Arabic, he explained on the first day that we walked together through the university, and his mother had been a slave from Somalia, but his father was the last of a long line of wazirs. During the days of the Sultanate on the Spice Coast, they had sat on the sultan's right hand advising him on how to run the kingdom and most of the time doing it themselves. The rule of the British was only an episode, and no one knew quite what would happen next, but it would depend, as ever, on the manipulation of political power, and political power was his heritage. He grinned when he said this, as though he was enjoying a great joke, but something in his voice told me that he meant what he was saying.

When I said that he reminded me of Padmore he gave me a sharp, sidelong look. 'You know Padmore?'

I told me then about how I'd met Osageyfo and his friends in Manchester, and he drew in his breath with surprise. 'I'll have to stick with you,' he said, laughing, 'you know some big men.'

After this he pressed me to tell him more about the conference, about Osageyfo, Padmore and Kenyatta. He was especially interested in Kenyatta, and if I had been longer in Moscow I'd have been suspicious enough to shut up, but at that time I was happy to talk. Even in the short time I'd been there I had begun to feel anonymous, a castaway adrift in a spinning world about which I knew nothing. Talking about those events gave me back my identity at least for a while.

In any case there wasn't much to tell. I knew no great political secrets. I didn't even know much about what happened, and what I knew it was hard to remember. In the years since then this meeting in Manchester of the Africans who were going to lead the struggle for independence became legendary. At the time I was half of my father's opinion, that they were dreamers unhinged and deceived by the education they had pursued among the whites. On the other hand, there was something extraordinary about this gathering of black men who were so conscious of their own importance, and of their mission. Makonnen had somehow persuaded the mayor of the city to open the conference, and I don't know whether he understood that the whole purpose of the participants was to kick white men on their asses out of the continent, but, flanked by Dr Milliard, the black doctor who had his surgery in Salford, and the writer James, he was effusive in his welcome. In any case, it was hard for the people of this time to take the prospect of colonial freedom seriously, even though they recognised the distinction of the visitors. This was years before Mau Mau became a familiar newspaper headline, and to see Kenyatta in that time it would have been impossible to guess at his future. I had no time for guessing, though. I was busy, running up and down, distributing flyers, criss-crossing the city with bundles of paper for the printers, and meeting people at the train station. I didn't receive any wages, although Mak sometimes gave me some pocket money. I ate at the Cosmopolitan and slept in a room at the top of the house where Osageyfo stayed. Kenyatta was also staying there, officially, but as I remember it he rarely slept in the place, spending late evenings in the Cosmopolitan or the Belle Étoile talking to a table of people who seemed to come over and over again just to listen to him, his booming roar echoing through the rooms. Afterwards he would disappear. Everyone knew he had women in the city and in various parts of the country, and he was famous for his sexual techniques, which, they said, caused women to swarm like bees. According to Mak, one of his best friends had been a white man, an anthropologist named Malinowski, who studied the customs of Africans, and was so fascinated by Kenyatta's stories about sex among the Kikuyu that he insisted on examining and measuring his penis.

These were the stupid stories I remembered and which I told Hussein as we strolled through the broad passageways and grand halls of the Moscow metro, a city beneath the city. On our way to visit Krasnya Ploschad, Red Square, we would descend at the University Station, heading in a straight line for Lubyanka and the centre of the city. At first I was alert, every sense tingling in anticipation of trouble. Being alone in a city of whites takes some getting used to, and I was never entirely at ease, but until I walked with Katya no one seemed to take any special notice of me, and moving among the throngs of people it struck me that I had met with more curious stares and furtive jostling as I walked through the streets of London.

'What happened to you?' Hussein asked abruptly.

We had just emerged from the well of the stairs into the vista which faced the golden domes of the Kremlin and St Basil's. Against the grey metal of the sky they shone as if they were being reached by invisible rays of light. It gave me a feeling I had not experienced since I stood with my father looking out over the stern of the ship at night. An immensity, strange and solemn, in which I shrank to a tiny speck, the world swaying and spinning beneath my feet. I would have liked to look at the scene in silence, but I knew that Hussein had seen it many times before and I struggled to find a response, although I hardly understood the question.

'Nothing happened. I was only a kind of messenger.'

'I don't mean that,' he said. 'I mean since then. From stoker on the boats to a student of history in Moscow is a big step.'

At last I understood. Perhaps he didn't mean to, but in that question Hussein sketched the gap between us, the descendant of Arab rulers and a man like myself, one foot still planted in the slums of Accra. In the days when Osageyfo employed me to run his errands around Manchester this had also been part of how I understood my role. He had kept me close to him, telling everyone that I was his countryman, and by implication, his protégé. A big man of his sort had to have followers. An urchin off the boats, an ignorant stoker's ignorant son, who dogged his footsteps, was like a demonstration of what he would come to be. For the moment I was a symbol for all those masses who would adore him later. I wasn't so ignorant that I didn't know he was patronising me, but I also knew instinctively that if he became my patron it would be my best chance in life.

This is how it had turned out. As it happened, the changes in the direction of my life were so gradual and seemingly random that I was hardly aware of where I was going, and talking to Hussein was, in fact, the first time I had seen it as a logical pattern where one thing led to the next. After the conference I went back on the boats and within three years I was a mess boy, working on a liner assisting the stewards, dressed in a white coat, barely sweating except in the hottest weather and far away from the hold. My father had only taken one more voyage with me, after which he remained in England, and it was the last time I saw him that I decided to leave the sea and take my chances on land. This was in the period after one of those moments that you remember always. It was a trivial occasion, an idle conversation when I had been talking to the chief steward, a man who had the reputation of being a strong supporter of the white seamen's union, although he had a kindly manner and spoke gently to the African boys. For some reason he took an interest in me, and one afternoon, sitting in the lounge where I took him his tea, he began to question me about myself and about where I had come from. I was already different to most of the other boys because my contacts with the politicians and intellectuals who flocked around Mak had, over the years, loosened my tongue and emboldened my spirit. When the chief steward asked me what my future would hold I told him that I wanted to be a steward. I don't know whether or not I meant it, but it seemed the only thing to say. He didn't tell me what he must have believed, which was that a black boy like me would never be a steward, a piece of discretion for which I was grateful when I remembered it much later. Instead, he raised his eyebrows in surprise, then smiled at me. 'You're a hard worker, Kofi,' he said, 'but if you want to get somewhere you'll need an education.' Later on I understood that these were mere words to him. To me it was like a signal for which I had been waiting. I had been more than six years on the boats. The opening of a new decade had come and gone. It was 1951. Time for a change.

At the end of that voyage I looked for my father. I found him at the Belle Vue Amusement Park in Manchester in a cage. I'd already heard that he had become some kind of performer. A kai show, they called it, and it was the career he had planned for himself even while we travelled to England on my first voyage. Although I didn't know it at the time the job he'd got for me then was his legacy. He knew, I suppose, that he would be leaving the coast for good, and he wanted to do something for me before he turned his back. It was a fortunate circumstance, because within a couple of years my mother had died of a tumour inside her, and then there was nothing to keep me in Accra. I'm grateful to my father now, and sometimes my pity for what he became brings tears to my eyes, but one of my permanent memories is the desperate anger which flooded through me as I stood in front of the cage in which he crouched below a sign – 'Wild Savage of the Fever Coast'. He was naked, except for a loincloth made of some spotted animal skin, and from time to time he leapt up at the bars, growling and barking. Watching this I was embarrassed, it is true, but more because his performance was grotesque, his animal imitations inconsistent and foolish, than because he was my father. Sometimes he waddled like a chimpanzee, sometimes he jumped and snarled like a tiger. No one except a very naïve child could have been convinced and it struck me that the pleasure of the spectacle must have been in observing his humiliation rather than because anyone imagined they were looking at a genuine 'wild savage'. I had arrived at the moment when he was due to be fed, a highlight of the show, and there was a mob of spectators, children, giggling couples and drunks, crowding the aisles, shouting ribald remarks and gasping at the sight. A bell chimed and the fat red-haired woman whom I knew later to be his wife appeared from round the back of the cage, dressed in a battered pith helmet and a faded safari jacket, and carrying a dish full of raw meat, which she proceeded to push through the bars, piece by piece. My father grabbed each one as she held it out, roaring and growling and tearing at the meat, rubbing the red juice over his face and looking up to snarl at his audience. In the meantime, three little ochre-skinned girls, my sisters, walked among the crowd holding out tin cans which they rattled as the coins piled up in them. I stood transfixed, an indescribable sensation in my chest, as if my heart was leaking blood. Had I been able to move I would have dashed the plate from the woman's hand and slapped her to the ground. I must turn away, I told myself, but my feet refused to stir from the spot. Instead, I took half a crown out of my pocket, all the money I was carrying, and dropped it into the tin that the smallest child was holding in front of me. At this moment my father looked up and saw me. His eyes flickered and for an instant his face fell and rearranged itself into its normal lines. I didn't wait to see any more, turning quickly and pushing my way out of the crowd which closed behind me like foliage in the jungle. That was the last time I saw him alive.

The place that my father had never quite occupied in my life was filled by Makonnen. Many of the Africans who knew him, in the West African style, addressed him as 'Father', in recognition of a philanthropy which had become more and more formidable, based as it was on a politics of African unity and solidarity. Whenever the boys on the boats had a problem it would be Mak who was their first port of call.

For the next couple of years I worked for Mak, and I found out that his generosity didn't extend only to Africans. The manager of the Cosmopolitan was a Hungarian Jew, and many of his employees were from the same origins, people who had fled from everywhere in Central Europe, along with Mediterraneans, Cypriots and the like. Being with Mak was like entering a new era in which the world came flocking to your door.

By this time Osageyfo and Kenyatta had been long gone. We read of them in the newspapers, of course. More and more often the men from the boats talked about Dr Nkrumah, then later his name became the single word, Osageyfo. Sometimes they brought letters to Mak which he would read in his office with the door shut. There were no messages from Kenyatta, and no one talked about him openly. We knew, though, that he had acquired a new name – Mzee. In the days soon after he left for Kenya, when women came to ask how to get in touch, Mak would shrug his shoulders and say he didn't know. This was a wise move, because over the next few years plainclothes policemen came repeatedly to ask whether he had heard from his friend Jomo, and from time to time they searched his house and examined his papers.

Padmore came sometimes, and I heard him say that Nancy was in Paris. Now that I was a grown man, in my early twenties, I would have loved to see her again and to try my luck, but she never came. I drifted, impatient and restless, uncertain of what to do with myself, when Osageyfo was imprisoned and released by the British for the first time. We demonstrated and celebrated in rapid succession. Then when they set up self-rule and he became prime minister I talked to Mak about going back. Mak must have written to him, because a note came in one of his letters. It said that he remembered me well, and as yet he had no useful role for me. The best thing was for me to complete my education in England and then in a few years return to serve my country. At that time he could promise me that I would be part of his plans.

The sentiment was so familiar that from the beginning I suspected Mak had written this, although it seemed to be the firm slant of Osageyfo's handwriting. On the other hand, I wanted to believe, and I did what I was told, enrolling in evening classes and planning a route to the point where I could join the university. I was still drifting but I was now able to persuade myself that I had a purpose. Not that it changed anything much about my life. The problem was my youth. In my mind time was an endless loop, and the honest truth is that I hardly ever thought more than a few days ahead, or imagined that events could abruptly alter the way I lived. When it happened it was like the blast of a grenade, an impact which tore up the ground beneath me and flung me off my feet.

I came back to the house one night and found Makonnen waiting. Without preamble he told me that I was one of a number of students chosen by the CPP, the Convention People's Party, to take up a scholarship abroad. Osageyfo himself had recommended me, and all that remained was for me to get on the plane to Moscow. I was more than shocked, and my first reaction was to say no, I knew nothing. Almost five years had gone by and I had five GCE passes, but I knew that this couldn't be enough to study in a foreign language in a new country. And why Moscow? I would have jumped at New York or Los Angeles or Paris, but Moscow was at the ends of the earth. Mak responded with impatience.

'This is a great opportunity,' he said brusquely. 'Osageyfo thinks you might make a diplomat, and we need our most trustworthy people in that city. We're not letting the Communists send anyone, and it's a soft option. They wouldn't let you into *those other places. Not yet, but in Moscow no one will question your qualifications because the graduates from Achimota and the boys at Oxbridge or the LSE won't want to go there. Never mind that. In ten years' time matters will be very different. The Russians will be fighting the British for trade and influence on the continent, and how many Ghanaians will there be who speak Russian? Don't be a fool. Grab it with both hands.'*

It was after I said yes that Mak told me he was about to sell up his properties and leave England to join Osageyfo. This too was a bolt from the blue, and it seemed then that I had no choice. Only a couple of months later I was standing beside Hussein in Red Square telling him the story of my life.

Hussein looked at me with searching eyes, as if trying to discern the qualities which had made me a favourite of the men I described.

'So that explains it,' he said. 'I thought there was something about you.'

'What do you mean?'

He looked at me thoughtfully, his eyes still weighing me up, and I guessed there was some revelation coming.

'They shifted things around a little before you came,' he said, 'and you ended up with Valery. That's interesting in itself. He's in Komsomol, the Party's youth wing, the cream of the cream. He spent a year in Komsomolsk, which goes to show you he's number one with the Party.' He caught my enquiring look. 'Sorry. Komsomolsk is a city in the East, up in that corner near Japan. About twenty years ago Komsomol got in a ship they called the Columbus and sailed up there to found a city in the middle of a big swamp. Now they're building secret aircraft there, new MIGs and Yaks, submarines and tanks, all that kind of thing. They don't let foreigners go anywhere near it. So you can see that he's trusted. He'll tell them everything they want to know about you, and stuff you don't know about yourself.'

'Who are "they" supposed to be? The police?'

It wasn't that I didn't believe him, but it was hard to imagine that there was anything about me which would repay so much *effort and planning. He shook his head from side to side, smiling as if amused at my ignorance.*

'The police? They'll be at the end of the list. There'll be the warden at Cheryomushki to begin with, then Komsomol and the regional Party people, the foreign ministry, the college administrators and maybe the KGB.'

He burst out laughing at the look on my face.

'You don't have to worry about the KGB. Not till you're ready to go back home. That's when they'll try and recruit you.' *The thought seemed to sober him up.* 'The point is that you're different. Most of the Africans here come through their party organisation. A lot of them are dunces grabbing a chance they won't get offered in Britain or the States. They do what they're told and go back home. The Party stays in charge. You've been sent by the people who're going to form the next government and the Party can't tell them what to do, but the foreign ministry wants a way in. If they had the chance they'd probably run every boy from the Gold Coast who could write his name through here. So you're in for the treatment. Take care.' *He paused, thinking about it.* 'Look. With a push from the big man you should do fine with whatever they've got in mind for you when you get back. As long as you can survive this place.'

I didn't know what he meant at the time, although when the first snows fell it was clear that surviving the winter would take more effort than I could ever have imagined. That afternoon I was walking back through the gates of the university with Valery. Ahead of us was the avenue of limes and birches leading to the nearby street market. Above us the skies were covered with a bruised and swollen blanket of dark clouds. There was a kind of dark, bluish-grey mist in the air. Suddenly, without warning there were flakes of snow, soft and plump like tiny feather cushions, tumbling straight down past the skeletal black arms of the trees. By the time we had walked the short distance to Noviye Cheryomushki, we were treading a soft white carpet of snow, the stuff gathering inches deep on our heads and shoulders, as if some giant hand had carefully sifted icing sugar over the figures on a cake. That morning Katya, the youngest of our teachers, had been drilling us in recognising the alphabet and pronouncing simple words. Many of the students, she told us, laughing, made mistakes which were hilarious to Russian ears. For instance, some of them persisted in reading Cyrillic as if the letters were English: 'Peck-to-pah,' she said, giggling. In English, of course, this was exactly what the word for restaurant looked like: РЕСТОРАН In Russian it was exactly the same word, restaurant, except that the letters were different. Listening to her and watching her bosom heave, and her lips sweetly framing the words, I had resolved to go back to Cheryomushki and practise my pronunciation. Instead I ended up sitting on my bed, hunched in a blanket, looking out at the whirling dance of the snow as it covered everything in a soft and glistening whiteness. It fell throughout that night, then in the morning it was freezing. It was worse than freezing. The cold was like being smashed over the head with a pickaxe handle, like walking into a brick wall naked and unprotected, like the all-out attack of a personal enemy, sudden, deadly and vicious. I had lived in England, a cold country, for more than half a dozen years and never experienced anything like it. Outside the door it was piled more than three feet deep. The world was silent, not the silence of night, but a sort of deep hush, the usual daytime noises of the street missing or muffled.

If I had not already been so crazy about Katya I would have stayed in the hostel all day, and to hell with the regulations. Instead I wrapped myself up and set out on what was now the long trek to the university. I would have walked through the fires of hell for that girl, although on that morning, ploughing waist deep through the snow was almost as terrible.

ELEVEN

Joseph was in no doubt that the events which occurred in Prague had been the most important of his life. It wasn't simply that he had discovered a brother about whose existence he had been unaware. It wasn't, either, the fact that his father seemed to be a different and more considerable person than he had previously imagined. What troubled him more than any of these things was the sense that his meeting with George had been the first step on an escalator of events whose speed or direction he had no hope of controlling.

After seeing Kofi that morning he had been plagued by another emotion, whose source he had no difficulty in locating because it was connected with one event which was still clear in his mind. This was the time, long ago, when he was still borrowing his mum's car and driving round London with all the unfettered exuberance of a seventeen-year-old with a new driving licence in his pocket. One evening he'd turned a corner at speed, and banged into a small grey cat. Alarmed at the impact and by its high-pitched screams, he'd stopped and got out just in time to see the animal's legs kick frantically, then stiffen and lie still. As he watched it heave the last breath, he felt a wave of grief and terror, which he knew even then was not for the cat. Instead, it was to do with the feeling that he had committed a final act, one which could never be called back or altered, and as a result his world would never again be the same. There was a similar shadow across Joseph's nerves during the day after he returned from Prague, and his meeting with his father had merely intensified the feeling of gloom which dominated his emotions.

His mood was complicated by the fact that he couldn't stop thinking about Radka. He felt guilty about doing so, because his thoughts of her were dominated by the urge to touch her, to feel the texture of the strands of hair straying down the side of her face, to hold her against him and feel her heart beating. Sitting in the car next to her he had felt the blood rushing through his veins and mad images ran through his head, her long white fingers stroking his cheek, her body unarmoured, supine and murmurous below him. These were pictures which, from time to time, piqued his imagination in a way that was both thrilling and unpleasant, like the unexpected pain of hot pepper on the tongue. He couldn't escape his guilt, because she was, after all, the wife of the man whom he now knew to be his brother. It would have been different, he thought, if they had met in London. If he had known for certain that George was his brother, he told himself, he would never have had these visions. It was the ambiguity of the situation which had shoved the unthinkable into his mind, because he had not been absolutely sure about George until he had come back and spoken to Kofi. He argued like this, trying to persuade himself that he had nothing to answer for, but at the same time he understood that he was merely making excuses.

Halfway through the afternoon he decided to obey one of his mother's axioms: confront the problem. Why was it that Radka had attracted him so strongly, and why was it that he continued to think about her? First was the fact that she had the kind of looks which had always attracted him; blonde hair, regular even features, not unlike his mother. She was also tall, slender with an impression of strength about her hips, reinforced by a coiling of the long muscles which ran down her thighs. But that wasn't enough. He had met women with the same kind of looks before. None of them, however, had her mystery or enigmatic presence. But that too was an illusion which reflected the fact that he knew hardly anything about her. Perhaps the truth was that the situation in which they had had their first encounter was the key. When he thought of her it was against a background of the city's medieval atmosphere, its tenebrous subtlety, its spires and the unexpected hollows which revealed themselves at every turn. At the end of a long journey, he had gone to her through a forest, climbed a winding staircase, and seen her face framed within the slate of ancient rooftops. She was his sleeping princess, and he saw her dreaming, her eyes closed, the long fair lashes tremulous, before the sheer foolishness of the vision struck him. For the first time that day he laughed out loud, amused at the effortless speed with which he had drifted into fantasy. Immediately, though, another more disturbing fancy arrived. George was the monster who possessed her, but perhaps the spark of jealousy which glowed inside him from the moment he knew the truth was something to do with how brothers felt about each other.

This idea added to Joseph's confusion. Hoping to hear something, anything, which might dispel the fog, he telephoned Kofi's flat a few times during the course of the afternoon, but there was no answer. He prowled restlessly up and down the house, unable to begin the task of re-inserting himself into the routine of his own life. Usually he would have been answering the letters and messages which had been piling up while he was away, or ringing round the TV companies to arrange freelance shifts editing film or videotape. Instead, when he could put Radka and George out of his mind, he kept thinking about the way Kofi had almost collapsed in the café. Up to that point he had thought of his father as someone who, in spite of his previous illnesses, looked irritatingly healthy. He actually showed few signs of ageing, except for the receding hairline and the dusting of grey which had crept over the tuft of beard on his chin. For Joseph it had been almost the biggest shock of the week to see Kofi slumped in his chair, his jaw slack, his eyes staring blindly into space.

After his fifth or sixth attempt to reach Kofi on the telephone he lost patience. It was already evening and the traffic was thinning out as he drove through Euston Road and Marylebone towards Paddington. The windows of his father's flat were dark, and he could hear the bell ringing with the desolate echo which told him there would be no answer. Frustrated, he gave up, then walked the nearest streets, looking into half a dozen pubs around Ladbroke Grove, but Kofi was nowhere to be seen. Eventually he gave up and drove back home.

Lena was waiting on the doorstep, and seeing her there Joseph felt the familiar mixture of guilt and irritation. She was carrying a bag, which meant she was planning to stay for the night, or for as long as he would let her.

'I left you a message,' she said, 'but you didn't reply, so I came anyway.'

He should have guessed, he thought, that there would be a message from Lena, and his only chance of heading her off would have been to telephone and tell her clearly that he didn't want to see her. The problem was that for almost a year he had failed to be honest with her, and she had exploited his lack of resolution to maintain the appearance of intimacy in a relationship which had long ago, on his side at least, grown mechanical and dispassionate.

He had met Lena when he went to talk about film and video editing at a weekend school in Bradford. This was close to the refugee camp where she had lived when she first arrived in Britain, but Joseph didn't know this until later.

He'd been aware of her right away, but at the time his mood was one of mild depression about the ideas of the students and the work he was seeing. There were about a dozen of them, all eager to make films or produce television programmes. His job was to teach them the techniques an editor employed in order to assemble a narrative from a series of images, and the tricks he used to create dramatic and emotional effects. Usually Joseph enjoyed showing off his skills, but on this occasion he found himself increasingly irritated by the fact that the ideas in their scripts and videos largely seemed to be secondhand versions of the stock clichés from the glossy magazines and downmarket TV chat shows. He spent most of the first day of the course discussing stories about New Age transcendentalism, about the threat of chemicals to the ecology, and about the role of women in the pop music industry. Some time in the late afternoon he put yet another cassette in the machine, started it with a feeling of weary resignation, and was riveted by a ten-minute video which consisted merely of a young woman addressing the camera. She was talking about her reaction on hearing the news that one of her relatives had been shot in Sarajevo. Occasionally her eyes filled with tears, but the impression Joseph received was that she had no interest in the gimmicks and theatricality which had characterised the other productions. Turning round to look at the woman who was sitting next to him, he realised that the director had been her own subject.

She was tall, a bit awkward in her movements, with beautifully glossy brown hair cut short over the nape of her neck. She was wearing a black sweater and a short tight denim skirt with a zip which opened a couple of inches at the hem as if designed to call attention to her bare thighs. At the end of the day he went for a drink with a group of the students and found himself, after closing time, in a little Kashmiri restaurant alone with Lena. She came from Sarajevo, she told him. Her father was a Croatian, her mother a Muslim, and they had escaped before the worst of the fighting had destroyed the city. When the Serbs arrived they had moved to the cellar of their building where they lived for the next six months, eventually leaving in a convoy with her brother, while her parents stayed behind. In the countryside they were halted for three days while the Serb militia moved through the vehicles, dragging away the young men to be shot and the young women to be raped. All day and all night they lay, clinging to each other, listening to the sound of gunfire and screams in the night. She and her brother had been lucky. They had discussed what to do beforehand, and under the eyes of the Serbs they pretended to be simpletons, drooling and spitting, grunting and moaning incomprehensible words. Crouched by the roadside, they had watched men being shot in the head, collapsing as if under their own weight, and even while their tears flowed they had maintained the pretence, grinning and grimacing and waving their hands in spastic gestures, gibbering like mad people. Remembering it, her face screwed up in a grimace of pain.

'Perhaps it wouldn't have worked if we'd been there longer, but after three days the UN took us through.'

They had ended up on the Croatian coast in a centre for refugees, from where they'd gone to Britain and another centre in Yorkshire. The rest of the family had been lucky, and although two of her uncles had been killed, her parents had survived, arriving in Britain two years later. It had taken her almost four years, she said, to reach the standard in English which would allow her to begin studying for the GCSE examinations, repeating the work she had already done before being forced to leave.

Joseph was as touched as he had ever been by her story, her moist brown eyes, and by the warmth of the rapport between them. Perhaps it was the fact that at her age, no more than twenty-one, she had seen and suffered so much. In the hour past midnight they went back to his hotel, and lying on the narrow bed, she showed him the shrapnel scars on her thigh and described the moment, outside the apartment block where she lived in Sarajevo, when she had felt the bomb which wounded her explode. She had been conscious all the time, and stretched on the ground she had felt a warm gob of flesh and blood splattering on to her neck.

'I was so lucky,' she said, her eyes staring, wide and fixed at the wall, 'so lucky.'

It was only a few days later that she telephoned him to say that she was coming down to London for the weekend. He had hesitated, half regretting the night they had spent together. Since separating from Liz he'd slept with a number of women, some of them for a period of several months. They had all been, he thought, essentially like himself, footloose and independent, people whose need for him was tentative and occasional. With the relationships which lasted longest, at the moment when intimacy became familiar and predictable, he had found himself growing bored and impatient, eager for a taste of new sensations. Oddly enough when this happened the boredom usually turned out to be mutual, the relationship which seemed so stable suddenly revealing itself as a cover for a distance which had never been explored. On these occasions the regret which followed a breakdown would be shot through with relief and a renewed pleasure in being alone. After a while it was as if Joseph's antennae were leading him unerringly to women who understood what would happen and were somehow prepared for this precise pattern of events.

Lena was different, her desire for him wrapped up with her hopes for the future and her plans for a new beginning. Seeing her now, Joseph felt the familiar prod of guilt. From the time of that first phone call he had known how it would end.

'How was it in Prague?' she called out from the kitchen.

She had gone there immediately, as she usually did, exploring the contents of the cupboards and deciding what they should eat that evening. Her visits always began like this, and invariably the entire weekend would be focused around preparing and eating meals. Afterwards she would disappear to the bathroom and emerge, the scents of the bath floating in front of her, half dressed, her long legs enticingly bare, her lips gleaming with fresh paint.

Once upon a time Joseph had anticipated the ritual with

172

pleasure. Now, its predictability irritated him. In any case he didn't want to talk about Prague, partly because he sensed that if he mentioned his brother's wife, Lena would subject him to innumerable questions about her. On the other hand, there was nothing else that he wanted to say. What he really wanted was to be alone, to telephone his father over and over again until he answered the phone, or to sit zapping back and forth between the channels on the television.

'Prague was fine,' he told Lena.

He heard her footsteps on the tiles and she appeared on the other side of the counter which marked the limit of the kitchen area.

'You never tell me anything,' she said.

'What do you want to know?'

Her forehead creased up and she bit her lip, a familiar indication that she was uncertain or apprehensive about his reaction. He had first seen that look when he told her that he didn't want her to come every week. This was the point at which, instead of turning up for a day or two at the weekend, she had taken to arriving halfway through the week and staying for several days. Eventually the suspicion grew in Joseph's mind that this was a prelude to her moving in permanently. The idea of having to share the house in which he had grown up with his mum was surprisingly unpleasant, and after a couple of months he'd had enough. The quarrel which followed had ended with his bellowing at her, and ordering her out. What he didn't want to think about was the fact that this was a moment which, for both of them, confirmed her status as a victim. When she packed her suitcase and walked out without a word he didn't try to stop her. Afterwards he felt a kind of freedom. He would have ended up bullying her and worse, he thought. When she telephoned during the next week he had tried to resist making it up, but she was so amenable, so understanding about what had happened that he found himself giving in. Within a fortnight she was back, her visit

173

opening with the declaration that she had only come for a couple of nights. She understood that he needed his space she said, in the phrase she had learnt. That night her eagerness exhausted him, and he woke later after only a couple of hours' sleep, to find her stroking his erect penis. 'Come on,' she muttered, 'come on.'

After that weekend everything seemed to have returned to normal, but he sensed that she had never forgotten the violence of the mood which had overtaken him. As he approached her shouting, she had cringed, her face screwing up as if in anticipation of a sudden blow. Somehow that moment had imposed a kind of pattern on what happened between them, and when she made a demand he was more and more likely to respond with some kind of challenge. Innocuous as the words were, they both knew that this was what was happening when he answered her question about his trip with a question of his own.

'What do you want to know?'

'I don't know,' she said, turning away from the counter.

Hearing the sullen note in her voice, he suddenly remembered Radka's tears as they sat in the car beneath the monument in Zizkov. Did she look like this when George shouted?

'Hey,' he called to her, relenting. 'Something happened. It's hard to talk about.'

She turned back towards him, her smile as eager and artless as a child.

'Tell me later. After our dinner.'

Later he lay sprawling on the sofa, while she sat on the floor at his feet, her head resting on his leg. It was time for the news, so he switched off the television. He knew by now that her eyes would grow dull and she would hang her head, expecting the inevitable sight of bodies laid out in a row and agonised faces. Once, she told him, she had seen a woman she knew from childhood talking about the torture and rape she had suffered.

174

'I met my brother for the first time in Prague,' he said.

She sat up staring at him.

'Your brother? I thought you had no brothers or sisters.'

'So did I.'

He told her most of it then. She listened in silence, her eyes wide and glowing. Occasionally she asked him a question. When he mentioned his brother's wife, she asked how old Radka was and whether she was pretty.

When he was finished, she got up on her knees and hugged him tight.

'I'm so happy,' she whispered in his ear, 'so happy that you found your brother.'

She hadn't shown any surprise or scepticism so far. If he had told this story to one of his English friends, he thought, they would probably have seen it as a kind of freakish coincidence – believe it or not, he could imagine someone saying. In comparison, Lena came from a landscape in whose history many families had separated and come together again.

'So happy,' she said again.

Her cheeks glowed pink and there were tears in her eyes. For a moment he wondered whether his story had triggered some terrible memory, then it struck him that she had taken it as evidence that she was his confidante, someone to whom he could tell his deepest secrets.

'Your father,' she said. 'What does he think?'

She had never met Kofi, and, for some reason he couldn't quite put his finger on, Joseph wanted to avoid telling her about how his father had reacted. He shrugged. Sensing a slight change in his mood she got up, lay beside him on the sofa and began to kiss him, with a gentle, teasing touch. He returned her kisses, pulling her closer, and she rolled over on top of him. This was the familiar prelude. The kissing would become longer and more intense. Soon they would touch each other, her hands sliding the skirt down over the smoothness of her thighs. Eventually they would get up, his fingers still entangled in her body, and shuffle to the bedroom. Typically, this was the way they almost always spent the first evening of her visit. This time, however, Joseph knew, something was different. Although he'd been, from time to time, bored or uneasy about the prospect of sex with Lena, when it came right down to it his body usually took over, his arousal would conquer his doubts, his thoughts focusing on the sensual pleasure of touching her, the blood pumping faster through his veins as she moved against him.

This evening, his reactions seemed to have changed. Her weight on his body brought no response, and instead of reaching down to fondle her thighs, he merely lay back, his hand trailing on the floor, his muscles passive and indifferent.

'What's the matter?' Lena asked.

'Nothing,' he replied. 'I'm tired.'

'I understand,' she whispered in his ear. 'You have things on your mind.'

She slid off him, sat down on the floor again and began stroking him gently. He lay back and closed his eyes as she traced the outline of his supine penis with her fingers, then tugged at the zipper on his trousers. Thoughts of Radka floated through his head as she stroked him into erection and he felt the first soft touch of her lips, but almost immediately he suppressed them, deliberately bringing up the image of the Roma woman Milena. Perhaps, he thought, it would have been like this with Milena. As for Radka, it would have been different between them. Somehow his imagination wouldn't go beyond taking her in his arms and kissing her. When they said goodbye in the car by the side of the street in Zizkov, she had pressed close to him, and her mouth had lingered on his cheek. It was Milena who had gripped his genitals and looked into his eyes.

He was close to orgasm when the doorbell rang. His instinct was to ignore it, but it rang again, two long insistent

176

bursts, and Lena pulled away from him. He looked up and she gave him an enquiring look.

'I'll just see who it is,' he muttered.

Kofi was standing on the doorstep.

'Ah,' he said. 'You were sleeping.'

'No,' Joseph told him. 'Come in.'

Kofi came through the door, moving cautiously, like an animal scenting a trap. Lena had scampered up the stairs as Joseph went to the door, but his father spotted the signs of her presence immediately, half-empty glasses, her shoes tumbled into a corner, the smell of perfume. He grinned at Joseph.

'You have a visitor. I came too late.'

'It's okay. It doesn't matter.'

Kofi sat down, refusing Joseph's offer of a drink. He was thinking about how to begin, but before he could open his mouth Lena came back into the room. She had changed into a long black dress and looking at her through his father's eyes Joseph saw, as if in the days when they first met, how attractive she was.

After she shook hands with Kofi she offered to make him some coffee and he accepted immediately.

'I thought you didn't want any,' Joseph reminded him.

'Ah,' Kofi exclaimed, beaming. 'When such a beautiful girl offers you refreshment you should never refuse.'

Joseph shook his head, laughing, but Lena made a triumphant face at him before marching off to the kitchen.

'I think I'll go to Germany,' Kofi said abruptly.

TWELVE

He had made the decision during the course of the day. After Joseph left him at lunchtime he'd continued sitting on the sofa. He was thinking about Katya, but, actually, a stream of images kept on pouring through his mind, some of which were connected with her, some of them not. The University Tower at Leninsky Gory kept on recurring, the red spark like a star in the night sky. He remembered, too, walking along the banks of the Moskva, staring up at the group of statues on top of the Kotelnicheskaya building, his head rearing back on his shoulders as if he was nursing a bleeding nose. In the metro approaching Lubyanka he had seen a woman, hair cropped short, but so light and glossy that it shone like a beacon in the artificial light. Her profile, flawless, a pale smooth skin, from which gleamed a bright blue eye. She had sensed him watching her, and she had turned a little towards him and smiled. If his Russian had been better he would have spoken to her, but in a couple of seconds the train pulled into the station and she had gone for ever. Looking at the photos of Katya with George in Germany he wondered whether the woman in the metro had survived and, if she had, whether she bore any resemblance now to the vision he had seen that day.

He must have sat motionless for a couple of hours, but eventually, he got up and went to the telephone. He dialled the number on the top of the letter he'd received, and as he did so, his heart seemed to thump and twitch unpleasantly. When the ringing suddenly stopped and Katya's voice answered, the ground lurched and if he had not been holding on to the back of the sofa he would have fallen. As it was he couldn't speak, and moving as if in a dream he lowered the receiver and put it carefully back in its cradle. Without sitting down again he went to put his overcoat on and left the house. At the library he realised that he was too agitated to work on his journal, so he gathered together a pile of novels he had read before, some of them more than two or three times. At last he settled on *War and Peace*, unable to begin at the beginning, but then forcing himself into concentration as he read about the march on Moscow, seeing in his mind the monument to Prince Bagration on the hill near the museum at Borodino. As they walked up the slope Katya, in a mournful voice, told him how many men had died there. The sun was shining, but as he listened to her, a chill seemed to settle in the air. 'We walk on their bones,' she said.

When the library closed he was still reading. At first he began walking back home, but his feet carried him to a pub on the corner, where he stood for a while nursing half a pint of lager. In normal circumstances the look of the place or the buzz of conversation would have been part of a background which he saw and heard without taking notice, but on this occasion he had found himself paying attention, listening to the words and gauging the quality of the sounds as if they were somehow important to him. Opposite where he stood, on the other side of the bar, a young couple sat, facing each other, their heads close together. On another day his eye would have passed over them, dismissing the pair as possessing no interest or distinction. The woman's hair was a mousy brown straggle, her profile thin-lipped and beaky. Her companion, whose gaze seemed always to be fixed on her eyes, was an exact male equivalent. Nothing special. As Kofi watched, he saw that their hands were clasped together on top of the table. This was a case of love, Kofi guessed, and he wondered whether he and Katya had looked like this in their time, obviously wrapped up in each other, and transported by the unpredictable surging of vagrant emotions. Of course, in public, he had never held her hand like this. That would have been foolish. Their intention, when they walked together in the city, was to look like teacher and student, Katya gravely reciting facts and figures or brief sketches of history while she pointed to various features of the buildings they passed. In the Central Market they walked closer together, and he ran his fingers along the back of her hand, or squeezed the crook of her elbow. Feeling his touch she would turn and smile. This was one of the places where they felt at ease. The traders were swarthy, leather-skinned brown people, or dark-eyed women, bulky in layers of padded cloth and trailing scarves, sometimes a family scurrying like ants round a stall piled with vegetables. Pushing through the fringe of women, while Kofi lingered, his eyes fixed on the smooth fall of her hair, Katya handled and squeezed peppers from Georgia, tomatoes from Kazakhstan, potatoes from the Ukraine. She stroked squashes and peered at jars of pickled fish and interrogated prices. When she looked back at him over her shoulder, her eyes sparkled and her cheeks were pink with pleasure.

Remembering this, Kofi felt a sudden catch in his breath, a spasm which was physically insignificant but, in his mind, seemed unexpected and dislocating, as shocking as the tremor of an earthquake, the ground threatening to slide away from under his feet. It was an effect which disturbed him without being astonishing because, before this event, he had viewed his life as a series of distinct and separate periods, each one of which he had left behind him, discarding it like the old skin of a moulting snake.

He had been born in Accra and spent his early life there. Then he had been incarcerated in the hold of a ship floating through the formless ocean. Then he had been Makonnen's apprentice, and later on a student. Then he became a diplomat, and after that a man who drifted, more or less, without a struggle into the contemplation of old age. These layers in his life had their existence in different countries, or in environments which were isolated from each other by moments of oblivion. In every

180

one of these periods he had been associated with one or another person who, for a time, had been everything to him but who had eventually disappeared, to be replaced by another. Sometimes when he encountered someone who had always lived in the same town or village, Kofi had a sensation of disbelief about the fact that their lives had been so static and unchanging. In fact the barriers of space and time between his present existence and his other lives gave him a feeling of safety and reassurance. On some occasions hearing a snatch of music or becoming aware of a scent, he would be thrown into a pool of memory in which he would float for a few minutes, halfway between sorrow and nostalgia. These incursions were like a breach in the stoicism which had become a necessary and inevitable part of his survival, and he would note them with a cautious interest, while he waited for the wound to heal.

On the other hand, since talking to Joseph that day, and since viewing the photographs of his son George, Kofi had been shaken and tormented by storms of unaccustomed emotion. Oddly enough, although these cataclysms were triggered by thoughts of Katya and by the sound of her voice, he knew that she wasn't their focus. He had long ago accommodated his separation from her, and now his recollections of that time were merely an alluvial sediment, a dark sludge of regret which weighed down his heart but which had no significance for the way that he lived. What he felt about George was entirely different. Looking at the photographs he had experienced a strange burst of hope and brightness. Although he was looking at the picture of a grown man, older than Joseph, it was as if this son had just been born, a tiny and vulnerable infant with the power to change his life.

In an instant he knew what he had to do, and as if triggered by the turmoil inside him, he put his glass down and walked out of the pub, then across the road into the tube station.

He reached Joseph's house without being entirely conscious of getting there, or what he had seen along the way. He had made his decision before leaving the pub, but faced with his son's incredulous expression, he found it next to impossible to describe the train of thought which had led him to it, or to defend what he wanted to do in the rational way that he knew Joseph would expect.

'What's brought this on?' Joseph asked. As he spoke he watched his father with narrowed eyes. Kofi guessed he was casting about in his mind for arguments which would make his disapproval sound reasonable and dispassionate.

'I telephoned,' Kofi said. 'I telephoned and I heard her voice.' He looked over at the kitchen where the sound of cups rattling seemed to be announcing Lena's return. A brief pause, then he lowered his voice and spoke with a rapid urgency, as if he wanted to get the words out before he had to stop. 'I thought I'd forgotten all of it. Even when you told me about George I wasn't too worried because I'll probably see him sooner or later, but there're other things that happened that I must know about. I have to see her and talk to her. I can't leave it like this.'

'Let's talk about it,' Joseph said quickly.

Seeing the expression of concern on Joseph's face, Kofi wondered whether he was thinking of George as a rival. If that was so, trying to reassure him might make things worse, but the truth was that although he loved Joseph, he was often uncertain of what he was thinking or how he would react. As a child Kofi had thought of his parents' role in his life as part of the structure of the world, predestined and unalterable as the sun rising. During that time he had hardly seen his father, and knew practically nothing about him. If he had it would have made very little difference, certainly not to his father, who, in any case, took his respect and submission for granted. In contrast Joseph had grown up in a world where the status of their relationship was conditional, subject to sudden reversals and dependent on the movement of unpredictable emotions. For years Kofi had struggled with the perception that Joseph, schooled by his mother, didn't know how to be a son. Meanwhile he suspected that Joseph believed that his father had no idea how to be a real parent, and whatever happened between them there would always be something missing. This was one of the reasons he now found it so difficult to say anything about the emotions stirred up by the sight of George's photograph. In some hidden recess of his heart he hoped that when he met George, they would be father and son.

'There's nothing to talk about,' he told Joseph. 'I'm going to see her. I can't leave it like this.'

THIRTEEN

DIARY OF DESIRE

The life and times of Kofi George Coker
Moscow 1957

In the depth of winter we went north to Kalinin where Valery said we could see the Volga, or if we were lucky, walk on its frozen surface. That never happened. The train journey was fine. We left early from the station where the trains set off for Novgorod and Leningrad, and within a few minutes we were passing through a landscape which looked like a fairy tale in a library book. All around the line the banks of snow stood up higher than our heads; beyond them a forest of black pillars topped with branches of dark green, all buried under a coating of white. Sometimes through a gap in the trees I could see the white fields stretching away into the distance. Sometimes we stopped while they cleared some obstruction along the line, and the only sound to be heard was the voices of the railway people shouting to each other, or strange music of metal striking frozen metal, or somewhere in the forest a muffled crash of falling snow.

The purpose was to walk in the forest; later on, on the way back we could see the town, he said, but we never did that, either. Instead we got lost. Valery had borrowed a pair of skis for me, but although he had given me a few lessons out on the hills I found it nearly an intolerable task trudging along behind him among the trees, my lungs bursting, my feet frozen, my legs close to collapse. Within a couple of hours we were lost, turning backwards and forwards in the middle of the silent trees. He said there were no wolves but as the sky darkened I had the feeling I could hear the padding of feet around us. My lips were too stiff to open and I had

*to speak through my teeth. If I survive this, I told him, never again.
Some time in the afternoon, we came to a stretch where the trees
grew thinner. It was snowing again, the flakes of white whirling
around our heads, covering us with white powder. Through the
white mist we saw a snowman working, digging in the snow,
behind the vague outline of a clump of huts. When he saw us he
straightened up slowly, shedding a shower of white as he moved,
and we saw that he was real. I suppose we were covered in snow
ourselves, and we must have looked like spirits emerging from the
woods, because he stared at us as if he was seeing ghosts. Valery
spoke with him and he laughed, shook our hands and led us into
the nearest* izba, *their name for the cabins in which they lived.*

*Inside it seemed like one large room, although when I got my
senses back I saw that there was a curtain covering the entrance
to another room, and towards the back a door which led to some
kind of stable. There was a stove in the middle of the wooden
floor around which the family sat, a woman nursing a baby
and three children, the eldest about ten. They put our coats into
a heap in the corner and brought us stools on which to sit. They
seemed friendly, and once the ice was broken the children gathered
round us, touching our clothes and asking questions. Valery talked
without stopping. I couldn't understand much of what he said, but
mostly it was about me. The peasant had a beard which gave him
a wild, strange look, but he sat opposite us and talked as if we were
ordinary visitors who had dropped in for the evening. We were on
a collective farm somewhere between Kalinin and Klin, he told us,
and we couldn't get to either place in time to catch the train for
Moscow. We would have to stay until the morning. 'Where do we
sleep?' I asked Valery. 'In the corner,' he told me, giving a look
which warned me to shut up. 'This is how the peasants live.' At
the time it struck me that the prospect pleased him.*

*We ate soup which the wife ladled out of the pot. We had eaten
the* kolbasa *and black bread we brought for the trip on the train
and now I was starving hungry. It was some kind of cabbage
soup as far as I can remember, with mushrooms and dumplings
floating in it. I didn't ask what was in them. It wasn't meat, a
fact for which I was grateful. Since my time on the boats, when*

185

they fed the crews whatever they could find, I always feared eating meat that I couldn't recognise.

We ate in silence, more or less. Afterwards the man produced a big bottle, a cork rammed into the top. He pulled the cork with his teeth, and without asking, poured the vodka into the bowls from which we'd eaten. Valery said he must have made it himself, and I was never sure it was actually vodka. It wasn't kvas, which was what I expected, and which is a mild-tasting watery drink a bit like ginger beer. Valery gulped his down as if it was kvas, but when I did the same I gasped and choked as it flooded down my throat – this was pure alcohol, liquid fire. No one seemed to notice and the peasant's only reaction was to pour some more into my bowl, which I sipped slowly, my head already beginning to spin. Time seemed to stop. The wife had been staring at me all the while, and as I sat swaying she suddenly asked me a question which I didn't understand. Before Valery could say anything the peasant turned to her and replied in a loud voice, which seemed to start some kind of argument in which the children joined. Valery listened, smiling. 'They're trying to work out,' he said, 'if you come from the same country as Paul Robeson.' That was my cue, and I started explaining, with Valery translating, where I came from. They listened politely, but talking about my life and about why I had come there seemed almost cruel, as if I was mocking their poverty. In the villages I had been to in my youth life had never been as hard. The rest of the night is lost in memory. I don't know where or how we slept, but in the morning it had stopped snowing and the peasant showed us a track which led to a village where the train stopped. We were back in our comfortable room in Cheryomushki by the afternoon.

Adventures like this made me firm friends with Valery. Hussein said I was naïve. He said as little as possible when Valery was around, and if we were talking in the room and he came in Hussein would take the first opportunity to leave. 'You can't trust him,' he would say. I didn't understand why it mattered, and, in any case, there were times when Hussein's cynicism annoyed me. I was enjoying everything, learning something new every day. Katya seemed to be taking an interest in me, which made going to the classes an excitement. At the time I had no idea what to do about my desire for her, apart from working hard at her lessons, but my pleasure was intense when she spoke only to me or came close to show me something in a book. The other boys noticed and began teasing me. Calvin, an Indian from the Caribbean, whenever he saw me silent or abstracted, would call out her full name softly in his strange accent. All this irritated Hussein as much as my friendship with Valery. One time he came into the room, picked up a book of Soviet history Katya had lent me, and flipped through the pages, laughing. 'Don't believe any of this,' he said. 'The Party invents history according to what they need.' The odd thing was that when he said this it gave me a kind of shock, if only because I found it hard to believe that an entire book, an official printed record, could tell lies. 'Look at Khrushchev's secret speech,' he continued. That made me look around, wishing that he'd lower his voice. Everyone knew about the speech in which Khrushchev had described Stalin's crimes against the people, but at our first meeting of the foreign students' union we had been addressed on this subject, among others, by the warden, who was also the deputy chairman of the regional committee. There were all kinds of rumours designed to demoralise the nation, he said, and it was therefore important, as guests of the Party and the state, not to gossip openly about internal politics. We could all read between the lines, and Hussein's sceptical language seemed exactly the kind of gossip which would disturb the authorities.

'They're busy rewriting the history of Comrade Stalin and Comrade Beria,' Hussein said, laughing. 'Just ask your precious Katya to lend you Stalin's book on politics. A year ago everyone had to read it. Now you would never know it existed.'

At times like this I felt as though there were currents running under my feet which I could hear, like rushing water under the ice, and in this mood I took every chance I could to avoid both Hussein and Valery. Calvin was my refuge. He hung out with a crazy Siberian called Dimitri, and they always seemed to know about places to go where there was drink and girls and dancing. One evening we went to the Komsomol college where they were having what seemed to be a combination of a picnic and a dance

187

out in the snow-covered grounds. They were playing some kind of game. It was one of those customs which in that strange country seemed more familiar to me than anything I encountered in England. It was the sort of game they might have played in villages on the coast, ploughing through the sand on the shore instead of snowdrifts. In this one the boys and girls all stood in a huge circle, singing and clapping their hands. In the middle one of them danced with a scarf, then dancing over to the circle, threw the scarf round the partner of their choice who would then come into the circle, exchange a kiss, and take up the dance, repeating the exercise until everyone in the circle was exhausted. Halfway through the proceedings half the boys in the circle would be drunk enough to fall over, and would be pulled up by their companions covered in snow to lurch unsteadily round the circle bellowing whatever music or chant came into their heads. The women were not far behind, either, throwing their legs up and tumbling over to show their legs up to the tops of the woollen stockings under the long overcoats and thick skirts. In these white nights the sight still comes back to me as if it was yesterday and sometimes I feel like shouting and singing in the faces of the old men around me – unforgettable, the boys and girls whirling as they kicked up the clouds of white powder, the shrieking of the women's voices, the feel of your partner's arms on either side clutching you tight as the circle moved like an irresistible turning wheel in which we pranced and kicked like tireless young ponies. In spite of everything, I remember these as the most joyous moments of my youth.

On this occasion there was a group of us from Cheryomushki, Calvin and Dimitri, a South African named Bloke, a big Yoruba named Olu, and a few more Africans from all over the place. We had half a dozen bottles between us, Stolichnaya, Moskovskaya, Pertsovka and Starka, and we were nipping steadily comparing the tastes, so it wasn't long before we were deep in the spirit of the thing. Before too long, one of the girls in the ring spotted Olu, probably the most conspicuous man in the ring. She threw her scarf round him and dragged him in, and they kissed, a luscious open-mouthed slobber which roused a riot of screeches and yells *all round the ring. When it was Olu's turn to choose he threw the scarf round a girl who was as physically notable in her way as he was in his. She was tall, a beauty with thick blonde hair which swirled in a cloud round her as she danced. In the circle Olu threw his arms round her, but when he thrust his lips forward she seemed to flinch and turning aside, kissed him on the cheek before breaking away. Olu tried to grapple with her again, but this time she thrust him away. He stood there for a moment then, moving deliberately, walked out of the circle. When we looked for him he had gone.*

This was the talk of Cheryomushki for a while. In the impromptu students' union meeting which took place the next day, Olu claimed that the girl had said, 'Abyezhyana' – monkey. Valery pointed out that this was so nekulturny *that a Komsomol student could never have said it. In public the other students were non-committal. In private Hussein said that this would teach some of us that the white man was the same whether he was in Nairobi or Moscow. Calvin and Dimitri said* nitchevo – *it doesn't matter. That same night, Calvin invited me to meet a girl to whom Dimitri had introduced him. She worked in one of the new fertiliser factories, but she had expensive tastes, for which her boyfriends paid. Calvin shrugged. 'Listen man,' he said. 'The thing is cheaper than these stuck up pussy at the college. I give her what she want, she give me what I want.' Sometimes, he said, a student from back home would bring bundles of stockings and cosmetics which the girl, Marina, loved, but a present of a few roubles would do. The allowances which the foreign students received were three times that of the Soviets, so we always had roubles to spare. Marina, he said, would greet me with open arms. The only snag was that visiting her required careful co-ordination, because although she lived in an apartment in Prospekt Kalinina near Novy Arbat, a district of shops and markets full of traders from the republics where a foreigner wouldn't stand out too much, she shared it with several of her family, and she was only available when her mother was absent and she was by herself, or when she could gain some privacy by locking the children of the house in their room.*

I said yes without thinking about it. The truth was that I had not touched a woman for months and the prospect filled me with lustful excitement. A few days later the visit was arranged. On the train to Arbatskaya we hardly spoke, although every time Calvin caught my eye he grinned and winked. It was already dark and we slipped without notice through the market as the traders packed up crowding the stalls for vodka and little snacks of pirozhki. At the apartment building we raced up the narrow stairs, and on the landing Calvin rapped softly on the door. On the way up we met no one, which was just as well because anyone who saw us would have known we were not supposed to be there. Marina opened it immediately and waved us inside without speaking. Behind her the apartment was a warren of small rooms to judge by the number of doors opening off the hallway which also seemed to serve as a bedroom, because there were a couple of cots leaning against the wall with a heap of folded blankets stacked next to them. Marina led us into a room at the end of the hall. It was neat and pretty, arranged like a bedsitter with a big double bed, a wardrobe, a table and a sink in one corner. The walls were lined with photographs which I guessed were her mother's. She was a short, dark-haired girl with big, wide blue eyes, short sturdy legs, big breasts and a smiling, vivacious manner. Calvin put his arms round her and they kissed, then he introduced me, his arm still clasping her proprietorially. She smiled and shook my hand, seemingly oblivious to the fact that by now Calvin was standing behind her with his hands under her sweater, squeezing and stroking her breasts. On the way to the apartment I had been wondering how Calvin conversed with the girl, because, although he had been in the country a year longer than me, his Russian was hardly any better than mine. As it happened she spoke a few words of English, and with the Russian we knew it was enough. In any case Calvin made it clear that he wasn't there to talk. He had wrapped some things in a package before we left, some presents he'd been saving up, he said, and now he took it out of his pocket and gave it to her. She opened it excitedly. There wasn't much, lipstick, creams, soap, a bra and pants and a pair of stockings, but Marina seemed thrilled, turning round to hug and kiss him. In return Calvin sat down on the bed and pulled *her down to him, his hand burrowing quickly under her skirt. From that point neither of them took much notice of my presence, except that Marina pulled back long enough to draw the blanket over them, concealing her body. In a minute Calvin was on top of her thrusting like a steam engine, both of them gasping and groaning as if they were completely alone. Under the cover I could see her knees raised and as the exercise became more vigorous her legs shot up, dislodging the blanket. This time she didn't bother about it and I watched them, my penis so erect that it was pressing painfully against my trousers. She was still wearing her stockings rolled round elastic bands high on her thighs, the muscles bulging and straining above them. Her legs circled Calvin's waist and she pressed with her heels on Calvin's buttocks. It seemed an age, but in a few minutes the thrusting quickened, Marina squirmed urgently and Calvin groaned, loud and agonised as if someone had jabbed him with a needle. He stopped moving, and Marina relaxed while Calvin rolled off her. He looked at me. 'Go ahead,' he muttered.*

Marina was smiling, her face flushing red, her legs slightly apart, the patch of dark hair at the bottom of her belly glistening. I got on the bed and she put her arms around me. Her body felt soft and welcoming and without my aiming it my penis slipped easily into her. She gave a high-pitched moan in my ear and gripped me tight. I don't suppose I took any longer about it than Calvin had, although I tried to prolong it, stretching out the incredible pleasure of being inside that tight warm crevice, pushing against the pressure of her flesh, the rush coming irresistibly from a distance like an express train. I was vaguely aware of Calvin sitting beside me on the bed, although what he was doing I didn't know or care. Later on he told me he was squeezing her breasts and working himself up for another go, but every time I slowed down trying to hold off the explosion Marina pushed against me, clutching me to her, squeezing me between her thighs, urging me on. It was over in what seemed like a couple of minutes. Afterwards I could hear again and I saw Calvin grinning at me. 'Boy,' he said. 'You needed that.' Marina laughed, slipped off the bed and pulling

her skirt down went out the door. Calvin stretched luxuriously.
'Good stuff, eh?'

I gave Marina most of the roubles I had in my pocket, embarrassed about doing so, but she took the money with a pretty smile and tucked it away without self-consciousness. Before we left, Calvin had her again, up against the wall next to the outer door this time, while I kept watch. All the way home he whistled and talked in a mood of infectious euphoria. I felt good too and that night I slept without dreams.

Prague

September 1999

FOURTEEN

George parked near the embankment, not far from the looming beehive of the National Theatre, and walked along to the Charles Bridge. He could have driven over the next bridge and parked on the left bank, but it was a bright cool evening and he wanted to take some time to reflect. Further up, the river made the rushing sound of a waterfall as it tumbled over the weir in long streams of feathery white. Below him the water lapped and sucked against the worn stone pilings. Halfway across George stopped and leant on the railing. From here he could see the back of the building where he was due to meet Liebl. George knew the café and it was far enough off the beaten track to be a quiet retreat. Tourists going to and from the castle stayed on the bridge, and there were few residents living in the immediate vicinity. Trade would be generally restricted to a small group of regulars, who, early in the evening, would still be working or on their way home. This, George presumed, was the reason Liebl had selected the place.

The phone had rung at nine in the morning, and, somehow, George hadn't been surprised to hear the familiar voice wheezing through the receiver. These messages had once been so much a part of his life that it seemed normal, as if the silence of the previous years had merely been a longer pause than usual. He was driving into Prague, Liebl had said, in order to see George, and he would say no more, except to name the time and place. That too, was as usual.

George had been certain, from the moment he picked up the phone, that what Liebl was after had something to do with the pictures, but none of the scenarios he outlined in his mind seemed satisfactory. Oddly enough, that period of his life, recent as it was, already seemed over and done with, ancient history. This was mostly because of the debacle in Hamburg. Afterwards they had decided that the whole enterprise was too dangerous to continue. For George the event had been earth-shattering, a trauma.

'I understand,' Valentin said. 'But there was nothing to be done. It was them or us.'

To George's surprise, both of his partners treated his distress with a kind of respect, almost as if they were humouring the nervousness of a raw recruit unexpectedly precipitated into a gun battle. They had disposed of the bodies without telling him where, but although Valentin maintained that they would never be found, the men's faces floated through his dreams from time to time. Somehow, putting a stop to the treadmill of thieving and smuggling seemed like a kind of expiation which gave him relief. His partners had agreed. Victor had enough money to begin winding up his motor business in Russia and complete the process of getting out. In any case, as he said, if he could keep the sums he had to pay out for protection he'd be a rich man, even in the West. The rest of the hoard could stay where it was. Valentin merely shrugged, his fertile mind already occupied with the prospects of the new and legitimate enterprise George had proposed. George had insisted on getting out of Germany and basing themselves in Prague, the nearest convenient location, because he assumed that, sooner or later, the Georgians' accomplices would work out what had happened and come looking. Nevertheless, after more than a year during which there had been no sign of trouble, he had begun to forget about the trail which must have connected the beheading in Smichov with the objects he had sold in Berlin. But it had always been there at the back of his mind. Liebl's reappearance was an unpleasant shock, but one which he had somehow been expecting, like a rotting corpse bobbing up from the depths of a lake.

As usual, Valentin seemed unaffected by the dread which had begun to churn inside George from the moment he heard Liebl's voice. In the end, he said coolly, all they could do was to hear what the man had to say. They had decided that George would go alone to the meeting. After all there was no point in letting Liebl know any more than he needed to about them. Valentin would come and find him afterwards.

He looked at his watch. He was now several minutes late, as he had intended, and he walked quickly on to the first flight of stairs off the bridge, which led on to Na Kampě. This was a short street lined with hotels and bars, ending in a postage-stamp park bordering the river. A long black limousine was parked immediately outside the door of the café. It was empty except for the driver, one tattooed arm crooked through the open window, blond hair cut close to his pink scalp. George guessed that this must be Liebl's vehicle, and he let his gaze rest on the driver's face, waiting for some sign of interest or recognition, but the man's only reaction was to give him an impassive glance before turning his head away.

The L-shaped interior of the café was a few steps down from street level, and the lighting gave it the impression of being dappled in shadow. It was too early for a crowd and Liebl was sitting by himself at one of the rectangular tables in the short base of the L. Another shaven-headed blond wearing a T-shirt, and built like a wrestler, was sitting a couple of tables away, between Liebl and the door. Ignoring him, George threaded his way between the tables and sat down on the bench opposite Liebl. The surface in front of the fat man was already covered in food and drink. The menu here contained the staple items to be found all over the country, pork, duck, beef, spinach, beetroot, cabbage, and dumplings made of potatoes or flour, the sort of bland, solid food which could see a farmer through the day. George had been reared on the German equivalent of these dishes and now he found the local cuisine boring and unappetising, but Liebl was chomping his way through the potato dumplings like someone in the middle of a banquet. He lifted his head and grunted an acknowledgement when George sat down, then raised his finger in a signal. The waiter, a skinny boy wearing an apron, arrived almost immediately, but George waved the menu away and told him to bring vodka. Liebl gave a muffled chuckle.

'To drink without eating is unhealthy,' he said.

George didn't bother to reply.

'What do you want?' he asked.

Liebl smiled. There was a ring of grease round his mouth and a little trickle of brown sauce on his chin. George looked away, only now remembering what a messy eater he had been. Around his plate there was a scattering of crumbled bread, a little pile of sticky bones was growing on a napkin in front of him, and there were splashes of sauce and beer on the surface of the table.

'I want to save your life,' Liebl announced. 'You're dealing with savages. Don't be fooled by their suits and ties. These people would enjoy cutting your head off.'

He knew about the killing in Smichov, George thought. This was what he had suspected all along. Liebl turning up out of the blue would have been just too much of a coincidence.

'I don't know what you're talking about,' George said.

Liebl lifted his glass and sucked down a half-litre of beer in one long fluent swallow. He lowered it, rapped it on the table to call the waiter, and wiped his mouth with the back of his hand. He pointed to the empty glass with his stubby finger, belched delicately, then turned his attention to George.

'Let me tell you a story,' he said.

George listened, his face impassive, but with a sinking feeling in his stomach, accompanied by a hot flush of rage at his own stupidity. What a fool he'd been to go to this man. The story Liebl told him sounded credible, but knowing him of old, George was certain that it was a concoction, made up of the truth, mingled with lies which it would be difficult or impossible to detect, and all of it would be intended to move him in one direction or the other.

A short while ago, Liebl said, an old friend had come to see him in Berlin. This was Zviad Abuladze, formerly a KGB officer, who also happened to be a Georgian. He was now a powerful and well connected businessman with interests in the security industry and links to several large corporations.

George knew exactly what that meant. The former KGB man, like many of his intelligence colleagues, would be a gang leader on a large scale, the ruthless and violent instrument of warring entrepreneurs. Over the last decade, as the large corporations jostled to repossess the resources of the Union, few of them could have survived or flourished without the services of the gangsters.

His friend, Liebl continued, had heard a disturbing rumour. Various pictures, and other valuable objects, looted from private houses, museums and churches in Georgia, were up for sale in the West. Such things had happened before and there was a continual stream of objects marching westwards from Russia and the former republics, but these appeared to come from the same source. Ownership was a difficult matter, and most of the pictures couldn't easily be authenticated in any case, but it was clear where they had come from. A number of other pictures and works of art had disappeared at the same time and were still unaccounted for. The Georgians guessed that the pictures they had seen on the market were only part of a hoard of loot. This was the cultural heritage of the fledgling state, they believed, and it could ill afford to lose its cultural artefacts, symbols of an ancient identity. This was the real issue. In normal circumstances these people had much more serious business to pursue than a few lost pictures, but the theft was the equivalent of stealing their souls, an extension of what the Russians had done to them for so many years.

'You can imagine,' Liebl said, 'what a terrible dilemma I faced.'

He pushed his plate aside and stared seriously at George. The man had come to him because they were old acquaintances, and they were, so to speak, in the same business. His request for information was also, in some sense, a commission to locate the hoard that he was certain existed, hidden somewhere in the territory of the former Union. By chance, Liebl continued, he was aware that a minor masterpiece had come into his friend Gunther's hands. So what was he to tell Abuladze?

'What did you tell him?' George asked.

'We made a deal. I offered to recover the goods. At a price, of course.' He paused, swigged at his beer, put it down and wiped his mouth. 'I'll make the same deal with you. Put the stuff in my hands and we'll share the profits. I'm talking about millions of marks.'

George shrugged.

'I had a few pictures. I sold them to Gunther. That's it. I can't help you. I wish I could.'

Liebl chuckled appreciatively.

'That's right,' he said. 'Think it over. You should talk about it with your Russian friends. But there is the problem of time. People talk and these rumours get around. I am not the only one now trying to find these things. The bees are searching for the honey. I hear they sent you a little message.'

Still smiling, he drew his finger across his throat. George stared back, focusing on the moist slits of Liebl's eyes.

'Was that you?'

Liebl shook his head.

'You know I don't work like that. But what you should know now is that the vultures are circling. You don't have much time.'

Valentin was waiting on the bridge. He fell into step beside George, and they walked across, meandering through the crowd of tourists, like two friends out for a stroll. Ahead of them the red sun, bisected by the cathedral spires, had begun to cast long shadows over the river.

'He knows everything,' George said.

Being with Valentin after such a meeting restored his equilibrium. When it came to these matters his cousin had a core of confidence which always surprised and sometimes delighted George. For instance, after the night of the Romanian's beheading, he had dealt with the police with an impressive calm, showing them round the factory, explaining the processes and offering them theories about the murder. They had been suspicious, of course, but both George and Valentin had several witnesses to the fact that they were miles away at the time of the killing. In any case, the authorities had recently come across several cases of the same kind of violence, all stemming from the criminal activities of the gangs that were pouring in from the East, and the dead man was a Romanian, a fact which made anything possible. On the other hand, it was no part of their business to harass respectable foreign investors unnecessarily, especially those who, like George and Valentin, had begun by establishing friendly relations with the local police, offering generous rates for part-time security work, and contributing gifts of spare parts and tyres when the occasion arose. By the end of the day the crime had gone down as one more unexplained event in the chain of mayhem inspired by the mafia from the East. All this was due to Valentin's self assurance, and it was clear that he wasn't yet prepared to take Liebl as seriously as George did.

'Maybe he's bluffing.'

George shook his head.

'I don't think so. What I think is that Liebl knows what we've got and his story about making a deal with Abuladze is exactly true. So I think in Hamburg it was Liebl who sent the Georgians, maybe Abuladze gave him a team to work with. If a gang had sent them the rest of their people would have come looking for them, and maybe they'd have

201

been all over us for the last year. I think Liebl worked out what happened and wrote them off. Since then he's been waiting. Somehow he kept the Georgians off our backs, or he didn't tell them where and who we were. When his men didn't come back he understood that we wouldn't be easy to take, and he didn't want us killed before he got his hands on the treasure. So he's been playing cat and mouse with us. But maybe he's tired of waiting or his bosses have told him to end the game.'

Liebl had denied that the break-in and the decapitation of the gypsy mechanic had been his work, but George was certain now that it was all part of a strategy designed to get the result he wanted.

'Liebl moves like a chess player,' he told Valentin. 'While you're worrying about protecting your queen he'll take a few pawns and then you'll suddenly find yourself fighting to avoid checkmate, but by then it will be too late.'

This was more or less what had happened when he had been Liebl's reluctant protégé. George had worked with him for a year, and, although he had become accustomed to the security chief's waddling incursions into his routine and his interminable questions, he had felt a distinct sensation of relief when Liebl announced that he was being transferred to the university. His mood changed, however, when he heard that he was also being transferred at the same time.

'The university?' George had asked incredulously. 'I'm not a professor.'

'Don't be silly,' Liebl chuckled. 'They have canteens there, too.'

'Why me?' George asked him. 'You already have people there.'

He was, in any case, struggling with a feeling of surprise. Liebl's job at the factory had been concerned with black market infractions, petty thievery and hooliganism. At the university there would be issues of ideology, public relations and espionage. Liebl must have pulled some strings to get the job. Even odder was the fact that they were allowing him to take a petty informant whose only contribution had been to relay a few items of routine gossip.

Liebl grinned at him.

'You're more important than you know,' he said. 'The university is full of comrades from fraternal socialist countries. We have to keep an eye on them, make sure that they stay fraternal. Vietnamese, Mozambicans, Angolans, Cubans, they're all here. But it's not like the old days. We bring them here, give them scholarships, educate them, and their response is distrust. They stay together, read banned books, write to their newspapers complaining about their treatment here, and now they even have meetings from which whites are excluded. We have to protect them, but we can't do that if we don't know what's happening.' He paused, as if to let the significance of what he was saying sink in. 'It should be easy for a man of your colour to speak with them, and, of course, you're one of us.'

From that moment George saw that there would be no point in arguing, but he made the attempt anyway.

'I can't do that,' he told Liebl. 'I want to stay here. I'm sure they'll keep me here if I tell them I want to stay.'

'If you do,' Liebl replied immediately, 'we'll bring you up in front of the conflict commission. You'll be on your way to some hole in the countryside in a couple of days. If you're lucky. They might want to arrest you.' The conflict commission decided the scale of punishments a worker could suffer for petty theft, as well as resolving disputes, but in particularly difficult cases they could call in the police, and if the security officials recommended it, they certainly would. Liebl paused for the threat to sink in. 'You don't want to be arrested.'

At this point George gave up his objections. As it turned out, the task wasn't difficult. Once he appeared on the campus African and Asian students came to him, their curiosity

203

piqued by his colour and his air of being at home in the city. They invited him to parties, asked for his help with translating and studying German texts, and harassed him for assistance in meeting and chatting with the women. George's English and French improved rapidly, and in a short while he was part of the social circle in which the students moved. To his surprise what he had to tell Liebl was not remarkably different from the sort of tittle tattle to which he had been accustomed at the factory. Some students brought in dope, which they smoked amongst themselves. Others smuggled in books and magazines, which soon disappeared. Most of them brought items which pleased the women they pursued; makeup, underwear, sweaters and skirts, scarves and cheap jewellery. The politics they discussed were intricate arguments about what was happening in their home countries, but they avoided talking about internal German matters. This was largely because they had very little interest in the personalities and events which featured in the environment around them. The incidents which caused a series of meetings and heated discussions were to do with the insults and beatings which were occurring with an increasing regularity when students strayed into the wrong areas of the city, or got into disputes with drunken youths.

George reported all this to Liebl without any sense that his information offered a serious risk to anyone. Liebl seemed pleased, and George noted that with his promotion his manner had become more dignified, echoing that of the academics among whom he was moving. At formal ceremonies and major guest lectures he stood at the back of the hall, flanked by plainclothes men he directed here and there with the air of a man engaged in important affairs of state.

It was several months before Liebl showed his true colours. By then George had persuaded himself that the security man was merely a fragment of the bureaucracy with which he had grown up, annoying, perhaps, and ruthless on occasion, but meaning no harm except to the fools and villains who asked for it.

As a result, when he walked into the café near the Friedrichstrasse station, on the evening of their first conversation about Silke, he felt no apprehension about what was to come.

'There is someone I want you to meet,' Liebl said.

'Who is it?' George asked. He looked around automatically. 'Are they coming here?'

'No. No. Nothing like that. I'm talking about Professor Elsner. Silke Elsner.'

George had heard the name, of course. She was one of the youngish, high-profile professors teaching in the departments of language and literature. Only about forty years old, but she was a recognised expert on Brecht who had acted as a consultant to the Berliner Ensemble. This had given her a platform of official approval which, it was said, she had used to tread a dangerously radical path. She had written famously about Günter Grass, walking a tightrope between admiration for his writing and condemnation of his anti-Communism. Her essays on authors published in the West, like Stefan Heym and Christa Wolf, were eagerly read and discussed, and she had even championed the satirist Volker Braun. The authorities had drawn a line at her interest in Solzhenitsyn, and in the last few years she had been forbidden permission to attend conferences abroad, even in countries like Yugoslavia and Czechoslovakia. At the same time her reputation protected her in the university, and her work continued to be published without interference.

'Professor Elsner?' George was genuinely startled. He had nothing in common with the woman and he couldn't imagine what they would have to say to each other. 'Why?'

Liebl gestured in resignation.

'She left her husband a little while ago. Now we have no one close to her. We need to know as much as we can about what she's doing.' He leant forward. 'The truth is that the state puts a high value on intellectuals like her right now. We don't want to lose her.'

That meant her husband had been Stasi's conduit to Elsner's private thoughts.

'What can I do with a woman like that? Why should she talk to me?'

Liebl grinned, his face creasing in folds of moist fat.

'Don't worry. All we want is for you to be part of her circle. We'll tell you what to say.'

All George had to do was to tell Elsner that he wanted her help. He was to follow this by saying that he was a fervent admirer of her work, and that he would love nothing more than to enter the university, but his race and his rebellious attitude had probably made the local authorities regard him as politically unreliable. Refusing to give up, he had worked his way into the job in the canteen in the hope of proving himself and becoming a student in her department.

'These intellectuals,' Liebl said, 'imagine that they are closer to the people than the people's own representatives. When she hears this from a black man who has served his time in the army and works in the canteens she'll embrace you with open arms.'

George understood now that the story was meant to trigger Elsner's empathy with rebellious underdogs and excite her guilt about the country's behaviour to racial minorities. As the icing on the cake she would get the opportunity to become the patron of a genuine proletarian outcast who would be her intellectual disciple and protégé.

'No liberal intellectual could want more,' Liebl said. 'She'll probably write a book about you.'

'And you'll ban it,' George told him.

He doubted, in any case, that Elsner would be so easy to deceive.

'Don't look so stubborn,' Liebl's tone was light, but he was watching George narrowly. 'No one will harm her, and if we know she's not going to do anything unpatriotic we can leave her free to do whatever work she wants.'

Later on, in the midst of his depression about Silke and what he'd done to her, George knew that he had never believed Liebl's assurances, and looking back, it was hard to explain, even to himself, why he had tamely agreed to do what had been asked of him. It was as if he had walked in his sleep into a tunnel from which there was no way back. All he could do was to go forward, hoping that one day he would see a light.

Once he had agreed, however, George felt a rising excitement about meeting and getting close to the famous intellectual. The story that Liebl had given him wasn't altogether fanciful, because he'd always had a sneaking desire to be, like the father Katya had told him about, a man who knew the world, and could win the respect of distinguished people. He had no intention of doing anything to hurt the professor, and it was possible that meeting her might open new doors for him. He prepared himself carefully, reading a couple of her essays and some of Brecht's plays. All this took a week, but he imagined himself dying with embarrassment if she exposed him with a few easy questions. In the meantime he made the acquaintance of Gisela, a skinny and intense woman from Meissen, who studied in Elsner's department. He had actually seen the professor walking past him with a couple of colleagues, and if he'd been so minded he could have gone up and spoken to her, but by now he was anxious to get it right, and seeing her, he averted his eyes and hurried past. He had confessed his interest in Elsner and his desire to meet her to Gisela, and within a fortnight she invited him to a private reading of one of Volker Braun's satires. The book had been published, but the print run was so small that hardly anyone at the university had got hold of it, so this was an eagerly awaited event. 'Not that I'm a supporter of his,' Gisela said, 'but everyone's talking about it.'

Afterwards there was a party at which the more senior

members of the staff were present. Gisela pointed out some of the well-known personalities to George, and soon enough she led him to where Professor Elsner was standing, a drink in one hand and a cigarette in the other.

She was a tall woman, only a few centimetres shorter than George, with a muscular, wiry body and a sweep of black hair which fell over her forehead. She shook his hand firmly, smiled broadly, then turned her head as if about to return to the conversation which Gisela had interrupted, but George stood his ground and hurriedly asked if he might speak with her for one moment. She frowned, then smiled again, a hint of resignation in her expression.

Within the next week he had visited her twice in her office. When he told her about his training as a boxer her eyes lit up, and she invited him to join her in jogging before breakfast. She too had been an athlete, and she tried to maintain her training, merely to keep fit, but recently she had lost the partner with whom she jogged. In the following weeks they ran together, and later on, walked for hours round the park in Pankow where she lived. George had begun talking to her about his imaginary studies, but in a short time he was telling her about his life and the experiences he had gone through. He was interested in English, he told her, at which she smiled knowingly. English studies had become the opium of the progressive young, she told him, even in the East. He almost pointed out that he was only about ten years younger, but he stopped himself in time, some instinct telling him that it was her sense of his youthfulness which drew her to him. Instead, he replied that his reasons were personal, and began telling her about his father. At this moment they were sitting on a bench beside an avenue in the Schlosspark, from where it was just possible to see the crucifixes which towered over the church nearby. As she listened her body seemed to grow softer, her weight shifting slightly towards him along the bench, and she put her hand on his arm, her forehead creased in an expression of concern.

208

The week after that, she travelled to Leipzig where she was due to lecture on Brecht. She was away for nearly a week, and George started to wonder whether she would have found a new protégé or whether, immersed in her routine, she would think that she had given him enough of her time. But the opposite was true. On her return she sent him a note asking him to dinner at her apartment in Pankow, and that night they made love for the first time.

During the act Silke was soft and passionate, clinging to him with every ounce of her strength and raking his back and shoulders with her fingernails so badly that he felt the sting for days as the cuts healed. Afterwards she sat naked on the side of the bed and talked about herself. She was a Berliner, born in the aftermath of the war. Her father had died soon after. Strangely, at this point, she laughed. Like many of that generation, she said, there was a little mystery about the dates of her birth and her father's death. It wasn't the same, she continued, but she understood how George must feel about his divided parentage. She crossed her arms over her breasts and looked down at him, her features shadowed and enigmatic in the twilight bedroom. Her husband, she told him, had been another professor, a distinguished sociologist, who had received permission to attend a conference in Austria six months ago. He had never returned, and she had heard nothing. In any case, as a senior academic she was officially classified as *Geheimnisträger*, someone who knew state secrets, and it was forbidden to communicate with a defector, but it was common knowledge that he was now on the staff of the Sorbonne. He had always been fascinated by Paris, but his defection made her life more difficult than it had been. Everything she did might be under scrutiny. Perhaps, she said, George should be careful about being in her company, because it might create more problems for him.

'I didn't mean this to happen,' she said. George curled his fingers round the soft flesh behind her knee and pulled her towards him, but she resisted for a moment, finishing

209

her sentence. 'But now it has it would be wise to be discreet and silent. Do you understand?'

She stared into his eyes, pressing her hand down on his chest to keep him pinned down, until he nodded his head in acquiescence.

'Of course.'

Suddenly inspiration struck him. He threw the sheet aside and holding his penis, he waggled it at her. '*Schultüte*!' he called out. In his mind was the present he had received like all little children in the republic received on their first day at school, a cone filled with sweets and tiny presents, and hearing the word, Silke gasped with laughter, then giggling uncontrollably threw herself on him.

After a couple of months George had more or less forgotten his anxiety about Liebl, along with his guilt about deceiving Silke. She knew, he reasoned, that she would be under surveillance and she was safe enough, because as far as he could tell she was not engaged in subversive activities of any sort. For instance, when, urged by Liebl, he showed her a copy of the banned magazine *Sputnik*, she merely looked at it and handed it back to him, with the comment that it was hardly literature. There was nothing to report, he told Liebl, secretly amused at the thought of so much official effort being expended for so little reason.

In later years, he sometimes woke in the night, sweating, groaning and berating himself for having been so naïve.

'I admire her,' he told Liebl recklessly. 'She believes in the ideals of the republic, and she's more brilliant than anyone I ever met.'

This was true. In the time he had known Silke he felt that he had learnt more than he ever had during his entire life. She talked about politics and culture in a way that he'd never heard, not grumbling about the shops or the size of her apartment. Instead she talked about time, and beauty and ugliness, and the work of her friends who were artists and writers. The only woman to whom he had ever listened with comparable attention was his mother, and sometimes, lying in bed with Silke, he thought he was feeling something of the sweet warmth he had known as a small child.

'I'm sure you're right about her brilliance,' Liebl said dryly, 'but I don't know anything about ideals.'

The end when it came was even worse for being unexpected. George turned up at Silke's apartment as he often did when he knew that she wasn't otherwise engaged. She opened the door, but instead of smiling or embracing him, she led the way, stern-faced, into the room where she usually sat at her desk, writing or reading in the pool of light cast by the lamp in front of her.

Sometimes he used to wake and find the bed empty, and looking in through the doorway he would see her profile, set and calm as she turned the pages of the book she was holding. Hearing him behind her, she would turn and smile.

On this occasion, however, the books and papers which usually littered her desk lay scattered on the floor, as if she had swept them away in one violent motion. In their place were several rows of photographs, laid out under the light as if she had been examining them carefully one by one. At first, looking at the shapes, George couldn't work out what they represented, then he realised that they were pictures of himself and Silke. Some of them were fuzzy and blurred, others sharp and clear, the difference, he assumed, was in the amount of light that was available. A few had been taken out of doors, and although they had never risked any intimate gestures in public, the camera had caught them touching or gazing into each other's eyes with a warmth that spoke volumes. The bulk of the photos had been taken indoors, in Silke's bedroom by a hidden camera, he supposed. Some had been taken at his small apartment, the furniture around them clearly recognisable. All of them were harshly outlined, the naked flesh giving the postures in which they were entwined an obscenity which startled him. In that moment he was, above all, surprised to see how it looked, Silke sprawled in front of him, his semen spurting on her skin, his buttocks poised, her mouth open in what looked like a scream. The photographs were dirty, ugly, with none of the charm or beauty of the experiences they depicted. All the camera registered was what they had done.

George, without knowing what he was saying, began to stammer something.

'Don't bother to lie,' Silke said sharply. 'Your friends told me. This was why they sent you. You've done your job.' She took a rapid intake of ragged breath. 'I don't blame you. Better men have done worse. But you don't know what you've done.'

'It wasn't like that,' George told her. His brain felt numb, and he couldn't look at her for fear of seeing the revulsion he knew would be in her eyes.

'I don't care,' she replied. 'I just wanted you to see these. Now go. Never speak to me again. Go.'

George's head roared, swelling with pain as if it was about to burst. He went straight to Liebl's office at the university. He had never been there before, neither of them wanting to be seen together. But now George climbed the stairs, rendered oblivious to consequence by the grief and anger tearing at his insides. It was already late in the evening and the place of the receptionist had been taken by two uniformed guards lolling in the outer office. George ignored them, and without knocking, opened the door of Liebl's sanctum. On his way up the stairs he hadn't known what he would do. In his mind was an image of himself punching Liebl to the ground and kicking his soft flesh until it gave way under his feet, but when he entered and saw the man sitting behind the desk, he hesitated.

'I've been expecting you,' Liebl said. He waved away the guard who had followed George in. 'Sit down.'

George ignored the invitation. Instead he leant on the desk, thrusting his face out towards Liebl.

'Why?' he asked. He couldn't trust himself to say more because he could feel his voice rising, and with another word, he knew, he would begin to shout, and then perhaps he would throw himself across the space between them.

'Sit down and I'll tell you,' Liebl said. 'I didn't make this choice. Understand that. I followed orders, just like you.'

'Don't say that to me,' George told him.

'Okay. Sit down and listen to me.'

George sat down, but he still leant forward on the desk, his eyes fixed on Liebl as if his limbs were locked into position, incapable of moving any further.

'She was about to leave. Her plan was to go through Yugoslavia. Those swine send people like her on to the West without thinking twice. From there she was going to join the professor in Paris. She already had a contract to publish three of her books in the West, translated into English and French and any other language that would bring a profit. We knew about this a long time ago.' He paused. 'Politics. We couldn't arrest her, because our bosses wanted her to stay here. They don't like it when the heroes of our culture skip. No one cares if some mechanic from Saxony goes over the Wall, but Professor Elsner.' He spread his hands. 'Arrest her and the Wessis would have bought her out. We'd have asked for a couple of million deutschmarks and they'd have paid it. She knew also that if Yugoslavia failed she had that option. Certain people didn't want that scandal to happen.'

Everyone knew that the government sold political prisoners for a price – 50,000 deutschmarks for a teacher, 200,000 for a doctor. Elsner would have fetched ten times the amount, but that would have been a clear defeat for Stasi public relations.

Liebl leant back in his chair, watching George as if gauging the effect of his words.

'I don't believe you!' George said furiously. 'Lies are your business.'

Liebl picked up a thin cardboard file lying in front of

him and handed it to George. There were two documents in it. They were photocopies, but the print was clear and George had no difficulty making them out. The first was a contract from a publisher with an address in Frankfurt. He recognised the signature immediately. The second, a single sheet of paper, was unsigned, but reading it, he knew who had written the letter. This was Silke, writing to her lover, the professor who had defected. In the letter she promised undying love and talked of her eagerness to rejoin him. From the first sentence George recognised her turn of phrase and even some of the words she used. They were the same endearments she had used with him.

'You wrote this yourself,' George said, throwing it back across the desk.

'Where do you think those papers came from?' Liebl asked him seriously. 'Do you imagine she left them lying around in her apartment?'

George guessed it all now. Once Liebl's bosses had got wind of the contract they had used the photographs to win over Silke's professor.

'We needed something,' Liebl said, 'that would open his mouth, and we needed an argument to persuade her. She will stay. She wasn't totally corrupted.'

The defector, George assumed, had rejected her after seeing the photographs. Remembering the impression they had made on him he didn't find that hard to imagine. He couldn't guess what methods Liebl's colleagues had used in persuading Silke to stay, but he supposed that they had used the threat of wider exposure and playing on her sense of shame and guilt.

'Don't blame us alone,' Liebl continued. 'She lied to you. One morning you would have woken up and found your training partner gone without a word. In the West she would have been drinking champagne and driving around in furs without one thought of you.'

George didn't believe that. He wondered whether she

had been trying to warn him on that first night, but the idea increased his misery.

'I'm telling you this, because I want you to remember that we're walking the same road, working for socialism. There was no betrayal. It was she who planned to betray us to the gang of cosmopolitan intellectuals.'

That was the end of it, but it was months before George could bring himself to reply to Liebl's enquiries. The fat man didn't bother to issue any threats or promises. Later on, George understood that Liebl knew he could afford to be patient, and like a fat spider he simply waited for his victim's rage to cool down. George caught glimpses of Elsner from time to time, but he never tried to speak to her. Over the next year he acquired a rapidly changing string of girlfriends, moving from Heike to Grete to Elke to Marianne to Birgit to Regine and Renate, before finally settling on Radka. In that time he had succeeded in expelling from his mind the image of Silke's face, set and grim, her light green eyes piercing him like arrows of contempt. He hadn't even heard her name for almost all that time when he bumped into Gisela in the courtyard of the Gethsemanekirche on the night the Wall came down.

'Have you heard about Elsner?' she asked. Her voice was innocent of intent.

'What about her?'

'She drowned. She went swimming in Rügen, and disappeared. They thought maybe she'd got away to Sweden, then they found her body.'

He barely had time to register his shock before a surge of the crowd carried her away. The next thing he knew he was marching along the Schönhauser Allee sandwiched in between Radka and Renate. The next time he saw Liebl, waddling along the Friedrichstrasse, a bulging briefcase in his hand, his appearance that of a man in flight, he told him without greeting or preamble that he ought to kill him.

Liebl had merely smiled his fat man's smile.

'You won't do that,' he said, before turning away.

It had been twelve years ago, but George felt the rage rising in him again as he thought about the way that Liebl had smiled the same smile while he sat watching him spraying food over the table. By the time he finished telling Valentin as much of the story as he could bear to repeat, the sun had disappeared. Behind them the river seemed to be chuckling softly.

'Fuck him,' Valentin said. 'We make no deals with this pig.'

'So what do we do now? Sooner or later they'll find it. Or they'll get to us somehow.'

Valentin clasped his hands together. He gave a grunt of impatience. George recognised his mood. Valentin hated the stasis of indecision. Stuck at a crossroads he would always choose, rather than sit around trying to figure out the puzzle.

'First thing,' he said, 'if they're looking for Victor's treasure it's only a matter of time before they find it.'

George shrugged.

'That's not our problem. We put all that behind us.'

Valentin looked at him sharply.

'This is different.' He used an American expression with a touch of pride: 'We're in a new ball game. They'll get to us sooner or later, but I don't care about that. We're Victor's partners, we can't leave him to fight this battle alone.'

Seeing the glitter in Valentin's eyes, George remembered his cousin talking about the feelings he shared with Victor about their experience as soldiers. Perhaps he should have listened more carefully.

'What can we do?'

Valentin grinned.

'Plenty. We can help Victor move the treasure and hide it somewhere else in another country. In Russia too many people know of it. I'll speak with Victor tonight. Then we do it. Afterwards we think about what to do with these animals. If they come, we'll be ready.'

London

September 1999

FIFTEEN

The extent to which Kofi's declaration disturbed him had been a surprise to Joseph. In Prague, when he promised Radka to persuade his father to see Katya, he'd been sincere, but later on, faced with the prospect, he felt torn by conflicting emotions. There was more to it than the strain which the trip might put on Kofi's health. There was, for instance, the way that so much of how he regarded his father had changed within the space of a few days. In recent times, when he thought about Kofi, it had been with a wearisome sense of obligation. His father, who he would have to visit from time to time, and who might fall ill again, imposing a burden of concern that he dreaded. Since being forced into a confrontation with Kofi's history, however, his feelings had altered radically. Although he had been looking at his father for many years he had never quite seen him as he was. In comparison, George and Radka had never met Kofi but they seemed to know more about him and to have clear ideas about what sort of person he was. The thought made Joseph feel angry and insecure, as if they were about to steal his father away from under his nose. What made it worse was the fact that only a couple of weeks ago he would never have imagined feeling like this.

'It's all a long time ago,' he had told Kofi.

Beside him he heard Lena stir, and without looking he imagined her lips shaping the word no. She was probably, he thought furiously, convinced that he was standing in the way of a forty-year-old romance, when in fact he was only being sensible.

'When you're my age,' Kofi said, 'every damn thing is a long time ago.'

Meeting his eyes Joseph knew that his own features were set in a discouraging mask, jaw set tight, an angry frown creasing his forehead, but he was, by now, beyond trying to conceal his disapproval.

'I was thinking about it today,' Kofi continued, 'sitting in the library. When I left Moscow I decided to forget about her, forget about what happened there. I had other things to do, and anyway I thought I knew everything that was going on. Now I know that I didn't. If she has a child by me, maybe nothing was the way it seemed.'

'It was over forty years ago,' Joseph muttered. 'Forty years.'

'I'll die sometime.' Watching Joseph's frown deepen, Kofi laughed as if it was an amusing idea. 'When I lie on the bed waiting I won't be thinking all this happened forty years ago. If I don't find out I'll think that I missed something. I don't know what it is. Maybe I never will, but I'll know that I missed it.'

What Joseph couldn't quite make out was the mystery of what had happened between Kofi and Katya before they parted. Kofi kept repeating that he wasn't sure and that he couldn't remember the details.

'I was being deported,' he said stubbornly. 'She was a Party member. That was enough.' He looked at Joseph and shrugged. 'I thought it was enough until you told me about this son. Now I don't know. I have to think.'

That was about all Joseph could get out of him, apart from his determination to go and see Katya. Suddenly it struck Joseph that Kofi had come to his door at that late hour because he wanted his help and support. In the usual run of things the old man was independent, almost stand-offish, and the idea that he might be looking for help with the mundane business of arranging to make the trip hadn't occurred to Joseph until that moment.

'Do you want to come with me?' Kofi asked. His tone was an attempt at being casual, as if he was half anticipating a refusal.

In the grip of his newly discovered feeling of possessiveness about Kofi Joseph had already determined that, if he couldn't persuade the old man not to go, he would accompany him.

Joseph telephoned Radka the next day. He'd been bracing himself, expecting her voice to reanimate the confusion of his thoughts about her. She sounded uncertain and distant, her accent stronger than he remembered. Rapidly, he told her about his conversation with Kofi, and about the fact that they were planning to come to Berlin for Katya's birthday.

'I did not expect it.' Her voice was warmer and more controlled. 'Thank you. Thank you.'

'Are you sure this is a good idea?' Joseph asked her. Now he'd agreed to co-operate, to join up for what he thought of as a moment of madness, his doubts had returned in full force.

'I'm completely sure,' she said firmly.

'What about George?'

'I don't know. He's not here. When he comes back I'll tell him.'

She told him the date. She would be leaving Prague with Serge in a few days. She wanted to keep the surprise from Katya, so she would telephone to find out the number of their flight and where they would be staying. She didn't mention George again.

During the next few days Joseph kept on hoping that Kofi would change his mind and bring it all to an end. Lena kept asking questions, which were more irritating because he didn't know the answers. He went through the motions, booking tickets and a hotel, forcing himself conscientiously to discuss the trip with Kofi, who seemed to have lost his inhibitions about visiting the house and turned up every other day. He didn't stay long, merely asking about the arrangements or whether Joseph had heard from George.

'Why don't you phone him yourself?' Joseph asked, to which his father shrugged, his eyes wavering away.

'I'll wait. It's only a few days. That will be better.'

Kofi seemed to have more to say to Lena. Sensing a slackening of Joseph's concentration she had simply stayed after the weekend. When he asked whether she wouldn't have problems at work, she told him that she was taking some time off and it didn't matter anyway. She worked in a department store in Leeds, which she considered beneath her. It was not the sort of job which the daughter of a teacher like herself would have taken in her city, and she thought of it as one of the punishments of her exile. Telling Joseph that it didn't matter whether or not she went back, she shrugged contemptuously.

Somehow he couldn't summon up the resolution to tell her to go, and, in any case, there was something about his mood which made him happy that she was in the house. It was only her attempts to establish a relationship with Kofi which irritated him. One day he came back to find her chatting on the telephone, smiling and giggling as if she was talking to one of her friends. When she put it down she smiled happily at him. 'Your father,' she said. 'He was in Sarajevo once. He was telling me about it.'

'Sarajevo.' Joseph was startled. Another thing he didn't know. 'When was this?'

'In 1950-something.' She made it sound like the Dark Ages. 'It was different then.'

That would have been before he was born, but the revelation gave him a sting of irritation. Here was another person who seemed able to get closer to Kofi in a few days than he'd ever managed in the course of a lifetime. If he hadn't already told her she could stay he might have suggested her leaving there and then.

'How is it,' he asked her, trying to keep his tone casual, 'that you and my dad have so much to say to each other?'

As he asked the question, she had given him a look out

222

of the corner of her eyes, something a little sly about her expression, as if hesitant about revealing what she knew.

'He's easy to talk to. Not like the English. He understands.'

'You talk to me,' Joseph pointed out.

She made a quick open-handed gesture.

'I know. I don't mean you.'

Joseph didn't believe her. Whenever they argued, she'd describe the features of his character that she disliked as being 'like the English', a phrase which he soon recognised she meant as a deadly insult. In any case she was now comparing him with Kofi, so that anything she had to say would probably be some kind of criticism.

'All right,' he snapped, not trying to conceal his irritation. 'He understands you, and he's not English. Forget I asked.'

She put her hand on his arm and peered at him, gauging his mood.

'I don't mean anything bad about you. You're different. But your father – it's not anything he says, it's what he is.' She paused, gathering her thoughts, feeling for the words. 'When I tell people here about myself they look at me like they're with a sick person. They're thinking, poor refugee, then they forget and they think, bloody foreigner. They're like children. When they hear that word they think they know everything about me. If you tell them about sitting in the dark waiting to die it's like something that happens on TV, and they hear without understanding and they really don't give a shit.' She was breathing faster, and Joseph could see that she was struggling to control her anger. 'It's not their fault,' she continued, 'because they don't know anything, but sometimes I hate them just because they don't know anything.'

Joseph had heard her say something similar before, and he felt an automatic tug of sympathy, but he was actually thinking about his brother. Did George find him ignorant and complacent in the way Lena was describing? After all

George had tried to embrace him and he had responded by thinking he was about to be conned.

'Your father had this experience,' Lena said. 'He knows how it feels.'

More than a week later, he remembered the conversation. They were about to take off from Heathrow, the sound of the jet engine swelling to a long screech.

'You never told me you were in Sarajevo,' he said.

Kofi nodded.

'I don't remember much about it.'

It was the sort of annoying reply that Joseph had feared he would get. Kofi wasn't habitually secretive, but, at times, when questions came up about places he'd visited or people he'd known, he would become close-mouthed. Joseph was accustomed to his reticence, but on this occasion he felt a sudden spurt of jealous anger. It was obvious, he thought, that his father assumed that he was too ignorant and insensitive for the memories he was willing to share with Lena, someone he'd only just met.

'You must remember something,' he told Kofi. 'You were chatting with Lena about Sarajevo. Like you remembered enough to convince someone who lived there.'

They had climbed above the clouds now and Kofi was watching the carpet of damp cotton wool below them, a dreamy look on his face, but caught by something in Joseph's tone he turned around and looked carefully at him.

'I really don't remember much,' he said. 'I was telling her a story, about what happened to me when I was there.'

'What was that?'

'Just some old stuff. You sure you want to hear it?'

'Of course,' Joseph told him.

Kofi nodded reflectively, as if considering the effect of his words.

'I was only there for a couple of days,' he said. 'When I was in Moscow, they used to send us on trips, festivals, conferences, that sort of thing. It was one of the ways we paid for our scholarships I suppose. So they sent me to a festival of youth in Sarajevo once. It was more crazy than most, although everyone usually had a good time. In those days life in the East was pretty drab and poor.' He paused, watching the stewardesses push a trolley full of drinks up the aisle. 'It was really poor. Stuff we take for granted was unimaginable. So every time they had one of these things people used to get as much out of it as they could. Drink and sex was what we looked forward to.' He grinned at Joseph. 'In England they like to pretend sex was only invented yesterday, but when I was on the boats England was no different to any other port. In those days sex wasn't complicated. You had people spouting about morality and respectability and then you had the way people were. The church people and the politicians said you shouldn't do it, then they went down to Tiger Bay and picked up a girl. Those were hypocrites, but if you were a working man or woman it was the only thing you could do for pleasure. It was the same all over Europe, but in the East it was special. They weren't puritans except about politics, and the Party had a high level of tolerance for human weakness, unless you were really senior. The highest had the most vices, but not many people knew that then. If you were just a cog in the machine you had a lot of latitude. You had to be careful what you said about politics, but when the partying started, as far as they were concerned you could drink as much as you could hold, and then go out and fuck a dog if you could find one that wasn't busy.' He was gazing out of the window, the dreamy smile back on his face. 'I was in the city two nights. Me and another boy from South Africa were the only black men there. By the end of the first night everyone was pissed and half a dozen girls came after us. I say girls, they varied in age, the youngest might have been seventeen, the oldest in her thirties or forties. They came from factories all over, I can't remember now, but what they said was that the only black man they'd ever seen was Paul Robeson, and they wanted to hear us sing.

225

I think they had the impression that all black people sang like Robeson, and they wanted to hear some spirituals. Well, we were all pickled and we agreed to give them a concert on condition that we could have sex with all of them. By the time we agreed the terms it was well after midnight and we'd got through a few more bottles. I'm talking vodka and *slivovice*, all kinds of brandy, we were out of our heads. So we started. I had to teach this South African guy the words of some of the songs, but he could really sing, and we had them, man. I was young and strong and it was like heaven. We were at it all night; first we'd sing, then we'd go with one of the girls, then we took it in turns to sing while the other one was on the job. Next day we had to find a corner to catch some sleep because they wouldn't let us back in the hostel rooms during the day, but that second night we were ready to repeat the whole thing again. There were only two of us, then we brought in a couple of guys from the Ukraine and another one from Siberia and we made up a little choir, which was a very good thing. When it was all over the boys said we'd been fucking on Stakhanovite principles, overfilling our quotas, because the word got round and we had a whole heap of women waiting to get in on the deal.'

Joseph was flabbergasted, and he wondered for a moment whether his father was making up the story.

'You told Lena all this?'

Kofi laughed, enjoying his son's astonishment.

'Yes. She loved it. I think she enjoyed hearing about the city before all the disasters started to happen. She said her grandfather talked about crazy things like that.'

'I didn't know it was all that crazy.'

Kofi laughed again.

'That was how we lived. Crazier things happened. Just before they built the Wall in Berlin an African student got shot dead going over the border after the whores who used to hang out in the bushes near the Tiergarten. He was the son of a prominent politician in West Africa, and they had to cover it up, make out it was an accident, because they couldn't tell the old man that his son had given his life for a quick one with a prostitute.'

Joseph took this in, almost bewildered. He had got used to the idea that there was a great deal more to his father than he had ever imagined, but, for the moment, he was more shaken than he wanted to admit.

'What about George's mother?' he asked. 'Was she there?'

Kofi shook his head.

'No. We didn't get together till later. She was different. She saw herself as a cultured intellectual. She was going to be part of the élite. The girls I'm talking about were like worker bees. All they wanted was a good time.'

Watching Kofi out of the corner of his eye, Joseph thought that his face was creased in a smile that he seemed never to have seen before, and he felt a sudden flood of tenderness for the old man.

'Are you looking forward to seeing her?' he asked.

As if he hadn't heard, Kofi turned his head towards the window and for a moment Joseph thought he wasn't going to answer.

'I don't know,' he said eventually. 'There's a lot of explaining to do, and I don't know what's going to happen. Maybe I should have talked to her on the phone. Maybe we shouldn't be going there.'

He frowned, his eyes looking out into the distance, fixed on some vision only he could see. Watching him, Joseph felt a stab of worry. He was sure now that, in one way or another, the trouble George was in would affect Kofi, and, thinking about the night in Prague, the silent garage, the puddles of blood, and the severed head of Milena's brother, he felt the hairs creeping on the back of his neck. On the surface they were simply going to see Kofi's old friend Katya, but Joseph had the feeling that whatever had been happening on that night wasn't over. He should have known, he reflected, that everything he had told Kofi would suck them both into a situation which he didn't understand and which might be full of unexpected dangers. If anything happens to my dad, he thought, just when I'm beginning to know him, I'll never forgive myself.

As if guessing Joseph's thoughts, Kofi turned and grinned widely at him.

'Don't worry,' he said. 'I can handle anything that comes along.'

SIXTEEN

DIARY OF DESIRE

The life and times of Kofi George Coker
Moscow 1957

I never went back to Marina's apartment, although I saw her a few times out with Calvin. I thought of her often enough during the next couple of weeks, masturbating like fury under my blanket, but by the time Calvin asked me again if I wanted to visit her, I was occupied with other matters. It was spring more or less, and although the snow and ice was still lying around, the rivers had begun to move and the birches were beginning to sprout green buds. Naturally my thoughts were focused on Katya – sexy teach, as Calvin called her, licking his lips. I suppose I might have got over it if I hadn't been obliged to see her practically every day, a provocation which was hard to bear. I don't know what I would have done in the end, but, as it happened, Fate stepped in and settled the matter without any effort on my part. This is a strange thing which has happened to me a few times during my life, and which I can't explain. Wanting something, I would worry at the problem, figuring this and that angle, then suddenly an event would occur which got me over every obstacle, as if a solution had been ordered and arranged by the spirits.

In this case the warden called me into his office when I got back one afternoon. He spoke English which, though not fluent, was still better than my Russian, and it allowed him to conduct his usual game of sly interrogation which, when the occasion required, he would alternate with outright intimidation. This time he was smiling.

'Comrade Coker,' he told me right away, 'I have good news for you.'

The good news was that there was going to be a festival of youth in Jelenia Gora. He showed me the place on the map on his wall. It was on the border between Poland and Czechoslovakia. A place of great natural beauty, the warden said, where Soviet youth mingled with each other, skiing, hiking and sharing fraternal discussions about the achievements of Soviet society. After thorough consultation I had been chosen as an appropriate candidate to join the delegation of foreign students. It had been Valery's doing, of course. He denied it, with a suspicious blandness, but he was also a member of the delegation, a fact which, according to Hussein, clinched the matter.

'He's got to keep an eye on you,' he said, chuckling. 'Can't leave you here to get up to mischief.'

'I'm not like you,' I told him. 'I'm not interested in their politics.'

As it happened I was alarmed by the 'opportunity'. A few months before this, as winter was closing in we had heard the news about the British and French invasion of Suez. After an address by some of the Komsomol cadres, the students' union at Cheryomushki had drawn up an indignant petition. The report that Soviet troops had been invited by the Hungarian government to restore order meant little to us at that point. It was only later, after the visit of a CPP delegation, that we understood more about what had also been happening in Hungary at the time of Suez. After that I had begun to approach everything political with a new sense of caution. The warden had warned me that I would have to make a fraternal speech, which, he said, had to be prepared in time to be translated. 'They need time to vet it,' Hussein said. So everything about the part they wanted me to play in this festival had me worried.

The next day all the worries vanished in a flash. After the class Katya told me that she would be leading the delegation to Jelenia Gora, and that she would be translating my speech into Russian and German. Everyone, it seemed, spoke one of those languages. After she told me this, I forgot my objections and set to work.

In the meantime Hussein invited me to meet a friend of his. A zek, he called him, a man who'd been in the labour camps, and when I hesitated he told me the man was black, now a Russian citizen, but originally from an island in the Caribbean.

'Don't worry,' he added. 'There'll be no trouble. His sentence was annulled last year and they let him come back to Moscow. He's only a sick old man. They're not interested in him.' He paused. 'But don't tell your roommate.'

I shrugged, but I didn't tell Valery. Next day we went to his house. We got out at Komsomolskaya and found ourselves in the middle of the group of railway stations. I recognised Leningradsky Vokzal from where the train had set out on my trip north with Valery, but I didn't mention it to Hussein. As we crossed the road we were passed by a group of short, thick-bodied men wearing fur hats and carrying big bundles, like donkeys loaded for the market.

Hussein paid no attention, heading straight on towards a massive white tower which looked almost exactly like the tower at the university but which he said was the Ministry of Transport. A little past the tower we turned a corner and then went through an alleyway which gave on to an empty square of muddy dirt, part stubborn grass, part rubbish. On the other side there was a row of old houses, shacks of crumbling brick and weatherbeaten plaster. Some of the windows were covered with tar paper, others were boarded up. I had seen houses like this before, but none of them quite so desolate. These had been run down when they were assembled, hasty, temporary structures which you would have imagined to be long abandoned.

'When you get to Jelenia Gora,' Hussein said, laughing, 'tell them about this.'

'I could tell them they're getting rid of all this.'

I was on firm ground here. The warden had taken us on a tour in the first week and outlined Khrushchev's crash programme of new housing. A couple of months later we were all familiar with the word Khrushcheby, a pun on their word for slum – truscheby, and it was true that sites like this were soon to be converted. I had seen it happening already, all over the city.

231

We crossed the rubbish dump, mud squelching beneath our shoes, and Hussein knocked at the door of one of the shacks. 'Vera', he shouted, 'Vera.'

An old woman opened the door slowly. She was bundled up in a scarf and a shapeless wad of a dress, babushka style, and when she recognised Hussein she smiled and turned her head to shout over her shoulder.

'Hussein. It's Hussein.'

Later on he told me that a knock on the door would terrify the old man until he knew who it was.

Inside, the old zek, Alexy, was sitting in a bed next to the stove. The room was dim and stuffy, a combination of smells, cabbage predominating, but it was warm and quiet. The walls had been pasted all over with old posters, newspapers and flyers so that everywhere you looked it was like being surrounded by a strange billboard, advertising meetings, railway timetables, and warnings about entering forbidden territory. On one side was a giant poster for the circus, which showed, in the middle of the picture, a clown balancing on a barrel, juggling a set of blazing clubs.

'See what he's doing?' The old man spoke English like an American, but also with the hint of a Russian accent. 'That's Russian life.'

'They call me Alexy,' he said. He had a light complexion, and a sturdy crop of white hair which seemed to run down the sides of his face and flower into the bush around his mouth and chin. I had never seen a black man with so much hair. 'You're the student Hussein told me about?' he asked me.

We drank the vodka Hussein had brought. I told him a bit about myself. He was interested in my experience on the boats, and he asked me about Padmore, whose photograph he had seen standing near Stalin at a parade in Red Square. Alexy had studied engineering in the USA and joined the Party there. In the early thirties he had travelled to Russia and found a job as an engineer on the railways. During the decade he married and became a Soviet citizen, but it all came to an end six years later, when at the height of the great purges in Moscow he was arrested and sentenced to a period of indefinite detention. Someone had

232

denounced him as a foreign spy, he couldn't say who, and in those days it was enough. He had been lucky to escape execution, but by that time the terror was slackening off in Moscow and they'd become more sparing with the death penalty. That was fifteen years ago.

'But you were innocent,' I said. In the face of his tragedy I felt sadness and guilt about being there in that place where such things happened, free and privileged as we foreign students were.

Alexy smiled broadly.

'Innocent? I don't know if you could be innocent then. I remember the year before going to a meeting and listening to Khrushchev. That same Khrushchev who has just condemned the excesses of former days. He was First Secretary of the Moscow Party then, and he gave a real fire and brimstone speech about the Trotskyists and the saboteurs, enemies raising their hands against Comrade Stalin.' He gave a chuckle which turned into a rumbling cough. 'There were about a quarter of a million people jammed into Krasnaya ploschad. Every one of them was shouting for the enemies of the people to be executed. We'd have cut their heads off and shoved them up their asses if we could, and I was shouting as loud as anyone.' He held his hand up, the finger pointing. Bony and curved, it looked like the prong of a claw. 'How many innocent people go to jail in the West? They're still lynching black men in the States. That won't stop. What they did here was no worse. The state had to defend itself. Mistakes were made. We shouldn't pretend that didn't happen. The vozhad and Beria used the situation. The innocent went with the guilty, but maybe that's how it had to be.'

Baffled, I glanced over at Hussein. He was watching Alexy closely, his face impassive.

'Did you never want to go back home?'

'Home? Where's that? I left when I was a boy. No one knows me. I don't know what I would do there. Maybe they wouldn't even let me in.' He laughed and coughed again. 'I'll die here, unless Nikita Sergeyevich gets me out of this hole and into one of his nice new apartments in time. Then I'll die there.'

On the way back to Cheryomushki I asked Hussein the question that had been on my mind while I listened to the old zek.

'How can he be so calm about what they did to him?'

'What else can he be? It would be much worse if he believed that all of it had been pointless.' He gave me an ironical look. 'You really don't understand. They're breeding a new kind of man here. That's what they believe. You think that because they're poor and life is tough they're just holding on. That's not how they look at it. They believe that it's possible for people to be moved by altruism rather than greed, and by love of their fellow men rather than hatred and suspicion.'

'So what's the KGB for?' I asked him.

'That's because people aren't perfect yet. If you think that things are going to reach their most extreme form before turning into their opposite, you have to control the effects. It's all about tomorrow. Today the misery and cruelty of life is normal. Tomorrow pays for all.'

The following week we set out for Poland. We were going by rail to Warsaw, and then by coach to the border. The train left around the middle of the afternoon and for the next twenty hours I was to be ensconced with Katya in a compartment for two. The sleeping arrangements were not segregated between men and women, and Katya had chosen me for her companion so that we could work on the speech. To say I was in ecstasy would be no exaggeration.

I was treading a tightrope in what I had written. Essentially I had made it a long account of the jobs I had done so far, moving on to a condemnation of colonialism and ending with a splurge of tribute to the Soviet Union. Katerina had no trouble translating it, but when it came to the final part of the speech she kept suggesting changes. I can't remember the details, but the general effect of them was to alter the language into something that the warden might have said, and towards the end it sounded as much of an arse-licking as any of the Party officials could desire. It might be a good idea, she told me at one point, to say that after the imperialists had been driven from the oppressed colonies, the youth of the world would be united in socialist friendship. I

234

didn't exactly argue with her, but I tried to keep it within the bounds of what I knew about, telling her that it wouldn't be convincing if I seemed to be saying things about which I was ignorant. On the other hand, I knew that the translation would probably say whatever she wanted.

All this took several hours. The attendant, an old lady with a seamed face and little black eyes like stones, kept bringing us tea, which she dispensed from a battered samovar, and from time to time, Valery appeared. His manner with Katya was not exactly unfriendly, but he wasn't warm towards her. Later on, when he knew more about how matters stood, he told me that Katya's father was high up in the region, one of those who supported Khrushchev in his struggles with Malenkov over the Virgin Lands programme. Instead of departing for Siberia to harvest wheat however, his daughter had found a nice little niche in Moscow.

None of this would have concerned me at the time. Katya was about the same age as me, and I was simply happy to be occupying the same space, listening to her talk and breathe. The seats were padded, but unlike British trains there were no gusts of warm air flowing from beneath them. It wasn't freezing but it was cold enough to keep our overcoats on, and when the samovar came, we warmed our hands beside it. She was wearing a long woollen dress below which I caught hints of her body, her soft breasts bouncing a little when the train went round a corner, or straining at the fabric when she stretched. There were dimples at the sides of her mouth which gave her a mischievous look when she smiled, but for most of the trip she was very much in earnest. Relaxing as the landscape outside disappeared into blackness, she told me that my speech would be significant because it would be an opportunity to demonstrate the importance of the Party's foreign aid policy. When she talked like this I found it difficult to meet her eyes, because I was torn between lust and boredom, and I didn't want her to see either. I couldn't work out at that moment, either, what she felt towards me. If I touched her would she turn away in revulsion or would she wrap her arms around me? Either one was possible, I thought. The strange thing was that, for the moment, I didn't want to find out. I was happy enough locked

235

into the box on wheels rushing through the night in which no one existed except for ourselves. In between arranging the words to her satisfaction I told her about myself. She asked me about my mother and my father, and what it had felt like to be at sea for weeks on end. That part of my experience fascinated her because she loved floating on the river, she told me. When she stopped talking about the oppressed people and the achievements of the Soviet Union she sounded like an innocent, naïve and sweetly curious about a world she didn't know.

It must have been close to midnight by the time we were finished. The seats folded down into beds and when she decided it was time for sleep she told me to wait outside. I walked down the corridor and went into the compartment which Valery was sharing with a couple of others. They were already wrapped in blankets, passing a bottle of vodka between them.

'I'm not coming back with you,' Valery told me.

On the way back he was going to leave early and make a stop in Kiev to see his relatives. That made me laugh at the thought of Hussein's face when I told him. So much for Valery keeping an eye on me.

When I got back to our compartment Katya was already buried under the blankets. I lay opposite her, listening to her breathe, wondering whether she was asleep and how I would get through the night, but in the time it took to think about it I was asleep too. I woke briefly when the train came to a halt in Minsk, and I remember promising myself that I would get out and try to look around on the way back. When I woke again it was light outside, and Katya had disappeared. She came back later, fully dressed, her hair gleaming as it swung round her face, and we drank our tea in companionable silence. Afterwards she made me read the speech we'd written, practising the speed and pausing for effect. It was funny. When she spoke to me as the teacher she seemed distant and bossy, almost looking down her nose at me, then she would change, and suddenly it was as if I was speaking to a shy and inquisitive child. The contrast was a little confusing, but it merely increased my excitement.

We had reached Warsaw about the middle of the day. I sat next to Katya on the bus. Turning to me to make some comment about the weather her voice was pitched low, for my ears only. It was as if we had become a couple overnight.

I don't remember much about the festival itself. At the back of my mind I'd had the idea that a festival had to be about music and dancing. But, of course, this one seemed to be about a series of interminable speeches. The delegates were scattered between the town and the top of the nearby mountain, on the other side of which was the Czech border. My dormitory was a big cabin up the mountain surrounded by pine trees. All through the day and night there was a sound of dripping water, and when you walked through the trees a kind of fine spray flew against your hands and face. It was beautiful. On the way to the conference hall on the first morning I paused and looked. I had never seen a landscape like this, the trees in different shades of green climbing up the hillside, parting to reveal occasional patches of snow, still pristine white as it melted.

In spite of the speeches there was a kind of holiday atmosphere around the entire site. As usual at these things the participants split into groups, the smallest consisting of those who were attending with a serious purpose in mind, the drafting of resolutions, meetings with colleagues, and various kinds of political collusions. Some of the delegates were already middle-aged and they formed a group with the serious Party people who went into a huddle at the beginning and the end of the day, occupying rooms with closed doors, from which they emerged scanning sheets of paper or talking earnestly amongst themselves. Everyone else seemed to be absenting themselves selectively, and you would come across groups of drunken young men and women in the woods or taking over entire dormitories for the night, singing, dancing and imbibing a steady flow of vodka.

Both Katya and Valery were among the groups of serious Party members and for a couple of days I didn't see much of them. On the morning of my speech, however, Katya told me that we would go out to celebrate later. She was nervous, I realised. It struck me that she was, in a sense, my patron, and it was possible that if I failed it would affect her standing in some way I couldn't understand.

237

Seeing that, I felt like doing my best for her, and when it was my turn to go to the rostrum I screwed myself up to sound as bold and confident as I could. It went well as far as I could tell, to judge by the applause, and when I went back to my seat, Katya squeezed my arm, her eyes shining and her expression more animated than I had ever seen. Afterwards we went to the canteen where they were serving Polish borshch. As it happened this gave me a fright next morning when I looked back at the toilet bowl and saw that it was stained dark red. I was on the point of running out to find a clinic when I realised that it was the beetroot working through my bowels.

After the meal we went down to the town and bought a couple of bottles of Zubrowka, a special Polish vodka the Russians said was the best. As we walked back she told me how well the comrades had received what I'd said.

I listened without interest. I had already made my own plans. Close by my cabin on the side of the mountain there was a spectacular view where you could sit, in a rough shelter, and look at the landscape. I led her there. The sun was going down and we watched the sky turn pink and grey and then dark. She drank from the bottle when I handed it to her. It was cold, but it was a calm spring evening and sitting there was bearable, especially with the vodka warming our insides. It was an anaesthetic against the cold, Hussein used to say. Sometimes when spring came and the snows melted they would begin to find the bodies of drunks who had lain down by the side of the road and been covered by the drifts, too paralysed to notice that they were freezing to death.

Thinking about this, I told her about getting lost in the forest with Valery, and imagining the peasant we found was a snowman. She laughed herself silly, and so did I. I hadn't found it funny until then, but we were at that stage when everything made us laugh. We were more than halfway through the bottle when the last gleam of sunshine began fading over the next ridge. It was dark around us and we had drawn close together, keeping each other warm against the cold air. I put my arm round her while she gulped from the bottle, and handing it back, she nestled closer. I turned and found her lips under mine. We kissed, awkwardly

238

at first, then our lips grew warmer and my hands reached for her soft breasts under the thick overcoat which seemed to have opened of its own accord. Looking back I can hardly believe that merely touching each other could generate so much passion in that climate. After a couple of minutes we nearly fell off the narrow plank of wood on which we were sitting, so we got up and stood amongst the roots of the big tree nearby. She leant against the trunk, pressing back against me, her arms tight around my neck. I lifted her skirt, scrabbling at the layers of cloth under it until I found her bare thighs. My hands were still cold and when I touched her she cried out quite loudly, 'Oh!' But she moved her feet apart and in that instant my fingers were playing in the soft warm place between her legs. In my head was the thought now or never, and I unbuttoned my trousers quickly with one hand, and releasing my erection pushed it into the heat. For a few seconds it seemed to blunder interminably, poking around in the hair at the bottom of her belly like a blind snake, then she moved, climbing up on one of the roots, and parting her boots wider, shuffling a little as she felt for a good grip, then she was standing a little higher, and then she leant over on my shoulders and it went in. I remember such things, the technical details, we called them, because I thought about them over and over again for a long while. I remember also the strangeness and the delight of the contrast between the cold air on my face and the furnace of her flesh where our bodies were joined. It was the sensation which was everything. At first I thought, at last, then I stopped thinking.

Afterwards she kissed me, then settled her clothes around her. We walked back through the woods in silence, hand in hand, smiling at each other from time to time. Back at my dormitory she put her hand on my arm.

'I have a secret. You must tell no one.' I nodded. 'Tomorrow,' she said, 'Nikita Sergeyevich will be here on a secret visit. I will make certain that you meet him.'

She stared at me, the colour high in her cheeks, her eyes shining.

Even then, I thought that was a little strange after our moment

239

in the woods. Had she been thinking about Nikita Sergeyevich while I poked her under the tree? I didn't want to think about it and there seemed nothing to say.

'Thank you,' I told her. 'I'll be there.'

Of course, when I did think about it I understood her excitement. Nikita Sergeyevich was a real hero, in many ways which I still think today; maybe not for the same reasons as someone like Katya. To her and her friends who thought of themselves as modern and enlightened, Khrushchev had thrown open the windows with his programme of reform and decentralisation, his uncovering of Stalin's crimes, even the Virgin Lands project which would make them independent of foreign grain. Some found pleasure in the wiliness he'd shown in shaming and defeating Beria, settling a million scores in the process. For many others it was a vindication of all they'd had to do to survive, a symbol of what it meant to spring from the black earth of the countryside, because this was the same man who had been treated as a jumped up peasant, a useful buffoon. He had held on through the years of terror and sycophancy, swallowing Stalin's murder of his son and the obliteration of friends and family. In the end he had survived it all, and now he was ready to begin transforming the world he had helped to shape. With his thick body and awkward walk and his face like a potato he was a sign of hope and vigour.

That was how it seemed, anyhow, during that morning on the mountain, although as with so many of the things I saw over there change was already on the way, carried along by currents which remained invisible, hidden below the ice.

It seemed that the secret had got out, because the hall was full to overflowing. Halfway through the second speech, delivered by a balding Komsomol member in a brown leather jacket, there was a bustle at the back and the comrade speaker threw his arm out dramatically and announced the presence of the First Secretary. We all went a bit crazy, standing and applauding for minutes on end and every time it seemed to be dying down it would start again as Khrushchev, grinning broadly, sure of his welcome, mounted the platform and stood waiting for the applause to stop. Eventually he spread his arms and waved them down, then he made a short speech. I didn't catch much of it, but I made out some of the phrases, like youth being the hope of the future, the triumph of Soviet science and technology, the promise of the Virgin Lands. It was a standard speech which I don't think said anything they didn't already know, but they loved it. Maybe it was more that they loved him.

I was standing in the hall applauding with the rest of the delegates when he got off the platform. It was clearly a flying visit, maybe one of many he was making that day. As he came close to the row where I was standing he looked round and caught my eye. I guess that wasn't difficult, since I was one of only half a dozen black men in the hall. He stopped short, with that rolling walk of his it was as if he'd suddenly stumbled, and he gestured to me. I pushed past the others in the row and emerged into the aisle to shake his hand. Around me the delegates applauded as if this was the climax of a summit meeting. He said something in Russian, then brought his other hand across to clasp mine in both of his. Close up his smile was infectious, a merry look which creased his face and made you want to smile back. I was dumb, all I could think of to say was one English word, 'Sir. Sir.' He grinned broadly and let my hand go and in a moment he was swallowed up by the crowd around him, moving quickly down the aisle and through the doors.

Turning round, I saw Katya standing by my side, her expression full of delight, almost exalted.

'What did he say?' I asked her.

'He said that it was nice to see you here, comrade, and he hoped you had many good memories to take home.'

It was a nice thing to say, I thought, and for a while I felt as if I was walking on air. I was twenty-seven. I was making my way in the strangest of distant lands, the leader of half the world had shaken my hand and wished me well, and I had just possessed the body of a beautiful woman who was the subject of my dreams. I was on top of the world.

Berlin

September 1999

SEVENTEEN

It was Radka who saw the fat man first. She and Katya had just emerged from the supermarket, a trip they had undertaken primarily for the purpose of buying cakes for Serge. Radka disapproved, of course, having been increasingly infected by American obsessions about diet and exercise, but Katya could always talk her round, and after a little wheedling and teasing from Serge she had consented to a shopping trip. This was about the third evening after their return from Prague, when Serge was just beginning to settle into the apartment, colonising it with the bleeping sound of his electronic toys and appearing at the earliest hours of the morning when Katya sat at the window sipping her coffee and watching the street come to life.

On this evening, Radka had been chattering about the gypsies who had flocked to Canada and England. It was TV Nova in Prague which had started it all, she said, with their programmes about how life was a paradise for gypsies in those countries. They were buying their audience, she said, as they always had with cheap and prejudiced nationalism, as if a constant diet of crap Hollywood movies wasn't enough.

Katya hardly noted her indignation, to which she was now accustomed. She had understood for a long time that these outbursts were a cornerstone of the friendship between them; and Radka let herself go on these matters to her mother-in-law because she assumed that, because of George and Serge, they shared a common loathing for the ethnic bigotry which pervaded everyday life. What interested her more was the fact that every turn in their conversation in the last few days had somehow led to the subject of Britain, and specifically London. If this had been the old days, Katya thought, she would have been certain that Radka was about to defect. As it was, she imagined that she understood why Radka's thoughts so frequently led off in that direction. It had to be the consequence of her mentioning the interview she had seen on the TV, with the young man who looked like George and said that his father's name was Kofi. Katya had tried to put the experience out of her mind, without success, but the more she thought about it, the more her feeling of doubt grew. Over the decades since she had last seen him, she had imagined more than once that she recognised Kofi in the turn of an African's head, or the image of a black man in the background of a scene on the TV news. For instance, when she heard the name of the UN chief, Kofi Annan, her heart had leapt dizzyingly, but in the next moment she realised that this couldn't be George's father. When she saw Joseph on TV, it had struck her, with the same kind of vertiginous rush, that he looked very much like George. Her first impulse was to go to Prague and see him in person, but George had persuaded her that it would be best if he saw the man and found out whether there was any substance to her intuition. On the phone he had said that the result was inconclusive. The young man was uncertain about the dates of his father's stay in Russia, and in any case, the name was a common one in Africa. According to George the boy had promised to speak to his father, who lived in London, but Katya had heard enough. She had endured similar disappointments before. Now, she thought, this would be like all those other times, and it was too late to upset herself needlessly over a ghost.

On the other hand, she found herself disturbed by Radka's prattle. She felt odd, uneasy, as if something was about to happen. During the period she had spent in Siberia, in Yekaterinburg before the time of George's birth, she had met miners who spoke about knowing when a mudslide would occur, and she had heard the same story about avalanches in the Northern Urals. It wasn't merely a question of the air going still, the sounds of nature quelled. There was something else which happened inside you, they told her, almost like a kind of trance in which your body began to predict the future.

In this mood Katya wasn't surprised to find herself shivering as they walked the supermarket aisles, but then she remembered that the air conditioning, together with the refrigeration, always affected her this way. She made a mental note to check on how she would feel when they got outside. In recent years she had returned to a routine concern about her health, visiting the doctor regularly and noting the variations in her physical well-being with interest. She supposed it was something to do with her release from behind the Wall. Since then she had begun to find herself interesting in a way that she couldn't have imagined before.

It was while they were loading the shopping into the boot of Radka's car that the big black limousine stopped immediately opposite, blocking the aisle of the car park. There were no cars in the way, and Katya, seeing Radka staring, and the shape of the car from the corner of her eye, assumed that someone known to one of them had paused to exchange a greeting. She turned to look, but all she saw was the glass on the rear window sliding down slowly, and behind it, the face of a fat man she could not remember ever having seen. She glanced at Radka, expecting some sign of recognition, but there was only puzzlement on her face.

'Hello,' Serge called out suddenly, in the cute way he sometimes had with strangers, and, slowly, the man's face creased up in a smile. Then the window closed, and the car drove on.

'Who was that?' Radka asked. 'Do you know him?'

'No,' Katya replied. 'I thought perhaps he was a friend of you and George.'

'No,' Radka said quickly. 'I've never seen him before.'

In the car as they drove away from the supermarket, she glanced sideways at Katya.

'It's funny,' she said. 'Now I think about it, there's something familiar about that man.'

Katya nodded her head in agreement, because she had been thinking precisely the same thing.

'George may know who he is,' she told Radka. 'We'll ask him when he gets here.'

The next day she took Serge to see the Rathaus in Schöneberg, which wasn't a long walk from her apartment. Radka had an errand to run, but in any case, Katya wanted to do this with Serge because the visit was intended to show him part of the city's history, and as a matter of course she took every opportunity to pass on to him all she knew about it. The previous night she had told him more about the Wall, and about Kennedy making his famous speech in front of the Rathaus. She hadn't been there, of course, and it was only a long time afterwards that she had heard about it. She had been living, at the time, in the East, off the Friedrichstrasse, not far from the university, in an apartment block for Soviet functionaries. That much she'd been promised when she came, and, in that respect at least, she had not been disappointed. She told Serge as much, but the truth was that she had developed no loyalty to the neighbourhood where she lived, isolated among the other Russians, and as soon as it was possible she had persuaded George to find the apartment in Schöneberg. Afterwards she spent most of her spare time exploring the western part of the city, walking in the Tiergarten or lingering over the exhibits in the Kunstgewerbemuseum nearby. Beyond the Brandenberg Gate she never ventured.

Sometimes, following her lead, George had taken Serge to explore the city, and to see the streets through which he had passed as a boy. They walked in famous places like the Unter Den Linden and Alexanderplatz, and once on a sunny day drove out to see the Soviet war memorial at Treptower Park. On these occasions Katya made no comment, but she invariably avoided accompanying them. Alone with Serge she confined herself to exploring neighbouring landmarks like the Rathaus, but, in fact, there wasn't much to see there and they'd probably end up walking in the little Volkspark next to it. During their travels she found as many stories as she could to tell her grandson about the city and its history, sometimes inventing funny monsters and comical heroes, but much of the interest she tried to communicate to him was equally contrived. In recent months she had come to realise that this counterfeit was a subterfuge, designed to assuage her unease about her inability to talk with him about her own parents. In much the same way she had said very little to George about his grandparents, evading his questions with bland generalisations and quaint stories about her childhood.

Radka, whose quick intuition matched her own, had spotted her evasions from the beginning, but it wasn't until Serge began asking questions about their respective families that she spoke up.

'Perhaps,' she suggested to Katya one day, 'he should be told about your life in Russia and about your parents. This is also part of his heritage. George tries to tell him about his name and where it came from, but he doesn't know much.'

Katya understood the hint. Serge's name had been her father's, and there were stories she might have told the little boy about him and what he had done in his life, but when she thought about what she might say, her mouth clamped shut against the words. In forty years her disillusion had hardly faded, and when she thought of her father she still remembered with bitterness the violence of his invective against Kofi, and the sheer obscenity of his tirades. He had never seen George, and he had died only half a dozen years later, before having time to repent. Her mother had followed shortly, but although Katya's grief had been intense, she also experienced a kind of freedom, as if their deaths had liberated her from the rage and despair of that time. In her mind her parents represented the collective will which had dominated her upbringing, and their deaths seemed to loosen the bonds which tied her to it. The consequence was a kind of amnesia, amplified by the distance from her birthplace. As a Russian working in the German state, her nationality gave her status and protection, while the petty restrictions she encountered seemed tedious rather than crushing; and although the freedom she experienced was tenuous and conditional, it was also concrete and tangible.

The problem of her later years had been George. Curiously enough, what worried her most of all as he grew up was the idea that, because he went to a German school, and mingled with young Germans every day, he would become a German. But there was practically no alternative. She wouldn't have dreamt of sending him back to stay with the relatives she still possessed in Moscow, even if they would have accepted him; and while there were tribal loyalties which tied the Soviet expatriates together, George, even as a toddler, was an obvious outsider. As a teenager he became his own man, and, for a time, they hardly spoke. When he brought Radka to meet her, Katya's first reaction was to be surprised, then she realised that in some way she hadn't perceived until she saw them together, he had become a man. From that moment Radka was a bridge between them. They liked each other, in any case. After some time Katya felt that Radka admired her independence and her firmness in cutting the knot between herself and her past. With Serge's arrival the relationship between them was firmly established, more like sisters she often thought, than a mother and her son's wife. Holding the little bundle, she could see herself, along with traces of Kofi, paler than in George, but still distinct, and her heart melted. She had been happy then, but in the previous couple of years she had begun to worry about George again. He seemed to have found his feet, but at the same time there was now a sullen undertone to his relationship with his wife. Neither of them would discuss the matter, and Katya's fears for George intensified after each occasion that she saw them together.

Standing in front of the Rathaus on the same day that Kofi and Joseph were flying into Berlin, Katya dismissed the sense of foreboding which had been stalking her for the last couple of days. Watching her grandson skipping over the pavement, she reflected that perhaps nothing would change, and that, at least until young Serge grew up, everything would be all right.

It was then that she looked up and saw the fat man's car on the other side of the street, its darkened windows blank and somehow menacing. She could see no one in it and she had no evidence that it was the same car because she hadn't noted the licence plate, but in the instant she saw it she had known. Immediately, she looked back at Serge, a few metres away, and called to him, her voice louder and sharper than she intended, and he stared at her curiously as he came to her side. For the merest moment it was George rather than Serge that she saw, a frown creasing his little forehead as he noted the terror in his mother's voice. That was how it had been years ago, and now she remembered the sensation of a fist clenching around her heart when she caught sight of her surveillance. It's all different now, she told herself urgently, and whatever this was the old days were over for good.

'Let's go home now,' she told Serge.

The sun was still high above them, but for Katya, it was as if a shadow had crossed the sky.

EIGHTEEN

When they got through the barrier at the airport, Radka saw them immediately. She was standing at the back of the crowd which was massed around the doors to the customs hall, but she could see the passengers emerging over the shoulders of the chauffeurs and taxi drivers holding up the placards which indicated who they were. She had dressed in a style which was both more casual and more Western than she usually affected, a pair of glasses which had a faint pink tint, black leather jacket and jeans, and, leaving the apartment she had realised with a faint sense of amusement at herself, that she was trying to make an impression. What kind of impression it was, she wasn't sure, but she recognised the feeling of anticipation which was hurrying her movements. It was the pleasure of looking forward to Katya's surprise, she told herself, but she also knew that this wasn't the way she would have dressed if Kofi had been the only person she was about to collect from the airport. She guessed instead that it was something to do with seeing Joseph again. Only an hour ago Katya had commented on how good her mood was that morning. What would her mother-in-law have thought, she wondered, if she had understood her excitement?

She didn't quite understand it herself. She knew, of course, that this meeting might be the prelude to a new life for all of them, and that was enough to provoke her exhilaration. At the same time, she had been touched by flurries of wayward emotion ever since receiving Joseph's phone call. Until then, she had begun to fancy that the entire episode had been a kind of dream. It had happened, of course, no doubt about that. George's brother had come to the apartment, they had met and talked. She had assumed, however, that hoping so eagerly for some change was a guarantee that it would not take place, and she had more or less resigned herself to hearing nothing more about the matter. Joseph's call had altered the equation, and suddenly, the visions she had been ready to dismiss as fantasies were the foundations of a new reality. Somewhere in the middle of all this was her first sight of Joseph, which memory, sometimes, for a fleeting moment, superimposed on her recall of the first time she had seen his brother George. It was possible, she guessed, that this confusion was the source of the daydreams which had been creeping, unannounced, through her mind.

Coming through the barrier at the airport, he was as she remembered. Tall, his skin a pale brown, curling black hair cut close to his scalp around the sides, a smile beginning to light up his features as he saw her. She was seeing, it occurred to her, a younger, sweeter version of George, as if some magic had swept over the image of the man she knew, erasing a corrosive patina of guilt and shame. Behind him she looked for Kofi, an erect figure with a loose, swinging walk, a face carved in black stone, topped with a brush of iron grey.

Close to her now Joseph fumbled a little, putting down his suitcase and making to kiss her on the cheek. Instead she put her arms round him and squeezed him.

'I'm glad to see you,' she whispered in his ear, the words unrehearsed, almost involuntary.

When she turned to Kofi, he was watching her, a thoughtful frown creasing his forehead, as if he was trying to work out who she was.

'This is Radka,' Joseph told him.

'My husband is George,' she said. She felt lightheaded, conscious that she was babbling. He knows who my husband is, she thought, and she took a deep breath, trying to calm down.

Kofi nodded with the same distant air.

'Where is he?'

Radka blinked, a little disconcerted by the question. Of course, they must have expected to see George, waiting.

'He's not here yet.'

In the car Kofi sat in the back seat, staring out of the window, his expression dreamy and abstracted. He answered Radka's polite questions, but it was as if he had removed himself into another world for the moment. Radka watched him in the driving mirror, remembering what Joseph had said about his health, and wondering whether she would recognise the symptoms if he began to show signs that the trip had been too much for him. Joseph must have been thinking similar thoughts because she noticed that he kept glancing at Kofi's reflection.

Serge was with his grandmother, she told them. She had considered bringing him but she couldn't be sure that he would keep the secret about his grandfather until Katya's birthday party the next day.

'Twenty-four hours is a long time in a little boy's life,' she said, smiling. 'I'm going to tell her in the morning. I thought maybe George should tell her, but if he doesn't come by then I must tell her before she sees you tomorrow. I don't want to give her too much of a surprise.'

The hotel Joseph had booked was in a side street off the Ku'damm, and Radka drove up the Bismarck Strasse so they could see the glass cage of the Zoo station. It was mid-afternoon and though the traffic was moderate for that part of the city, it was still enough to stop them within sight of the building. At that moment a group of Africans walked across the street in front of the car, and seeing Joseph and Kofi in its interior, they stared curiously. She met their gaze with a pleasant expression but refrained from smiling, because after one or two disagreeable experiences she now feared that her attempts at friendliness might be misinterpreted. Apart from this she was marvelling over their resemblance to her husband's father. There was the shade of their skin, to begin with. Unlike the negroes she

254

saw on TV or the cinema screen their colour was glaringly dark, more black than brown. Then there was their hair, black wire piled like a carpet, and their large flaccid lips. She couldn't resist a look into the mirror, seeing Kofi's tired face like a reflection of the faces in front of her. The strange thing was that, in normal circumstances, her mind hardly ever linked her husband or her son together with such faces, and doing so now gave her an uneasy, almost frightened feeling. It reminded her of going with George for the first time to Prague to meet her mother, who persisted until her death in giving his name a French pronunciation. Her nerves had been tighter and tighter the closer she got to the city, as if she was developing eyes in the back of her head to catch the expressions on the faces of the other passengers as they looked at her and George. In Berlin people stared less. George's dress and manner marked him out as a native, like a camouflage for his colour. In Prague it was different. People feigned indifference, but they looked twice, seeing her with George.

Her mother had been, as usual, talking about her teaching job from which she was soon due to retire. She would receive the usual medal for her long service, she said angrily. This was how they had treated her brother, who had worked, before his death, in the petrochemical complex at Litvinoff. His skin had been wasted and discoloured, his lungs rotted, but the swine had given him a medal. Nothing else, just a medal. Her mother could go on like this for hours, and in any case she showed little curiosity about George. She knew better than to ask him too many questions about his own background and work. For over a decade she had survived by close-mouthed discretion, her personality resembling a surface which offered no reflection. In the circumstances she would refuse to know too much detail, even about her own son-in-law. It was afterwards, when they were alone towards the end of the visit that she ventured something which hinted at her thoughts.

'He's not very dark-skinned,' she remarked thoughtfully. 'In Romania no one would notice him.'

Remembering the conversation Radka smiled at the thought of what her mother would make of Kofi. By this time she was driving into the curving forecourt of the hotel.

'Shall I come and help you check in?' she asked Joseph.

He shook his head. Even from the outside it was clear that this was the sort of establishment where the staff would speak English, and as if to emphasise the point a young man dressed in a neat waistcoat and a white shirt emerged and began unloading the suitcases from the boot of the car. Joseph grinned at her.

'They probably speak better English than we do.' He took her hand. 'What are you doing later?' Radka felt like gasping for breath and she didn't trust herself to speak, so she shook her head. 'Let's meet later. My dad's tired. He'll probably go to bed early, but we need to talk.'

On the way back to Schöneberg, the district where Katya lived, Radka realised that she was feeling elated at the prospect of being out alone with Joseph, her mood pervaded by a kind of frivolous gaiety she hadn't experienced in a long while. This was how she had been with Renate as they walked out for the evening, or getting ready to meet someone new. In her mind now, her emotions about George were exhausted, as if he had been her opponent in a long struggle which neither of them could win. When they talked it was without revelation, and George's mind seemed closed to her, their intimacy a mere habit which left her feeling solitary and vulnerable. In comparison Joseph was like an open book. When she embraced him his body had been taut and edgy, the uncertainty in his eyes when they met hers like a confession. On the telephone she had heard something in his voice, but she hadn't been certain until she had touched him at the airport. Thinking about his reaction she felt the heat rising in her face, and, involuntarily, she found herself wondering how to behave when she met him later. If she was cold and distant, perhaps they would never be friends.

Ten years ago, this had been how she felt about seeing George, the air charged with bubbles, and the sense that something momentous, she didn't know what, would happen before the night was over. The thought conjured up the image of his face when she had first seen him across the room, younger than Joseph's, brooding with a hint of pain. It had been Renate who took the initiative and spoke to him on that occasion. This had been at the party after the group of African poets performing in the Freundschaft Hall had finished their final reading. Renate nudged Radka to make sure they were looking at the same person.

'Oh yes,' Radka breathed into her friend's ear.

This was typical of how they operated. Renate was the bolder one of the pair, making deadpan jokes and flashing the dark Mediterranean eyes she had inherited from her mother. Radka went along with her, throwing fuel on whatever fires her friend lit. This was the way they confronted George, Renate weaving through the crush of students, dragging Radka by the hand behind her. Radka smiled, remembering the look on George's face, halfway between surprise and pleasure, as he raised his head to see them bearing down on him.

She had been the best of friends with Renate then. This was in the time of calm before the storm. It was true that no one knew for certain that the regime was dying, but there was something in the air, a hint of expectancy which seemed to make their hearts beat faster. Both of them had agreed that they would never settle for men who were contented with things as they were, or who wanted to stagnate in some niche until they were worn smooth like stepping stones in concrete.

George, she knew from the beginning, would never be a dull and spineless functionary. He had been born, in a manner of speaking, out of uniform, and everything about him seemed to announce that he belonged elsewhere.

Walking along the Friedrichstrasse with him on that first night Radka indulged herself in the daydream of a new life, in which George would be her guide. Beyond the Wall anything would be possible, she thought, George could probably become a millionaire, and their children would be happy and unafraid, brown and beautiful, treading the white sands of faraway beaches.

The reality was very different. Everyone knew the facts, but in the years which followed the first rush of exhilaration about their new freedom, most of her friends and acquaintances struggled with a growing sense of disappointment and frustration. Some found it easier than others. Renate, for example, wangled a job with the Greens. They suffered a defeat in the federal elections a year later, and she switched to working for a Christian Democrat deputy. In a couple of years she was indistinguishable from any other Wessi, with an apartment in Bonn, and too busy for more than an occasional expedition to her parents' house in Saxony. On the other hand, George, whom she had vaguely imagined would take to the atmosphere of the West like a salmon swimming upriver, seemed depressed and fatigued by the effort of finding work and shelter. As for Renate, they had drifted further and further apart, and it was after a long period of silence, in the wake of the baby's arrival, that Renate had reappeared to drop her bombshell about George. It must have been a kind of revenge, Radka thought at the time. But up to that moment she had still regarded Renate as her best friend, and her revelations seemed to cast a cloud over Radka's entire life. Worst of all was the sense that just as she had been deceived about George in the past, her visions about their future were an illusion. Renate had talked about the Stasi agent who had recruited herself and George as if he had somehow sapped their will to resist, and although Radka had often heard something similar about people who had spent years spying on their family and friends, the idea offered her no comfort. Renate had described the agent, trying to jog her memory, a fat man whom Radka had seen around the university a couple of times without registering, but the truth was that she didn't want to hear about it, and she didn't want to remember.

As this memory played itself back through her mind, Radka was making a right turn towards Schöneberg, and she paused, her foot frozen on the brake pedal, hardly hearing the angry blasts of horns behind her. All of a sudden, she remembered the smile and the grotesque round face, and, in a flash, she realised why the fat man who had stopped to smile at her outside the supermarket had seemed familiar. She had, for the moment, no idea why he had appeared or what he wanted, but she was now certain that the man she had seen peering out of the big black car was the same agent who had wound his tentacles round her husband and her best friend.

NINETEEN

Upstairs on the third floor of the hotel, Joseph unpacked his suitcase, had a shower and made himself a cup of coffee. Alone in the room he felt liberated, as if he'd been carrying Kofi around on his back all day. With a feeling of luxury he drank his coffee, zapped through the TV stations and stared through the window at the quiet street below. They were close enough to the Ku'damm to hear its bustle, but in this street there seemed to be hardly more than a few pedestrians, and, although both sides were lined with parked cars, the stream of vehicles was sparse and intermittent.

After a while he crossed the corridor and knocked on the door of the room opposite. Kofi had taken his coat off and was lying on the bed, watching a game of football with the sound turned off. Joseph guessed that it was a local match, because he didn't recognise the colours or any of the players.

'What do you think?' he asked.

'It's a nice room.'

'Not the room.' Joseph hesitated, then went for it. 'I mean what do you think about tomorrow? Katya and the birthday party.'

'I don't know. I wanted to come and see her, but I don't know about all that. But if they think that's the best thing to do, that's okay with me.'

He didn't take his eyes off the television screen. Joseph hovered uncertainly. He wanted to say something that would bring him closer to Kofi's thoughts, to cut through the barriers between them, but he didn't know what.

'I've been lying here,' Kofi said, 'thinking about Moscow.

Being abroad reminds me. Existence shapes consciousness. Consciousness determines existence. The one thing
is linked with the other. Katya said that. It was in all
the books. In the end I understood that it was a kind
of reasoning that accounted for everything.' He propped
himself up on one elbow and looked at Joseph. 'You see,
when I went there I didn't know how different people
could be. I only really understood it when I had to leave.
That's why I was never too worried about finding out what
was happening with Katya. I thought I knew. Being here
it's hit me that the world has changed, been changing a
long time. I mean I saw some of it on TV but that's not
personal you know.'

He was rambling, Joseph thought.

'Are you up to it?'

'It's complicated,' Kofi continued as if he hadn't heard
the question. 'At the time I didn't think that anything I
did would last for a long time. What I mean is this. My
life was over some time ago. I eat and drink and sleep, go
to the library, talk to people. None of it matters except for
you, and I'm like a shadow, even to you.'

'No,' Joseph said quickly. Kofi smiled.

'I'm glad you said that, but it's true. Some years ago I
realised that nothing would happen any more *because* of
me, and all the things that happened to me before are like
that. Osageyfo has died and so has everyone else who was
there, or else they're old men like me. I thought Katya had
died somewhere or as good as. Everyone who knew me as
a real person.'

'That can't be true,' Joseph protested automatically. 'You
know a lot of people.'

'That's not what I mean,' Kofi said. 'What I mean is
about understanding that you're real.' He looked at Joseph,
chuckling a little at the puzzled look on his son's face.
'Everything about the life I lived as a young man is a
memory now, pictures in a box like the television. I got
used to that, watching that person I used to be walking

around and talking with all the other memories, like a shadow of something that wasn't there any more. I stopped remembering a long time ago. I really couldn't recall the colour of her eyes, or how long her hair was, and when I thought about those times there were even things blended in there that happened to other people, and when I stopped to think about it I realised that I'd taken them over as if they'd happened to me.'

He chuckled again, and it struck Joseph that his father was laughing at himself this time.

'When you told me,' he continued, 'it was like the first time in a long while that I remembered that something real had happened, and that those were real people out there, instead of dreams in my head. That's what I'm doing now, trying to get a grip on the reality.'

'You need a rest,' Joseph told him. He couldn't think of anything else to say.

'This isn't easy,' Kofi said. 'I was just thinking when you came in that if I had my way I would lie here until it was time to go home.'

'You need a rest,' Joseph said again.

To his surprise, Kofi nodded obediently.

'Yes. I think I'll take a rest.'

He closed his eyes and lay back, as if preparing to go to sleep.

'I don't know what to make of it,' Joseph confessed to Radka later on.

They were sitting in an Indian restaurant on the Kantstrasse. By some coincidence it had exactly the appearance of an Indian restaurant he sometimes went to in Bayswater, and waiting for the meal he had the momentary and absurd delusion that if he walked out the door he would find himself walking towards Notting Hill. The illusion was strengthened by the fact that the waiters spoke English, not with the fluency of an English Asian, but with an accent he hadn't heard since he was a child.

262

'They speak German in the same way,' Radka said. 'I think they haven't been here long.'

'Their German is still better than mine,' he told her. 'Anyway they've been here long enough to invent currywurst.'

Perhaps, he thought, it was something to do with the familiarity of the place which made him feel as if everything was so – he searched for the word in his mind – normal, as if he was out for an evening in London with a friend. In England, he told Radka, the equivalent of currywurst was called chicken tikka masala. She repeated the words carefully, giggling as she did so.

'In a hundred years,' Joseph said, 'everyone will have forgotten where those words came from.'

She was wearing a black dress, and a pair of gold earrings dangled by her neck, swaying and trembling as she moved. Joseph had been prepared for anything, but to his surprise the atmosphere between them had been light and flirtatious from the moment he took her hand in the hotel lobby and they began walking towards Savignyplatz.

It was like the first outing with a new woman, with the knowledge that after this evening anything was possible. She told him more about herself without urging. She worked part-time at a research institute at Charles University. Mostly what she did was to translate texts. There was always work for a good translator. Lately she had begun to work for an English language publisher who gave her work she could do at home so she could spend more time with Serge. Moving around as they did he had few opportunities to make friends.

Listening to her, Joseph began to feel that he knew and understood her. He felt relaxed, in control of himself. They didn't talk about George until the meal was finished.

'I don't know where he is,' she told Joseph. 'He was pleased about us leaving Prague and coming back here and crazy to see his father. But he spends most of his time with Valentin.'

She didn't have a good relationship with Valentin, she

263

said, even though he was George's cousin and Katya liked him. Ever since he appeared there had been trouble between herself and George. There was something about him, in any case, as if he brought with him the violence and chaos that was Russia. Even without the mysteries in which he had involved George she probably wouldn't like him.

'Because he's Russian?' Joseph asked her.

She hesitated.

'Yes.'

'What about Katya?'

'The women are different,' she replied immediately.

George had said that he would be there on Katya's birthday, but that was all she knew.

'How do you stay with someone who tells you so little?' Joseph asked.

The question seemed to have slipped out of his mouth before he could stop it. They were walking back towards the hotel, along a quiet cross-street. It was lined with the lighted windows of closed shops, and at the end of it he could see the traffic of pedestrians flowing up and down the Ku'damm. Radka hadn't replied, and for a moment he wondered whether she was angry. She looked round at him, her eyes glowing with the reflections of the street.

'I grew up in a kind of silence,' she said. 'There were many things I didn't know. Secrets were normal.' She paused, then she smiled quizzically, as if something new had occurred to her. 'Do you tell your wife everything?'

There hadn't been much to tell. Liz had left him, rather than the other way round, and she was the one who had led a secret life for more than a year before that. Even so she had accused him of being distant, impossible to live with, because he kept his thoughts and emotions to himself. On that occasion she had spoken with a cold, vicious contempt which left him feeling whipped and humiliated. George, he thought, would probably never have married a woman like Liz.

264

'I'm not married,' he replied.

'Right. I forgot.'

She gave him a wry grin and he laughed, charmed and inexplicably excited by the idea that his brother possessed this woman who was so beautiful and at the same time so amiable and compliant. Almost without thinking he put his arm round her and she leant towards him without resistance. Walking on, their hips bumped in rhythm. In a couple of minutes they reached her car. She leant against it, head back, a pose of exhausted languor. Joseph watched her, thinking that if she had wanted to go she would have simply opened the door and stepped into the car.

'If only you weren't married to my brother,' he heard himself say. She turned her head gradually, like a puppet being pulled by slow wires, and the greenish glinting of her eyes in the reflected light seemed to ignite the air between them. Her eyes opened wider still, and for a moment he thought that he had shocked or offended her, then behind him he heard a voice calling out. Radka frowned, lowering her head to stare past him.

'George.'

There were two of them a few metres away, tall and bulky, wearing black leather jackets and blond crewcuts. Joseph grinned at them, making a gesture of denial. These must be a couple of George's weirder friends, he thought.

'You'd better tell them they're making a mistake,' he told Radka.

She said something, in a peremptory and dismissive tone, but instead of moving off the men loomed closer.

'I'm not George,' Joseph insisted. The men didn't look like old friends of anyone at all, and they were moving with a menacing purpose, but hearing Joseph speak in English the nearest man paused, staring, a puzzled frown creasing his forehead. Radka snapped out something which Joseph didn't understand, but he caught the word '*polizei*'. His guess was that she had threatened them with calling the police if they didn't go away, but that didn't seem to impress the two men. Instead, one of them took a quick stride that brought him close enough for Joseph to catch the sour smell of beer on his breath. For a long moment they stared into each other's eyes.

'What do you want?' Joseph asked, trying to keep his voice level and calm.

Radka spoke again, louder, her voice shrill, and Joseph heard the word for brother repeated a couple of times. The man didn't reply. He clamped his lips together and nodded his head as if coming to some conclusion, then, suddenly, whirled round, grabbed Radka by the shoulders, pinning her against the side of the car, and spat out some words in a fierce, angry mutter.

'Let her go!' Joseph shouted. It was as if he'd come to life, the blood coursing through his veins and driving him to the attack. 'Let her go!'

He hit out automatically, punching the man's arm just above the biceps, connecting with a satisfying thud on the solid muscle. The man let Radka go and she stumbled against the car, reaching out to stop herself falling. This was all he had time to see because, in the next instant, the world exploded in a kaleidoscope of colours. He didn't lose consciousness, but his legs would no longer hold him upright and he sagged to the ground. All he could see was a blur.

'Joseph,' Radka said loudly. 'Joseph. Can you hear me?'

She was kneeling above him, her hands supporting his head. He lolled against her breasts, feeling warm and drowsy, ready to drift off to sleep. Time seemed to have stopped and he had no idea how long he'd been there.

'Can you get up?'

She tugged at him and he got up slowly, beginning to feel a stinging pain in his ear. As he stood, he staggered, leant on Radka for support, and then he pressed his hand to his side, feeling the pain in his ribs.

'He kicked you,' she said, seeing the gesture.

His nose was bleeding, and she gave him a wad of

tissues. He walked upright through the lobby, Radka's arm holding him up, the bloody tissues clutched to his face, and somehow she got him into the hotel and up to his room. His vision was clear now, but he felt weak and distant as though an invisible curtain had come down between himself and his surroundings. In his room he lay on the bed while she called the reception, and, speaking in an urgent and authoritative voice, asked them for a doctor. He sat up. The pain had dwindled to a dull throbbing.

'I don't need a doctor.'

'To be safe,' she said. She hesitated. 'Do you want to make a report to the police?'

'No,' he replied automatically.

In London his reaction would have been the same. In normal circumstances the police were unpredictable and difficult. In a country where he spoke only a few words of the language he recoiled instinctively from the prospect. For all he knew the men who had attacked him could have been policemen themselves. The other complication was the fact that they had called out George's name.

'Who were those men? What did they want?'

She shrugged.

'They said George's name,' he insisted.

'I don't know. I told them you were George's brother.'

'He said something to you.' He took a guess. 'A message for George?'

'I don't know what he was talking about.'

'What did he say?'

She didn't reply and he tried again.

'The least you can do is tell me why I got punched.'

'I think it was all a mistake,' she said. 'It makes no sense. He said to tell George they were waiting.'

The doctor came in a short while. He examined Joseph, told him there was no serious damage, and gave him a few aspirins.

'I must go,' Radka said when the doctor left. 'Shall I get Kofi?'

267

He shook his head. At that moment he couldn't face the idea of coping with his father.

'No. Stay for a little while.'

'I have to speak with Katya,' she said. 'To tell her you're here.'

'Good,' Joseph told her. Radka's plan had always struck him as risky. No one really knew whether Katya would want to see Kofi, and even if she said she did, she might well change her mind when she knew he was nearby.

Radka sat on the bed facing him.

'Just for a few minutes,' she said vaguely.

Joseph began fumbling with the buttons of the bloody shirt. The doctor had opened it to look at his chest, then, ridiculously, carefully buttoned it up again.

'Let me help you,' Radka said.

She unbuttoned his shirt and drew it over his head. As she did this she didn't meet his eyes and, feeling the delicate touch of her hands, he wondered whether she was thinking about George. She held the shirt by the arm and threw it across the room. She gasped and wiped her hand on the bedspread. She was breathing faster, the blood drained from her face.

'Blood,' she said angrily. 'I hate to see blood. It frightens me.'

Her fingers traced the bruise on his ribcage.

'Your skin is very pale here,' she said. 'Just like George.'

For an instant, George's face flashed through his mind, then he dismissed the image. He put his hand over hers, pressing it close against his skin. He drew her gently, and inclining gradually towards him, she touched her lips to his face. They kissed, her body still tumbling down on his, with the endless slowness of a hallucination. They stayed like this for a few minutes, then when he touched her breasts, stroking them through the fabric of her dress, she opened her eyes, gazing into his.

'I must go,' she whispered.

'Yes.'

They kissed again. Joseph's body was tense and humming, his pain forgotten. He was more excited than he expected or wanted to be. Time vanished. They lay facing each other, their bodies entwined, and he was moving slowly, feeling himself like a great bulk inside her.

'George,' she whispered. '*Liebling.*'

He was lying dazed and half asleep when he felt her swing off the bed and he heard the noise of water running in the bathroom. When he opened his eyes again, she was standing beside the bed. In the reflected light from the open door he could see that she was fully dressed.

'I have to go,' she said.

She bent over and kissed him quickly on the cheek. Then she was gone.

TWENTY

DIARY OF DESIRE

The life and times of Kofi George Coker
Moscow 1957

*That winter seemed to be going on for ever. It did not, of course,
it was simply that the arrival of the spring didn't mean the end
of snow and ice. But after our visit to Jelenia Gora I hardly
noticed the weather. Katya and I were in love, and we didn't
think of much apart from each other. In those days we were
like tigers in the snow, leaping to each other whenever the
opportunity offered. We must have made love every day for
weeks, underneath convenient trees, against freezing walls, knee
deep in snow, once in a tunnel near Komsomolskaya, once while
she bent with her back to me over the railing of a bridge over the
Moskva, then we walked over the bridge down Kotelnicheskaya
Naberezhnaya, went into the archway that led into the massive
apartment building they called the Visoky Zdaniye, and then did
it all over again, facing each other this time. Another time we did
it on the floor of the empty classroom at the college. Under her
skirt, during that period, she wore two or three slips. When I
lifted them under her coat I could feel her naked belly heaving
against me. Sometimes, it seemed, I thought of nothing else except
the next time.*

*The snow was wet underfoot when she invited me to meet her
parents. By this time I had begun to acquire a grasp of what
the people were like. For instance, talking to Valery about Katya
showed me a picture of her that was new to me. He'd noticed
how often we were together, of course, although I was careful
not to say too much about how we spent our time. Like all the*

others, he guessed. Calvin's 'jokes' about 'educational pussy' and 'bringing teacher a banana' would have told him, in any case. When I mentioned that I had been invited to Katya's apartment he laughed as if I'd said something funny. Her father, he told me, was one of those who had survived the purges and travelled with Khrushchev to the Ukraine in order to repeat the entire process. They knew him well there.

As usual, I had to read the meaning of Valery's comments between the lines, and I had the feeling he was trying to tell me to be cautious about this visit, or perhaps not to go, but, in the end, I closed my ears.

As it happened there seemed to be nothing very alarming about Katya's family. They lived to the west of the city, near Kutuzovsky Prospekt. The apartment was on the first floor of a quiet block at the end of a crooked lane pitted with holes and ruts, which were full of cracked ice and muddy slush. Inside, the place seemed like an explosion of colour and decoration, packed to bursting with objects, and it took my eyes a little time to adjust. The floor was covered with fringed carpets, mostly red, the walls were lined with shelves, full of books, dolls, little brass knick-knacks and wooden statuettes. Stepping across the threshold I was hit by a strong smell, some kind of herb I had never encountered before.

Katya led me through the hallway into the room next to the kitchen. Her father was sitting at a desk. I had expected someone who looked meaner, but he appeared to be jovial, with a cheerful round face, topped by a fringe of blond hair, going white in streaks. Put a beard and a red hood on him and he'd look like Santa Claus, I thought. Later on, when I told Hussein this he nearly fell over laughing.

'You haven't really seen him yet,' he said, and this was true, because the next time I caught sight of Vladimir Andreyevich he was wearing a huge black overcoat and a black hat and he was getting out of a big black car surrounded by a group of men who looked exactly the same, and according to Hussein this was what he really looked like.

When I first met him, though, the questions he asked me seemed natural and harmless, just the sort of thing that any concerned

271

father would ask of a young man who came home for dinner with his daughter. 'Oochenik,' he called me with a burst of laughter. That meant pupil and it seemed to be a family joke, because he kept on addressing Katya as oocheetyelneetsa *– teacher – drawing out the syllables ironically. It made her laugh, for some reason, and I laughed along with her, and we all seemed to be getting on like a house on fire. Katya's mother was, in contrast to her husband, a stern-looking woman, lean and greying with little round spectacles perched on her nose. She worked in one of the ministries, I gathered. The odd thing was that they were the reverse of what I expected – the woman cool and gloomy, the man warm and welcoming. After dinner he brought out a bottle of Polish Zubrowka and we began talking seriously. Katya sat next to me on the sofa, her face covered in smiles, translating quickly the words I didn't understand and phrasing my replies to her father. Her mother, who spoke barely two words for the whole of the evening, sat at a little distance from us behind a table on which was a pile of books with some sort of journal propped up against them. She was reading it most of the time, but occasionally she would lay it down and listen to what we were saying, her chin resting in her open palm, her eyes magnified and bulging behind the glasses, switching from one to the other of us.*

Vladimir Andreyevich looked like a bit of an idiot, but he knew a lot, I'll say that for him. He asked me what I thought about Nasser, and he asked me to describe Dr Nkrumah. Nikita Sergeyevich, he told me, had proved to the colonial leaders that he was the real friend of Africa and Asia when he forced Eisenhower to call for the withdrawal of Britain and France from Egypt. It wouldn't be long, he said, before my people realised that their true interests lay in alliance with the socialist countries against the bullying and oppression of the capitalist world. I kept my thoughts to myself. I already knew the depth of our politicians' scepticism about Khrushchev's intentions. I had the feeling that Vladimir knew it too, but if he was trying to draw out my opinions about such matters as Suez and Hungary and their implications for my country, he would have to wait a long time.

To prove his point he told me a few stories about China. He had been part of a delegation to Beijing, which had been headed by Nikita Sergeyevich and Nikolai Aleksandrovich. The Chinese were very polite people who couldn't do enough for their comfort, but after a time, everyone in the Russian party began to be depressed by the sheer quantities of tea they had to drink. Every time they drained their cups the Chinese would refill them. If it had been vodka, of course, it would have been different, but so much tea was intolerable, especially for Nikita Sergeyevich who had to keep getting up in the middle of negotiations to empty his bladder. In the end he simply refused to drink any more tea. Half the delegation followed his example. The other half modelled themselves on Bulganin who continued to drink the innumerable cups of tea, and as a result was out of the room when many important matters were being decided.

At the end of this story, Vladimir leant over and refilled my glass. I told him that for a foreigner like myself tea might be easier to cope with. He found this hilarious, but it didn't stop him pouring the vodka. By the time I left I was only just able to walk. Maybe Katya's father knew what he was doing, because at the beginning of the evening it had crossed my mind that later on we might have a quick bout in the dark stairway. That night, however, I was only capable of lurching slowly to the metro station.

After this our relationship was more open, that is to say, we took less trouble to hide it, and, as if the two things went together, the desperation of our attacks on each other's bodies grew less intense.

Valery and Hussein issued warnings couched in their different styles. Valery's comments were in code. He took to speaking ironically about Party apparatchiks, quoting fragments about hypocrisy from Khrushchev's speeches, and so on. Hussein was more open. 'Be careful with these people,' he said. All this meant little to me. The fact is that I was too happy, uncaring in my ignorance, like a blind man strolling towards a cliff, his face turned upwards to the sun. The disaster, when it came, was sudden and definitive.

*   *   *

That evening we had been walking around the Kremlin, St Basil's and Red Square. I remember wanting to see the domes against the beams of the setting sun. It was the kind of romantic idea which astonishes me now when I think about it, but we walked there for more than an hour. After dark we headed for the embankment, savouring the fresh cool spring breeze blowing off the river. It wasn't late, but it was an ordinary working day, and by this time of night there were few pedestrians in this part of the town. We were walking past some railings as I remember it. There was an old church or a building which used to be a monastery. The area was littered with them. In the gardens the birches were budding. In the reflected light they shone with a pale translucent and unearthly green. Ahead of us a red star lit up the top of the Visoky Zdaniye. Everywhere you looked there was something to see. I seem to remember that Katya was describing a letter she'd received that day from her brother, who was a rocket engineer, full of excitement about some tests they were doing. By the end of the year he had said, Soviet science would overtake all the achievements of the West. I was frankly sceptical, but of course, Katya was right about that because soon enough they produced the triumph of Sputnik. Deep in the argument, we didn't notice the young men following us until we heard the voices. At first I couldn't distinguish what they were saying. Then I heard the words 'abyezhyana' and 'chornim'. I'd been called a black monkey in the streets before, but usually I had been with one of the other boys or a group of students when some drunk started to bellow abuse. There was something about the situation and the sound of the voices which told me that this was different. The four boys behind us didn't sound drunk or mad. I was familiar with the feel of it, because the vibrations, the passion aroused by the mere sight of a black man and a white woman swinging along hand in hand, were the same in any language. The last time I'd experienced it was coming out of a pub in Wilmslow Road, late on Saturday and bumping into a crowd of white men. The girl with me needed no telling and she'd whipped off her high heels and started running before I had time to think. Remembering this I grabbed Katya by the arm and began urging her along,

274

looking around for a convenient building or a house to which we could run. Unfortunately, I reckoned without her sense of security – 'arrogance' Hussein called it later, but the fact was that this was new to her. The girl who ran with me that night in Wilmslow Road knew that being with me put her beyond the pale. In Katya's case running away from hooligan elements within sight of the Kremlin simply wasn't in her nature. I was poised for flight when I realised that she had swung around and started berating the boys. It was all too fast and agitated for me to understand, but I moved back to her side, trying to ease her away. Of course I couldn't leave her to it, but it was a mistake. As I reached for her, one of the young men hit out at me. He was blond and wearing a leather jacket, which is about all I remembered later. I swayed back, but Katya kept trying to get in front of me, which meant that we got tangled in each other's feet and by the time I could set myself to push her aside I had been surrounded. One of the youths held me from behind, the others set to work hitting me. They weren't experts. I think they meant to beat me up. Instead they knocked me unconscious with only a few blows. I must have been out for a few minutes, and I woke up to find myself still lying on the ground, cradled in Katya's arms. My jaw felt as though it had been broken, and I could feel my face growing agonisingly tight as it swelled.

'Don't move,' she kept saying, but there wasn't much prospect of that, and in a few seconds I passed out again.

I was aware of being put on a stretcher and driven away, although I kept falling asleep. I guess that they must have given me some kind of drug, because I felt no pain. I was floating above the city, watching my ambulance speeding along the embankment. Ahead of me the red star loomed, and I felt like laughing.

Next morning when I woke up in the hospital Hussein and Valery were both there, standing round my bed. When I tried to speak it hurt, but I could feel that there was nothing broken.

'Is Katya okay?' I asked them.

'She's back at work this morning,' Hussein said. 'They didn't touch her.'

That was true, and I was relieved but not totally surprised.

What surprised me was how much the incident changed our relationship. I didn't see Katya until my face was getting back to normal and I could walk without limping. I didn't go to my classes, and she didn't show up at Cheryomushki. This was as expected. I was foreign and one of her students, so there was a flavour of transgression about our relationship which would have made it difficult for her to confront the warden. She wrote me a letter which Valery delivered with a shrug and a flick of his eyebrows. It was a careful message, saying how sorry she was and how she hoped I would be better soon, and that she was looking forward to resuming my instruction. I knew this last bit was her real message to me, put in a way that she knew would make me laugh, so I felt better right away. This was a relief because I was having to deal with another matter about which I was in two minds.

After I returned to Cheryomushki I found that I had become the focus of attention among my fellow students, a fact which didn't altogether please me. On my second day back the students' union held a meeting at which I was invited to speak about my unfortunate experience. The problem was that afterwards, Hussein proposed a resolution to be sent to the regional committee condemning this example of racial violence directed against comrade students from abroad in the shadow of Lenin's tomb. I knew he was making mischief. I wasn't certain why, but he hardly ever attended the students' meetings and he had often sneered in private about the language in which his resolution was framed. Predictably, the subsequent debate split the student body in half. Hussein had talked to a number of the boys about his intentions during the day and most of them had already discussed it and decided to abstain. I couldn't be sure whether the warden had spoken to them, but everyone knew by now what his line was on such attacks. He had come to see me in my room after I got back and told me that I'd had the misfortune to come across some drunken hooligans. My impression that they had called me a black monkey was incorrect. According to Vladimir Andreyevich, Katya's father, she had heard no such comment. The brawl was a misunderstanding provoked by my ignorance of the language. Repeating my story would merely lower the morale of my comrades in Cheryomushki and give ammunition to the enemies of the Soviet Union's forward-looking policy of aiding the oppressed colonies.

Towards the end of the student meeting, Calvin of all people got up and put this argument. Hussein watched him with an ironical smile curving his lips, but when he asked for someone to second the motion there was no response. Hussein looked at me. 'Leave it,' I told him. I knew by then the resolution would be defeated, and there seemed no point in pursuing it, even if I had been certain that I wanted to.

Next day I asked Hussein why he had bothered. He must have known that our flock of sheep would refuse to pass such a resolution. He grinned at me, triumphant.

'I want to go home,' he said. 'I really do. I've had enough. My work is more or less finished. I don't need to be here, but if I just went I'd be in some trouble when I got back. They've spent quite a bit on my research. Now they've revoked my scholarship they've got no claims on me.' He took in my astonished expression, still grinning. 'The warden told me this morning. They're kicking me out. I'll be in London in a couple of days.' He clapped me on the back. 'Thanks.'

'Thanks?'

'It was all your doing. You gave me the idea when we were talking about Padmore. If I'm going to work in the West it will help me a lot to have been kicked out of Moscow. I don't want anyone to think I'm some kind of Party plant. But I had to wait for a good excuse. Nothing too serious, something that everyone can find understandable. You gave it to me.'

'I'm glad,' I told him, unable to restrain my resentment at that moment, 'that you found my getting beaten in the street so useful.'

Hussein looked at me seriously.

'Let me tell you something,' he said. 'That was nothing. To those men you were probably a symbol of privilege, and you are. In their existence the richness and variety of your life is unimaginable. What they did to you is their revenge on the

277

world. Everyone knows that. Misery is relative. The point is that there is nothing the Party can do about it, and it will get worse. I've been studying the Virgin Lands programme. Remember? It won't work. But Siberia's the next big thing. The Russians will do the same there. Invent some crazy way of extracting as many resources as possible, take as much as they can out of it, send it to the centre and use it for whatever they want, and then leave the place in a state worse than they found it. What does that sound like to you? Colonialism, right? The thing is they can see how it ends up right now in Africa and Asia, but they won't take any notice. At this moment imperialism looks good to the Party, and by the time they understand the real cost it will be too late. They think that the West is getting out of the business because they're decadent. Believe me that's what Nikita Sergeyevich was brought up to think, and what he won't understand is that Western Europe is running for cover, so he's going to maintain Stalin's imperialist system in the republics and Eastern Europe, and one day some bunch of nationalists is going to get up and start killing Russians and then it will get worse. These people are in for a very bad time. My resolution was a bad joke, but the tragedy here isn't yours. Be glad you're what you are. In my country and yours within a few years we'll be driving limousines and ordering executions the way the big men do here. Save your sense of justice for that.'

The following week I walked with Katya around the university campus under the shadow of the tower and asked her why she'd given her father a false version of the incident. She gazed at me with astonishment. 'I didn't say that.' The warden must have invented it all, she said. I should have known, I thought. He'd said what he had to in order to confuse matters and keep me quiet. Now I knew the truth it was too late. Katya sighed and told me she was sorry. The worst of it, she told me, was that at the end of the week, she was going off to Komsomolsk to see her brother. The visit had been promised for months, but this was his first and perhaps his last break for a while, so he wanted her to come now. If she refused he would be hurt and she might not see him for a long time. I told her I understood. When we said goodbye, I didn't know that I would only see her one more time.

She was still away when a delegation arrived from London. They consisted of the Party officials who were responsible for supervising some of the scholarships, and they were treated as important dignitaries. There was a black man from the Caribbean in the group, who was their troubleshooter for the problems of the blacks. The rumour was that Hussein's expulsion had caused a great stir and the delegation had come to restore calm and instruct their clients in how to behave. For a few days I saw him going backwards and forwards, interviewing various students. He seemed nice enough, and when he asked to see me I agreed. As I expected he asked me about the incident in which I had been assaulted, and I told him the details exactly as they had happened. 'If you're going to stay here, my brother,' he said at the end of my account, 'you'll have to forget about it.'

I didn't argue with him, because I had come to the same conclusion. In any case, the anger and confusion I had felt was beginning to fade. The truth was that to be abused or attacked because of the colour of my skin was something to which I had become accustomed long before, and the excitement which the incident had caused struck me as exaggerated and false. If so many people had not been so concerned I would have succeeded in putting it out of my mind in a few days. As it was, something about the way that they were trying to cover up the whole business had started to infuriate me. The black man from London was no different. I sensed that he believed everything I said, but I sensed also that his job, unnecessarily as it happened, was to shut me up. 'There's always a problem,' he said in a confiding tone, 'with the women.' I didn't reply, and he must have thought he was getting somewhere. He lowered his voice. 'This girl of yours,' he whispered. 'There's no question of your marrying her. The parents would block it. I met the father. He's a nice guy, but there're problems. These are important people and they expect a lot of her. You're not even in the Party.'

'We never discussed marriage,' I told him.

He shrugged.

'Well, it's been mentioned.' He hesitated. 'There's a lot of ignorance even here,' he continued, 'although the Party is working

279

hard to educate people. There was a story in one of the papers recently about an African who got permission to marry his Russian girlfriend and take her back with him. They said that when he got back he sold her.' He gave me a sorrowful look and shook his head. 'Of course it wasn't true. We made a hell of a protest, but it's the kind of rumour that gets around and causes trouble.' He raised his finger and pointed. 'We're going to take up your case behind the scenes, but we have to work with the Party. Once you go public with resolutions and petitions you just hurt the country and it doesn't do any good.'

I nodded, because I agreed with the last bit and he squeezed my hand warmly before he went away. That was the last of it, but, although I didn't know it, the attack had been the first step in my expulsion.

Katya returned shortly afterwards. In the evening we went out to Leninsky Gory and walked through the new grass up the slopes. There were a few couples strolling about in the twilight and a wedding party climbing the hill. As they went past a few of the men called out and one of them came towards us. The sound of his voice and his manner was boisterous and friendly, but it was all I could do not to back away. He held out a bottle, and I took it and drank. Then he shook our hands and went away, jogging after his comrades. Unable to stop myself I told her what the official from London had said about the prospects for our getting married.

'I think he's right,' Katya said.

Her tone was calm and dispassionate, as if she was talking about someone else.

'Did your father talk to you about it? What makes them think we want to get married?' She didn't answer. 'It would be impossible in this country anyway,' I told her.

We walked on in silence.

'I can go to Paris next month,' Katya said. 'There's a conference and they've asked me.'

Hearing the words was as if someone had switched on the lights in a dark room. Up to that time it had not occurred to me that we might be together in some other place, and when I thought about her there had been no expectation of any future beyond the next time we would meet. Suddenly it was possible to imagine her with me years away from the Lenin Hills.

Walking up the slope we began planning. There had been no need for her to ask me, because her assumption that I would want to be there with her in Paris was entirely correct. We didn't talk about what would happen there or whether there was any question of her leaving permanently. At the back of both our minds was the thought that no one could stop us getting married in another country. The odd thing was that the whole idea might not have come up at all if it hadn't been put there, between us, by the intervention of others. Without saying anything, we both knew that being together in Paris would be the first step on a path which might carry us anywhere. The first snag, of course, was that in order to avert any suspicion we would have to stop seeing each other. In the circumstances it wouldn't take much for them to cancel her trip.

'The next time I see you,' Katya said, 'will be in the shadow of the Eiffel Tower.'

I don't know what would have happened if everything had been as normal. Instead, I was on edge, nervous and agitated. I wrote to Makonnen saying that my father had been in poor health when I left and that I hadn't heard from him. It was preying on my mind to the point where I couldn't concentrate on my studies, and I wanted him to get me permission and to pay for the fares so that I could go back for a couple of weeks to sort matters out. Mak had lost touch with my father years ago, and in any case, he was a mere toiler, a sparrow whose fall no one would have noticed, but I trusted that my patron would take the hint. The story about my father was the safety net. If they thought this was a journey of compassion and that I was coming back, no one would connect my leaving with Katya.

The arrangements were made faster than I thought possible. Ghana had by now established an embassy in Kitay-Gorod and Mak had sent a message through the ambassador. I think that the warden was pleased at the thought that I would have a holiday *and return refreshed. Since my 'accident' I had discussed the matter with him twice, pretending to slowly come round to his point of view. I had met with worse things in England, I told him, and I had no intention of confusing the issues by allowing myself to be used as a tool of propaganda by anyone. He nodded approvingly, and returning my passport to me, shook my hand warmly.*

I went to see Hussein's friend, Alexy, the black zek, before I left. He was still sitting up in bed, as if he hadn't moved since my last visit. I gave Vera the bottle I had brought and sat beside him.

'I wanted to tell you something,' he said. 'Hussein told me about what happened to you. Don't judge us because of that. In twenty-five years nothing has ever happened to me, because of my colour, even in the camps. But even if it had, it wouldn't matter. When you go back to Africa tell them that this system offers more freedom to more people. If they imitate the West what they'll have is a ruling class working for the Americans. The hope is here.' He paused. 'Without Stalin and Beria this would have been a paradise.'

This time I couldn't restrain my curiosity.

'So you're still a Communist?'

'Of course. When comrades come here from the West they expect perfection. What they never understand is that this is a state which is still on the way to changing the world.'

I half expected Valery to lecture me too, but he had said very little since my accident, which I appreciated. In spite of the suspicions Hussein planted in my mind, we had been good friends, sharing many thoughts, as young men do. When the time came for me to leave he held my hand in his and looked straight into my eyes. 'Are you coming back?'

Something inside me refused to lie to him, although I couldn't tell the truth either. 'Maybe,' I told him. 'I'll see how it goes.'

I got one letter from Katya with one word written on a sheet of paper. I knew it was her from the handwriting, although it was unsigned. 'Abyssinia', it said. It was a childish code I had learnt from a girl in England: 'I'll be seeing you'. No one would guess its meaning but I hid it away among my papers, and I still have that letter, the ink faded, the paper creased and falling apart.

It is all I have. She never came to Paris in the spring. I waited, haunting the hotel where the Russians were staying, perusing the faces at the conference long after I knew she wasn't there, and I didn't give up until they left. In desperation, finally, I arranged to bump into one of the delegates whom I recognised from the Komsomol college. I explained that I was doing a brief period of research in Paris, and asked after Katya. The delegate looked surprised. Katya had not been part of the delegation. They left the following day and I returned to London, where I got a summons from the Ghanaian embassy. The Russians had revoked my scholarship and withdrawn my visa, the attaché told me. He looked at me with obvious disapproval. 'You're not the first,' he said, 'to get into trouble over these women. But we expected more discipline from you.'

Coming out of the embassy there were tears in my eyes, and I walked the pavements between the high stone buildings without knowing or caring where I was going. In my mind I was wondering what had happened to her, and whether I would ever see her again, and what to do with the rest of my life.

TWENTY-ONE

Joseph and his father ate breakfast together, Kofi picking at a couple of rolls and drinking cup after cup of black coffee. He had noticed Joseph's bruises and the stiffness of his movements immediately. Joseph told him a version of the story, editing out any mention of George. At the end Kofi reached out, and, holding Joseph's chin in his hand, turned his head from side to side as if examining a small child.

'You're okay,' he said finally. 'I heard Berlin was bad. You should be careful.'

'You too,' Joseph told him. He was oddly irritated by his father's coolness.

'I've been in worse places,' Kofi replied.

He had secured an English newspaper from somewhere and he read it carefully, replying laconically to Joseph's comments. For his part Joseph stopped talking as soon as it was apparent that Kofi was in no mood for conversation, and, in any case, he was relieved not to be forced into elaborating on what had happened. What he really wanted was to sit and daydream about Radka, and the way her naked body had felt against his. His heart skipped a beat when he thought about the fact that he would be seeing her soon.

Ironically he was more nervous and on edge than Kofi seemed to be. Walking in the Tiergarten his father seemed to have recovered from whatever had ailed him, striding with his shoulders back, his head angled upwards as if he was trying to get his share of the fresh air in the park. He was still in a distant and abstracted mood, but Joseph couldn't resist asking him once more about Katya and what it had been like with her. Oddly enough, he wanted to tell Kofi about Radka and what had happened between them, but the instant it came into his mind it also occurred to him that Kofi might explode with indignation. 'Your brother's wife? You fucked your brother's wife?' He imagined his father saying it, and then he wondered how George would take the fact that his brother and his wife had betrayed him so completely. The idea gave him a peculiar little shiver, and, catching something in the corner of his eye, Kofi turned his head to look at him.

'Are you looking forward to it then, Dad?' he said, forcing a smile.

Kofi shrugged.

'I don't know,' he replied. 'We have a lot to talk about.'

'Do you think she had something to do with your being expelled?'

This was a thought which had been at the back of his mind, since Kofi had said what he did about Katya being a Party member.

Kofi shrugged again.

'I don't know. Why would she?'

Joseph didn't know the answer to that, but somehow the thought that she might have been untrustworthy didn't displease him.

'I'm surprised you're so trusting,' he said. For some reason, he realised, without being able to stop himself, he was trying to needle the old man. 'You were always telling me not to trust white people.'

Kofi flicked him a quick dangerous glance, and they had walked on for a few steps before he replied.

'When I told you that, you were a child, and I told it to you because you did.'

It was the middle of the day when Radka came to fetch them. It was a short trip, she said. George hadn't arrived yet, but they were expecting him soon.

'How did she take the surprise?' he asked her.

285

She pursed her lips in a non-committal grimace.

'Okay,' she said. 'She is looking forward to seeing you.' She paused. 'Her feelings are complicated. It's natural.'

Her tone was friendly, but distant, which disappointed Joseph. He knew, of course, that in Kofi's presence she was unlikely to let slip any clues, but nevertheless her manner was like a dash of cold water in the face, as cool as if he was a business acquaintance. If anything she was warmer towards Kofi, fussing round and asking whether he was comfortable as she settled him in the back of the car.

They were there in less than a quarter of an hour, turning off the broad thoroughfare of the Bundesallee into a criss-cross pattern of quiet streets. There was something solidly comfortable about the look of these houses and apartment blocks, dull red brick faced in gleaming white, with lines of trees dotting the pavements. Unintentionally Joseph found himself comparing the district with the street in London where his father lived.

'Very nice,' he murmured.

Radka gave him a quick impersonal smile.

'It's new. They rebuilt all this after the war.'

Katya's apartment was on the first floor of a block, the entrance to which was reached through an archway which gave on to a paved courtyard. In the middle were a couple of trees surrounded by benches. They walked in single file, Radka leading the way and Kofi bringing up the rear, his footsteps seeming to slow down and drag as they climbed the stairs. On the landing Radka paused and looked around. Then she put the key in the lock and turned it. As she did so they heard the high-pitched piping of Serge's voice – 'Matka.' Immediately, the sound of his feet thundered along the corridor and before they could get past the threshold, he had hurled himself at Radka, clinging to her legs, laughing and hooting and talking rapidly, all at the same time. She picked him up and hoisted him in her arms, putting her finger over his lips.

'Wo ist deine Oma?'

By this time Serge had seen Joseph and Kofi and he squirmed around to watch them, his eyes wide and his mouth dropping open slightly.

'Babushka?' he whispered, his eyes still fixed on the visitors.

'Ja. Das ist eine Überraschung.'

'Ah.'

The boy's eyes seemed to grow wider and rounder as he contemplated the nature of the surprise his mother had brought home. Joseph felt the urge to laugh. They'd used three different languages in as many sentences. With himself and his father in the room it would be four.

Serge pointed to the open doorway from which he'd emerged. Radka touched her fingers to her own lips this time, looking round at Joseph and Kofi, then beckoned them to follow her. The room at the end of the hallway was big, with tall French windows leading to a small balcony overlooking the courtyard. It was a pleasant room, the sort of room where Joseph could imagine sitting and whiling away the afternoon. The walls were light grey and with a faint pattern of tiny maroon flowers. There were two armchairs, one of them in soft worn brown leather, opposite it against the wall a piano with the lid open. Above it a line of photographs. In some of them he caught sight of his own face looking back at him. Katya was sitting in an armchair facing the window, warming herself in the bright oblong of sunlight which slanted through the glass.

Joseph had expected someone older, or rather someone who looked more aged, a shapeless old babushka with a watery gaze. Instead, the woman who turned to look at him had a kind of vigour and sharpness about her which made her seem younger than she must have been. Her grey slacks were buckled at her narrow waist, and her white hair curled round her face in a soft cloud. Around her mouth the dimples were etched deeper, along with the tracery of lines beside her eyes, but she was still pretty, with an easy smile and bright clear eyes.

'Georgi,' she called out, beginning to get out of the chair, then her smile faded as she realised that it wasn't her son, and she was about to say something, Joseph never knew what, when she saw Kofi coming through the door behind him. She stared for a few seconds, and behind him Joseph felt his father's silence, motionless.

'*Hier ist mein Onkel*,' Serge said loudly. He looked at Radka for approval and she smiled, drawing him towards her.

'You know who this is?' she asked Katya in English.

Katya nodded slowly, still staring at him. Then she sat back in the armchair as if her legs had given way. The colour had drained out of her and her eyes blazed at Kofi.

'I never believed,' she said, speaking the unfamiliar words slowly, 'that I would see you again.'

She began to cry, sobbing helplessly, curling up in the chair as if trying to hide herself away. The little boy stared at her for a moment, then he too began to cry, a huge wail, his face buried in his mother's dress. She began speaking to him soothingly. Kofi pushed past Joseph and knelt by Katya's chair.

'Hey,' he said, his voice light and jocular. He held her hands between his. 'I don't look that bad, do I?'

Katya looked at him and laughed, then she cried again while he put his arms round her and they hugged each other. Radka had turned around and gone out of the room with Serge and he could hear their muffled voices somewhere outside. For the moment Joseph felt like a voyeur, an intruder in an intensely private scene, but there didn't seem to be anything else he could do, so he sat down and watched his father and Katya hugging each other. He found the sight both touching and disturbing. In a curious way, seeing his father's emotion he felt pleased for him. At the same time he found himself wondering whether it was the depth of Kofi's feelings for this woman which had made the separation from his mother inevitable.

After a while Radka and Serge came back, pushing

288

between them a trolley loaded with cakes and pastries. The couple stood up and Kofi led her by the hand to Joseph's side.

'This is my son, Joseph,' he told her.

'I know him.' She had dried her eyes and now her face was all smiles. 'I saw him speak on the television. He looks like George.'

She hugged and kissed him. Joseph smiled stiffly, wondering how he was expected to behave. Fortunately, their attention focused almost immediately on Serge who, carried by his mother close to Kofi, clung round her neck and drew back from his reach. Kofi laughed unselfconsciously, cooing and making a clown's face at the boy, who, recollecting Radka's instructions, suddenly put out his hand.

'Hello, Grandfather,' he said hesitantly in English.

'Oh, bravo!' Katya cried out, clapping her hands. 'Bravo.'

After this they behaved as if it was a normal everyday occasion, Kofi and Katya smiling and touching each other like a couple who had only been separated for a few weeks. They talked about the old days and about places and people they'd known, but they sounded to Joseph like a pair of pensioners at a reunion. If there were undercurrents to be explored they clearly intended to keep them hidden for the moment. Joseph stuck it out for another hour, then he said he was expecting a phone call at the hotel. Something to do with his work.

'But you must wait for George,' Katya said.

'I'll be back soon,' he said. 'Besides, you two have plenty to talk about. I'll see you later.'

Radka came to the door with him. Now her eyes met his and she smiled softly.

'You'll come back?' Her voice was pitched low and she spoke quietly, giving the question an undertone of intimacy.

'Later,' he told her.

She reached out and squeezed his arm and he lifted

her hand to his lips, feeling like a traitor, because he had no intention of going back, not that evening. No one was thinking about how he might feel, he thought unreasonably, walking back along the Bundesallee, and suddenly he experienced a desperate urge to be relaxing in his own house, waiting, perhaps, for Lena to come into the room and sit quietly beside him.

Back in his hotel room he lay on the bed, drinking beer and watching the news, followed by a football match between two South American teams. He must have fallen asleep before it came to an end, because he woke up to the sound of the telephone ringing. The sun was low on the horizon, the tall blocks in the centre of the city casting long shadows. He fumbled for the phone, knocked it over, and picked it up blearily.

'Mr Coker,' the voice said, 'I have a message for you.'

'A message?' he repeated, astonished. He knew no one in the city, apart from George and his family.

'From your brother. He is waiting for you.'

'Waiting for me?'

'Yes. He is sending a taxi.'

Joseph shook his head.

'Wait a minute. What are you talking about?'

'You are Mr Coker?'

'Yes.'

'Mr George Coker is sending you a taxi. He wants you to meet him. He wishes to speak with you.'

'Where is he? Let me speak to him.'

'That is not possible. He's on his way here.'

'Where?'

'Kreuzberg. The taxi will bring you here. You will find it waiting outside the hotel.'

There was a click and in a moment Joseph heard the dialling tone.

He hesitated, in two minds about what to do. His instinct was simply to go downstairs and get into the taxi. He had become accustomed, during the conferences and festivals he'd attended abroad, to being ferried around in buses or cars, and there was an easy familiarity about an impersonal phone call warning him that there was a vehicle waiting. This was different and after his experience of the previous night his caution was automatic.

He picked up the telephone and dialled Katya's number, and when she answered he asked whether George had arrived.

'No. We haven't heard from him yet. When are you coming back?'

He said he would join them later, and he was on the verge of telling her that he was going to meet George when it struck him that if his brother wanted to see him alone he might be about to reveal something that he wanted kept from his wife and mother. Kofi was the same. There were times, he had said to Joseph once, when men should keep their conversations hidden from women. Joseph was about thirteen then, and hearing this he had smiled, thinking what an antique his father sounded but not wanting to say it. George had not telephoned his mother's apartment, but that might well be par for the course, and his brother, a man who kept his comings and goings secret even from his wife, would probably regard his telling Katya as some breach of male etiquette.

The car was waiting in front of the hotel, as the voice on the telephone had promised. It didn't look like a taxi, but he knew that meant nothing. The driver, a nondescript middle-aged man wearing a peaked hat, looked up from his newspaper as Joseph approached.

'Herr Coker?'

'Where are we going?' Joseph asked him.

In reply the man shrugged and gestured, as if indicating that he spoke no English. He reached behind him and pushed open the rear door, but instead of getting in Joseph beckoned to the young man hovering by the entrance who had carried his baggage in the day before.

'Ask him where we're going.'

A brief exchange.

'He says a bar in Kreuzberg. Near Dresdenstrasse.' He paused. 'There are many bars there.'

Indecisive, Joseph caught an ironic twitch on the boy's face, and suddenly his fears seemed ridiculous. It was still broad daylight, the rays of the red sun slanting across the entrance. Hearing that he had been too apprehensive to get into a taxi in front of his hotel, Kofi would probably smile sarcastically, and George would make a joke about the bourgeois timidity of the English. Joseph made up his mind.

'Let's go,' he told the driver.

TWENTY-TWO

It was early evening when George telephoned Radka from a bar in the Prenzlauer Berg to tell her he was back. The news that his father and brother had arrived left him troubled and restless, so he had another drink with Valentin before heading for Schöneberg.

'I want to see this fabulous African,' Valentin declared.

George could see that he meant what he said. Over the years Kofi had become part of the mythology of their family, a curious and secret romance which Valentin had heard and only half believed from the time he was a toddler. In his childish mind, he told George, Katya had been an innocent princess lured away by a dark magician, and when he arrived in Berlin to embrace his aunt, it was if he had walked through the entrance to a forgotten fairy tale.

George was by now accustomed to Valentin's rhetoric which went in one ear and out the other. He was thinking about Radka, who had sounded disgruntled and irritable on the telephone. Perhaps she was annoyed about being left by herself to cope with his relatives. She had wanted him with her in Berlin, and when he told her that he wouldn't get there for a few days she had been furious. It was a matter of business, he kept insisting, and eventually she had retreated into a sullen silence. On the other hand, they'd been through rows of that kind before. She was used to his absences, and it didn't take too long for her to come round. Her bad temper was probably more to do with the fact that he was with Valentin. Radka hated the bond between them, and in recent times, when he talked about his cousin, she tended to withdraw into a sudden silence. She'd had an idea that what they were doing was illegal and dangerous, but that wasn't the real problem, the difficulty was what she felt about Valentin. George couldn't understand it. When they argued about his cousin, it all came back to the same thing. This was a paradox which grew more difficult as time went by. For Radka George's association with Valentin represented a kind of failure on his part. If he was going to engage in business, she said once, why not take the opportunity to become a proper Western businessman, instead of getting into shady dealings with Valentin? Unable to crawl out of the mud, she shouted, he had dragged George in with him. In his turn, George accused her of double standards. In the West business was even more crooked, he told her. She was simply deceived by the skill with which they covered their tracks, and everything she said revealed the typical mentality of the old comrades to whom any kind of enterprise was a crime.

This was an argument which made her even more angry and he knew that, in any case, her dislike of Valentin had never been altogether rational. The way Radka felt about his cousin, he pointed out, was very similar to the deep prejudices he'd read about which the whites held against negroes in the American South. This was hitting below the belt, and her eyes filled with tears. The negroes, she argued, had never done anything to her, and she could never sympathise with those who wished to murder and ill-treat them simply because of their colour. Russians were different. It was they who had ruined her father's life and caused his premature death. It was they who had separated and destroyed families, looted her country and every other country in the region, it was they who had raped and tortured and massacred, and it was they who had perverted entire societies.

In this mood she reduced George to silence. In her heart, he thought, Radka believed that Russians were capable of anything bad. She was polite enough to Valentin, but

George suspected that she really thought of him as a peasant with snow on his boots. At first he had taken it as a joke, but the closer he got to Valentin the wider the distance between himself and Radka seemed to grow. It had been worse in Prague, partly because building up the new business had taken almost all of his time, and partly because he was spending all of that time with Valentin. The problem was that Prague was a place where a Russian could enjoy himself. It wasn't depressed like the capitals in Romania or Bulgaria, or untrustworthy like Budapest, or dull like the Scandinavian cities – 'like St Petersburg with no style,' Valentin said. As for Poland, forget it, in Warsaw and Lodz they took your money but made their resentment obvious, and Berlin was an enigma. You never knew where you were with the Germans. The Czechs were different. These were people who knew how to enjoy themselves. Valentin set himself up nicely with a house in a quiet street in Holesovice and he was at home from the first day. George spent most of his spare time in the house. Radka refused to accompany him on his outings with Valentin, and he abandoned the attempt to persuade her after a short while because it had become part of the life that he lived for himself, without her. For instance, the house seemed to be stocked with an endless supply of women, travellers from everywhere, young Americans with rucksacks on their backs, Hungarian and Bulgarian women passing through the city, and visiting Russians. Sometimes they were pals of Milena's, working girls from massage parlours and bars, sometimes they were ordinary Czech women who Valentin had encountered at an office or a party. The house was usually full, a party every weekend, and a few times in summer they took to the woods, waving champagne bottles and screeching like birds. George had never lived with such flagrant and reckless enjoyment. He loved it and he hated it, alternating between moments of wild ecstasy and periods of guilt and gloom, which he imagined sometimes was the product of his Russian blood. In any case, the life his cousin had made for him was like a drug. Going home to Radka he felt bored and restless, and lying in bed next to her he found himself musing about the dusting of freckles across the breasts of a girl from Kansas, or the wet rasp of Milena's tongue on his foreskin. One drunken night Valentin hugged him so tight that his ribs almost cracked.

'You are Russian!' he shouted in George's ear, 'and I think Kofi was Russian too.'

'He was African,' he shouted back.

'I forgive him,' Valentin said grandly.

Thinking about it, George grinned. Only Valentin could have said this to him without offence. The truth was that Valentin was most of the things Radka said she despised about the Russians, a loudmouth, unreliable, unpredictable, but being with him had brought out an aspect of George's personality which had, for many long years, been suppressed. Now he couldn't imagine giving up his cousin's company. When Valentin talked about returning to Russia to move Victor's treasure he seemed to assume that George was coming. George told himself that the sensible thing would be to say no, but once the arrangements were made he also knew that he couldn't leave his partner to make the trip without him.

They had driven the two trucks over nearly three thousand kilometres in a few days, crossing late at night at the posts where Valentin had distributed his bribes. They'd lashed a few old chairs and a chest of drawers on to the back of the load so as not to cause embarrassment and since they were not carrying drugs, they'd ridden through the inspections with ease. The German border was the hardest, but they'd come through escorted by a British army captain who'd cost Valentin a fortune. After that they'd driven from East to West, skirting Dresden and Düsseldorf, ending the journey fifty kilometres from the Dutch border. There was an old Luftwaffe base there, now occupied by the British air force, but a third of the

296

runways and hangars were disused. They lay within the former perimeter fence which was not patrolled or linked into the security system, although it was guaranteed to keep out casual passers-by. At two in the morning they'd driven along the dirt road which wound through the woods bordering the site, cut their way through the wire and driven the trucks into one of the old hangars, then left the way they'd come, carefully weaving the fence back into place with new lengths of wire.

Victor stayed nearby. He would get himself a place in Düsseldorf, he said, and until they worked out how to dispose of the hoard or found a better hiding place, he would drive out from time to time to inspect the fence. During the journey they had discussed what to do. The idea was to get rid of it all at once, and to take a reasonable price from anyone who would take it off their hands. The problem was finding a buyer who could be trusted not to rob them or cut their throats before the deal was done. The alternative was to park the goods somewhere innocuous, like a furniture warehouse where no one would suspect their presence, until things cooled down.

'Someone will find it, wherever it is,' Victor said with a gloomy air.

Valentin raised his eyebrows at George and smiled. Victor simply wanted to get the money. His dream was to go to California with a few millions in his pocket. There he would meet Sharon Stone or someone who looked exactly like her.

They were no closer to finding a solution by the time they got back to Berlin. But confronted by his father's presence and the prospect of meeting him, George resolved to put the problem out of his mind. In front of his mother's apartment he paused for a minute before getting out of the car, checking his appearance in the driving mirror. As he climbed the stairs his footsteps dragged. In his heart he was eager, wanting to fly like a bird to his father's side, but there was, at the same time, another emotion weighing him down, a kind of fear about what he might encounter at the top of the stairs, and about how he would behave.

His mother met him at the door, and she hugged him fiercely. She seemed normal, but her eyes, he noticed, were red and tearful.

'Guess who is here,' she said loudly.

Kofi was sitting in an armchair near the window, one arm around Serge, who stood by him, leaning against the chair. When the boy saw George come into the room he shouted, twisted away, ran to his father and hugged him, then climbed on to his back, arms draped round his neck.

'That's my grandfather,' he announced.

Kofi got up, came towards George, and, a little awkwardly, embraced him, pressing his cheek to his son's. Seeing his father's face close to him, George felt the prickle of tears behind his eyelids.

'At last,' he murmured. 'At last.'

He sat next to Radka, still hugging Serge, who immediately broke away and went to stand by his grandfather again. Radka gave him a strained smile, then turned her head away.

'Time to get ready for bed,' she told Serge. 'You've had a long day.'

The boy pouted, but after she promised Kofi would be back he went quietly enough.

'I'm very happy to see you,' Kofi said. 'If I'd known I would have come sooner. But I'm here now.'

'I thought you must be dead,' George told him, 'until I saw Joseph. Then I knew.'

His voice choked and Kofi got up again, came to the sofa, sat down and put his arm around George, who hung his head, feeling the tears start behind his eyes. For a few seconds George felt Katya watching him, and he seemed to see himself from the outside cringing like a tearful child. In that instant he felt bewildered and embarrassed, struggling with the waves of emotion which flooded through him, then he gave in and rested his head against Kofi's shoulder.

He heard Katya leave the room and he sat up, looking at Kofi who was watching him with a gentle smile. George, controlling his features, smiled back. He was thinking, with a feeling of surprise, that at first sight, Kofi looked nothing like himself or Joseph. He had, of course, seen his mother's photograph of Kofi, but he had often tried to guess what his father would look like as an older man, forty years later. He had various pictures in his head, most of them assembled from glimpses of Africans on the TV screen, but he had always imagined him as looking like himself with a darker skin. Now he realised that the photo, a black-and-white snap in which all the tones were really shades of grey, had not prepared him for the vivid impression that his father's appearance would make: the velvet-black undertones of Kofi's skin, the contrast of his greying hair, his gleaming white teeth had a visual power which struck George almost like a physical sensation.

'Your mother did a good job,' Kofi said, his mouth still curved in a smile. 'You look great.'

George felt the same smile on his own face, noting a resemblance for the first time. The middle of Kofi's upper lip curved upwards in a peak, like Joseph's, and he had always seen the same shape when he looked in the mirror. He ducked his head, not knowing quite what to say. For as long as he could remember he had talked privately to his father in his head, especially in moments of stress or anguish, knowing instinctively that Kofi was a man who would understand and sympathise. Now he could think of nothing to say. As if reading his mind, Kofi patted his arm.

'There'll be plenty of time for us to talk,' he said.

As it turned out, when Katya came back a dam seemed to have burst, and they talked with hardly a pause for the next few hours. Kofi told them the story of his life since he had seen Katya. He had hoped to be part of changing the world, he said, then found himself trapped in a bubble, around which the world changed without his help. Katya told George about the days when she had first met Kofi, a wide-eyed and innocent African, whose hair she had wanted to touch to see whether it felt the same as sheep's wool. Kofi asked George about how he had fared during his schooldays, and George found himself reciting the tale of precisely those times when, alone and mad with frustration, he had wished for Kofi's presence.

It was a couple of hours later when George asked about Joseph.

'He had some trouble last night. Radka was there.'

Kofi's tone was nonchalant, and it seemed to George that whatever had happened to Joseph hadn't made a huge impression on him.

'There isn't much to tell,' Radka said quickly.

She told him the outlines of the event. They had been approached by a couple of men who had hit Joseph. She had got him up to his room and called a doctor before leaving. During the day he'd been fine, so there was no real damage done.

'Shit,' George exclaimed. 'It's getting worse.'

Kofi shrugged. What had happened to Joseph, he seemed to be saying, was part of the occupational risk of being a black man walking around a white city. George knew that, but there was something about the impersonal manner in which Radka had told the story that worried him.

'Don't worry,' Katya said. 'He telephoned before you came. He'll be here later.'

'I'll call him anyway,' George told them.

He got up and went to the room which Katya had decorated with some of his things: a poster of Mohammed Ali, a block of concrete from the Wall still spray-painted with part of a sketch, blown-up photos of himself in the ring, a couple of shelves of classic English books – Robert Louis Stevenson, Dickens and others, the paper yellow and curling. Radka had taken some of these objects down and added her own touches, but he still thought of it as his room.

He rang Joseph's hotel from his mobile, but there was no reply when he got through to the room. He switched the phone off with an irritable flick, suddenly realising that the news of Joseph's beating had crystallised a kind of guilt he was feeling. He had nothing to lose, he thought, by this reunion, but perhaps it might seem to Joseph that for the first time in his life he would have to share with a brother he had never known. In Prague he had put Joseph's stiffness down to English reserve, but, thinking about it now he began to wonder whether his brother's coolness had in fact been concealed anger. On top of that he had come to Berlin only to be attacked in the street.

George was about to try the number again when Radka came in and shut the door, standing with her back to it as if she wanted to stop him getting out.

'I didn't tell you everything about last night,' she said. 'Those men attacked us because they thought Joseph was you. They gave me a message for you.'

She gave the rest of the details then, and as he listened he felt a cold certainty that Liebl had been behind it all. His fists clenched with rage. Blackmail and intimidation had always been Liebl's favourite weapons.

'I saw that fat bastard as well,' Radka said. 'The one who worked for the Stasi. Coming out of the supermarket, he was waiting for us. He looked and smiled as if he knew something about me.' She paused and when he didn't reply, she stared at him, her eyes wild with an angry resentment he thought had been buried long ago. 'I thought all that was over. You promised me.'

'It is over,' George told her. 'This time it's different. I'm going to put a stop to it tonight.'

Before Radka could reply the mobile warbled in his hand. Gripped by some premonition, he put it to his ear, knowing who the caller was even before he heard the wheezing intake of breath.

'This is Liebl,' the familiar voice said.

301

TWENTY-THREE

During the ride to Kreuzberg Joseph tried asking a couple of questions in English but the driver simply shrugged, so he gave up and contented himself with peering through the windows, noting the landmarks he recognised. The car stopped in a narrow street and the driver got out, opened the door and when he got out, led the way across the pavement to the doorway of what looked like a shop. He pushed open the door and gestured.

'This isn't a bar,' Joseph said.

The driver gestured again. There was a light behind the blacked-out glass front, and he peered in through the door trying to make out what was inside, but he could see nothing beyond the shape of a giant stuffed animal which stood near the entrance. Joseph had a vision of a smoky back room in which George would be sitting surrounded by his cronies, and feeling a sudden flush of anger he walked past the driver and went in. A bell chimed as he crossed the threshold. There was a narrow corridor running between the exhibits which crowded the space, and he walked along it, brushing past some uniforms hanging from the ceiling towards the man standing behind the glass case at the back of the shop.

He was short, balding, with a little beard on his chin. He wore a neat black suit over a black vest, and he watched Joseph approach without making a sign of greeting or recognition. There seemed to be no one else in the shop.

'I'm here to meet George,' Joseph told him curtly.

He was ready now to hear that there had been some mistake, and he was wondering whether the man would call him a taxi so he could get back to the hotel or to Katya's apartment.

'George Coker is your brother?'

The man's tone had an authoritative rasp, like an official asking about his passport, and Joseph felt like telling him to mind his own business.

'Yes. That's right,' he said. 'Where is he?'

'I'm sorry,' the man replied. 'He's not here.'

Joseph made up his mind. He had no intention of waiting around in this crowded little hole.

'When he gets here,' he said, 'tell him I came.'

He turned to begin retracing his steps, but within a few paces of the doorway he stopped abruptly. There was a dog standing on the carpet in front of him. At first glance it looked innocuous. It didn't growl or snarl. It simply stood there, its little red eyes above the funny squashed up muzzle staring intently.

'Please don't move,' the man said behind him. 'These dogs go for the crotch and it's very hard to persuade them to let go.'

'What's this all about?' Joseph asked. 'My brother sent a car for me. That's why I came. I'm going now. Just get your dog out of the way.'

He had been bewildered and angry; now he was beginning to realise that he had been stupid to come here. He could hear the sound of voices and traffic from outside, but inside the shop the atmosphere was suddenly dark and oppressive.

'I sent the car.' The man's voice had a dispassionate, lecturing tone. He spoke excellent English, with a touch of what sounded like an American accent. 'There is someone who wishes to speak with you. It won't take long.'

'I don't know anything about my brother's business,' Joseph said, turning to look at him. 'I only arrived in Berlin yesterday. You've got the wrong man.'

'I don't think so,' the man said.

'I don't give a shit,' Joseph told him. 'I'm going.'

303

He was angry enough to ignore the dog, and he turned away, intending to skirt a path through the piles of junk, but the man must have made a signal then, because suddenly, without warning, Joseph felt an excruciating agony, a jolt which shocked him in the muscles of his right calf and spread through his body. He screamed, trying to pull away from the dog which was attached to his leg, and he felt the creature's claws scrabbling on the floor as it fought for its balance.

'Get it off me!' he shouted. 'Fucking get it off!'

Through the fog of pain which blurred his sight, he realised that there were two more men in the shop. He didn't see where they'd come from and he didn't care. His entire being was focused now on the spasms of pain which were coursing through his body. The man behind the counter pointed his hand. It made a clicking sound and the brute let go. Joseph nearly fell over, but just in time he grabbed one of the stands next to him and clung on, just managing to stay on his feet. He could feel the blood running down his leg into his shoe. The pain was less intense now, but the entire right side of his body was still permeated by the agonising sensation which flowed from the segment of torn flesh where the monster's fangs had gripped.

His tormentor held up his hand. In it there was something that looked like a child's toy.

'This makes a click,' he said. 'If I click it the dog will attack. Please go with these men. They will take you to a house where you will wait for our friends. There is another dog there. Not so tame as this one. Don't cause a problem.'

The warning was unnecessary. Joseph was in no condition to cause trouble. The two men who came towards him were huge, in any case, with broad chests and shoulders to match, like walking beer barrels. They both had long brown hair, twisted into a ponytail, and a moustache. They looked almost identical, like a tag wrestling team. They gripped him effortlessly by each arm, but instead of taking him out of the door they went towards the back of the shop. Joseph's panic mounted, but limping between the men he tried to clear the fog in his head. Calm yourself, work out what to do, he thought, but for the moment no inspiration came, and he hobbled obediently through the back of the shop. They came out into an area littered with dustbins, at the end of it another building which turned out to be an empty shopfront with an entrance in another street. There was a car waiting at the kerb. As they crossed the pavement the car flashed its lights and gave an electronic beep. Without a pause one of the men opened the door and pushed Joseph in.

As the car sped away Joseph reached up and tried the door cautiously. Locked. In the front seat the two men paid no attention, so he guessed that the car was locked centrally. He sat up, trying to take note of where they were going, but the street names went by so quickly that he couldn't decipher any of them.

'Where are we going?' he asked.

There was no reply.

'I'm in pain,' Joseph said loudly. 'If my fucking leg gets infected I'll be in no condition to talk to anyone. I need antiseptic and bandages and aspirin.'

Still no reply.

'I don't suppose either of you dumb shits speak English?' he muttered.

The car stopped suddenly, with a screech of brakes. Without looking round one of the men got out and walked quickly across the street. Joseph tried the door again. It was still locked, and in the mirror the driver watched him without expression. Up ahead a big road sign indicated POTSDAM. Joseph's heart sank. He guessed the sign meant that they were going on to the highway out of Berlin. This was probably his best chance, he thought, and he began rehearsing in his mind a quick grab for the driver's throat, when the other man came back into sight running towards the car. He got in, and turning to face Joseph he held up the plastic bag he was carrying.

'Antiseptic,' he said in clear English, 'bandage and aspirins. When we get there you can use them.'

In a couple of minutes they were speeding along a three-lane highway. Thoughts and plans chased through Joseph's head, to be instantly discarded. At the same time he felt curiously listless and devoid of energy. He lay back bracing himself against the raging pain in his leg. See what happens, he told himself. If they intended to kill him they wouldn't have been interested in whether or not his leg was infected. At the same time, the image of the grinning head in the garage in Smichov came into his mind.

'Where are we going?' he asked again, and when neither of the men replied he asked again.

'Shut your fucking mouth,' the driver said.

Joseph closed his eyes against the dark treeline rushing past the sides of the road, and opened them again when he felt the surface under the car change. They were crossing a long bridge, and in another few minutes the car swung off into what looked like a suburban street, the houses wide apart and guarded from the outside by trees and high walls. Halfway along the street the car turned into a curving driveway at the end of which stood a big, squat, two-storey house. The driver pulled up in front of the door, got out, then opened the back door for Joseph.

'Out,' he said.

Joseph got out. This was the moment in which he had planned to make a break for it, but, as his feet hit the ground, he staggered and he would have fallen if the other man had not taken his arm and steadied him. He felt light-headed and dizzy, but he would still have tried to run had it not been for the two Dobermans who had appeared from nowhere and squatted down a few yards away, motionless as statues, their eyes intent on his every movement.

From the outside the house appeared to be crumbling,

306

the paint peeling and a couple of the windows on the upper floor boarded up. Inside it was no better. The floor of the massive hallway was covered with dirty carpet from which the pattern had long disappeared, and there was litter dotted around, bits of old newspapers, a torn and empty suitcase, and a cardboard tub which had once held a jumbo-size order of McDonald's chicken nuggets.

Joseph's guards led him through the hallway and up the stairs. At the top they unlocked a door which opened to show a small square room in which the only furniture was a single bed against the wall, the bare new mattress still covered with a sheet of plastic. There was a window, but behind the glass it had been boarded up from the outside. Joseph hesitated, but someone pushed him from behind and he lost his balance, sprawling forwards on to the floor. By the time he picked himself up the door had closed. Getting up he banged on the door and shouted, but nothing happened. He put his shoulder to it and shoved, but nothing gave. It was made of some kind of metal, and the effort sent a spray of stabbing pains shooting through his body. Eventually he hobbled over to the bed, rolled up his trouser leg and stripped off his shoes and socks to get a good look at the damage. His calf was red and swollen, the area round the row of weeping punctures already inflamed and painful to the touch. He poured antiseptic over the wounds, wiping them carefully with the cotton wool he found in the bag, and swallowed a couple of the aspirins they'd given him. Then he tried to wrap a bandage round his leg, but his hands shook and it kept unravelling. After a while he gave up and sat back against the wall. His body ached and he felt too exhausted to think. He wondered whether George knew what had happened to him and what he would do if he did. The reason he was here must be something to do with his brother, but he couldn't begin to guess what it was. Perhaps George owed money, and this was a way of compelling payment. They would probably tell him sooner or later, but whatever the motives were it was obvious that unless some miracle happened his fate was in George's hands. A few weeks ago he had never heard of the man. Now he was trapped in a nightmare.

He heard someone fumble at the lock and the door opened. An old man came in. Behind him Joseph saw one of the men who had brought him from the shop, and then it closed.

'Who are you?' Joseph asked him.

He was short with a spare neat frame, bony features and a light brown skin, and he was wearing a tight grey suit, the tie round his neck fastened by a fat old-fashioned knot.

'Salim,' the old man said. 'They want me to look at you.'

'Are you a doctor?'

The old man laughed.

'No, but I've seen plenty of wounds.'

He sat down beside Joseph and began to examine his leg.

'What am I doing here?' Joseph asked. 'Did you bring me here?'

The old man laughed again. Somehow it was infectious. Ridiculously, Joseph felt a light-headed grin spreading on his own face.

'No,' the old man said. 'This is nothing to do with me. I am only doing them a favour.'

'Who are they?'

'I don't know.'

Joseph jerked his leg away from the old man's probing hands.

'Leave me alone,' he said. His tongue felt heavy in his mouth. 'Tell them I don't know anything. If they want me to talk to them I'll talk. No problem. But I want to get out of here.'

The old man was looking at him as if his words meant nothing.

'I want to get out of here!' Joseph shouted.

'Me too,' Salim said. 'But we have to wait.'

This was Alice in Wonderland, Joseph thought.

'What are we waiting for?'

'The trucks, of course. Where are you going?'

'I don't know what you mean.'

The old man seemed to be babbling but whoever he was, Joseph thought, he wasn't one of the kidnappers.

'Can you get a message out for me?' he asked. 'I'll pay you whatever you want. I don't know who you are, but they brought me here as a prisoner. All I want is a phone call to tell my father where I am.'

'Don't tell me,' Salim replied. 'Please. They don't want to hurt you. They told me. And your money is no good to me. No one knows I'm here. When I leave I'll get in a container. They'll open the doors and I'll be in England. No one will know that I'm there, either.'

'You're a refugee,' Joseph said.

The old man nodded.

'I used to be a refugee. Now they call me illegal. The government wants to send me to a swamp in Iraq, where I was born. I would never survive, but I have two sons in London. Once I get there I'll be safe.' He began wrapping the bandage round Joseph's leg, little gouts of flame seeming to follow the touch of his fingers as he pulled it tight. 'In this house we're waiting. Soon we'll be gone. If the police came here now they would send us all back, Bosnians, Kurds, Africans, we have nowhere else to go.' He paused. 'They won't hurt you,' he repeated. 'They're crooks, of course, but when you pay them they do what they promise. Some of the others are evil. I've heard of people paying their money and then being killed. These ones are honest. They are the only people who will help us. I wouldn't do anything against them even if I could. What else can I do?'

Joseph lay back, defeated. The old man's voice took on a soothing, almost hypnotic tone, telling a story which he had obviously gone through many times before. He had been educated in Egypt and travelled in many parts of the world teaching English. He had once lived and studied in England, and he could have stayed at that time, but the travel bug got to him. In the last ten years he'd made his way from Beirut, through a number of different countries, and ended up in Germany. He had seen everything a man should see, he said, the black stone in Mecca, the aurora borealis burning in the northern skies, the crimson circle of the sun dipping into a pool of red fire far across the Indian ocean.

'Now I'm crouching like a rat in a cellar.' He laughed. 'After all this.'

Joseph chuckled sleepily. Somehow the old man's voice was causing him to drift off. He felt a sudden edge of panic. He couldn't afford to sleep. Beside him Salim picked up the bottle of pills and looked at them. He took one out and tasted it.

'This is not aspirin,' he told Joseph. 'I think you'll sleep.'

Joseph nodded. It was true that he could hardly move a muscle, but his mind was still racing. He'd only taken two, and perhaps he could fight it off. He sat up and shook his head. The door opened, and Salim stood up.

'Help me,' Joseph said slowly, not caring who heard him.

'I'm sorry,' Salim replied. 'I wish I could help you, but I don't exist.'

TWENTY-FOUR

George was parked a couple of hundred metres from Gunther's shop, facing away from the Dresdenstrasse, but from there he could see the doorway. Most of the shops and offices were already closed, and this was a side street with few passers-by so he had a clear and uninterrupted view. It was still early evening and Valentin arrived shortly after George had got there. He opened the door of the car and slid in without a word of greeting.

'He's still there,' George told him.

Valentin grunted. He was unusually quiet tonight, George thought, then he realised that Valentin was anxious about Joseph and how he was faring. Joseph was too soft for anything serious, he had told George on the mobile phone. George agreed, but it was too late to worry about that now, he'd replied. He was actually feeling the same kind of anxiety, because all this was his own fault for underestimating what he was up against. Joseph had been with him in Prague, and now he had turned up in Berlin. Anyone watching him could have made the connection, and, in any case, Radka had told the men who attacked Joseph who he was.

As usual Liebl had outflanked him; when George had answered the call in his room at Katya's apartment the fat man had sounded pleased with himself.

'All this time,' he said, 'I didn't know you had a brother.'

'Where is he?'

'Don't worry about him. At this moment he's my guest. You can pick him up when we make the deal.'

'I can't make any deals with you,' George said. 'I don't know where to get any more pictures.'

311

Beside him he heard Radka stir. Out of the corner of his eye he saw her sitting forward, staring at him, her face clasped between the palms of her hands.

'I don't believe you,' Liebl told him. George heard his breath wheezing. 'I don't want to hurry you. You can let me know tomorrow.' He paused. 'Don't leave it too long.'

The phone went dead.

'What is it?' Radka asked.

'I've got to go,' George told her.

'What's the matter with you?' she asked angrily. 'Your father's only just arrived.'

'It's Joseph,' he said. 'I have no time to explain. He's in trouble.'

He walked out then, ignoring the sound of her voice calling to him, paused in the doorway of the sitting room and told Kofi that he was going to meet Joseph.

'I'll come with you,' Kofi said, getting up.

'No. No. You still have plenty to talk about.'

That had been a couple of hours ago. George had driven directly to Liebl's office in the Prenzlauer Berg. The neon sign was lit, but the door was locked and although he shouted and knocked on the glass no one appeared. He got back in the car, his brain churning, and drove to Joseph's hotel. It had suddenly occurred to him, hoping against hope, that this might simply be one of Liebl's tricks, designed to break his nerve. He rang Joseph's room from the lobby, but there was no answer. Still moved by the fast receding hope that Joseph might suddenly appear fresh from a walk around the city, he approached the porter standing by the entrance.

'I was looking for my brother,' he said. 'He speaks English, and he looks like me.'

In other circumstances saying that would have given him a quiet pleasure.

'Ah yes,' the boy said, his eyes surveying George in a single sweep. 'I saw him today. He was going to Kreuzberg.'

Back in the car George telephoned Valentin and told him

312

about Joseph getting into the taxi and where the boy said he'd been going.

'Who do we know in Kreuzberg, a man who knows both you and Liebl?' Valentin asked.

George had been thinking along the same lines. Since the meeting in Prague, they had known that Liebl was getting his information from Gunther. At the beginning George had assumed that Gunther was merely one of Liebl's many casual contacts. Later on, doing business with various other dealers, he had picked up hints which told him that Gunther's connection with Liebl was something altogether different. As a Stasi agent Liebl's style had been to intimidate or blackmail people into doing what he wanted. Nothing had changed. On their first meeting George had let Gunther know that he could lay his hands on as many objects as he could market. That would have been enough for Liebl.

'Meet me in Kreuzberg,' he told Valentin.

They sat in silence for a few minutes, watching the front of Gunther's shop. Nothing happened.

'What are we waiting for?' Valentin said. 'Let's go and take a look.'

He dug into the pocket of his overcoat and took out the Beretta he always carried nowadays. Out of habit George had locked the one that Valentin had given him 'for protection' in the boot, and for a moment he wondered whether to take it with him, then decided that one gun between them was enough. Valentin pulled the slide back with a snap, checked that the chamber was clear and slammed the magazine in.

'Okay,' he said, draping his overcoat over the gun. He looked round and smiled at George. 'I think it might be time for a little crude violence.'

They got out and walked up the road towards the shop. The blinds were drawn down over the glass pane in the door, but they could see that there were still lights on in the interior. George turned the handle and pushed but nothing happened. He looked at Valentin and shook his head. Valentin looked around. The street was quiet. They had seen a couple of men coming out of the video store next door, but apart from that there was no one close by. Valentin swung the butt of the Beretta and knocked a hole in the glass, then losing patience, kicked a big hole in the middle of the pane and pushing the blind aside, stepped in. Following him in, George saw Gunther bending behind the counter. There was a clicking sound and a scrabbling of paws. A dog came round the counter, already running, the brown body streaking towards them. He was a couple of feet away in the seconds it took to see him coming, and Valentin, caught by surprise, without enough time to raise the gun and aim, shot him from low down by his side. The bullet took him somewhere in the body, throwing him up in the air and into a stand packed with military overcoats. For an instant he thrashed among the clothes, snapping and growling, then he came again, dragging his hind legs along the floor, emitting a sobbing whine, his muzzle dripping blood and gaping open with the lust to kill. Valentin took careful aim and fired again, blood spraying over the floor as the bullets splattered into the animal's flesh, but the dog, relentless as a robot, didn't stop moving, trying to drag himself forward, until the third shot. Valentin walked forward, took aim again and shot him in the head.

'*Arschloch*!' Gunther screamed. '*Arschloch*! You didn't have to kill him.'

His voice was high pitched. It sounded hysterical, and George realised, with a shock, that he was crying, the tears running down his face in an uncontrollable stream. He came from behind the counter and knelt by the dog. '*Arschloch*,' he muttered.

Valentin took him by the collar and pushed the gun under his chin so that Gunther was looking up at him.

'You're next,' he said calmly, 'unless you tell us what we want to know. We don't have time to waste.'

'It's nothing to do with me,' Gunther said immediately.

'Liebl told me to telephone and ask him to come here. I thought he wanted to talk to him but he sent two wrestlers to pick him up. I think they took him to Potsdam.'

'Get the car,' Valentin told George. 'Let's get out of here.'

George walked quickly up the road. If anyone had noticed what was happening at Gunther's shop they were minding their own business. In this part of the city discretion was the rule, and short of a struggle out in the open, the other residents would mind their own business. It was a safe bet also that the neighbours were well accustomed to peculiar comings and goings in the junk shop. In this street if Gunther had been a Turk or Kurdish it might have been a different matter, but as it was the pavements stayed empty. George drove the car in front of the entrance and parked. With the blinds drawn and the lights out no one would notice the hole in the door until the morning, he thought, and if Gunther co-operated he'd be back patching it up before anyone could walk off with his stock.

Before George could get out Valentin emerged from the doorway, pushing Gunther ahead of him. They got in the back and George stepped on the accelerator and took off.

'*Langsam bitte,*' Valentin said in an affected voice which was his ironic reprise of George's habitual request for him to drive more slowly. 'No one is chasing us. *Langsam bitte,*' he said again, teasing.

'Where are we going?' George asked, pretending not to notice.

'Potsdam. Our friend is going to show us the way.'

Gunther had been carrying a tangle of leather straps and a coil of what looked like nylon clothesline.

'What's all that for?' George asked him.

Valentin held up the leather straps as if demonstrating a household product.

'These are dog leashes. He says there are dogs there. He knows them, and he doesn't want me to kill them. So he's going to tie them up when we get there.'

315

Valentin burst out laughing as he said this. In the driving mirror Gunther's eyes blazed in fury.

'What about the rope?'

Valentin laughed again.

'You'll see.'

'You didn't have to kill him,' Gunther repeated, his voice choking.

'Yes, I did,' Valentin told him. 'We had these little bastards in the army, and I know what that clicking shit means. Killing him was the only way. So shut up about the fucking dog.'

'Who's Liebl working for?' George asked Gunther.

'I don't know,' Gunther said snappishly. He folded his arms and turned his tear-streaked face towards the window, looking out into the darkness. Valentin grimaced at George and put his hand on Gunther's neck.

'I don't have time,' he said. 'And I don't have patience. George is your friend. I am not. If you don't tell us everything you know I'm going to squeeze your puny little neck. First it hurts, then you're unconscious, then you die, but I'm not going to kill you. I'm going to squeeze you till you pass out, then I'll wake you up and do it again.' His voice turned reflective. 'Of course, I may make a mistake.'

'Okay, okay,' Gunther snapped. He sounded more peevish than frightened. 'I'll tell you everything I know, but I warn you I know nothing.'

The Russians had come to his shop a few days ago. He corrected himself. They were Georgians, not Russians, but it was really all the same to him. Liebl had sent them. They said that the paintings he'd been passing on belonged to them. They wanted to get in touch with the black Russian who'd given them to him. They only wanted to talk to him, they said. George heard the echo of Gunther's terror, and he guessed that sending a couple of Georgians had been one of Liebl's little touches, intended to produce precisely that effect.

316

'How much did they pay you?' George asked.

'Nothing.' He hesitated. 'They said there would be a reward if I succeeded in reaching you. But I had no choice. They threatened to kill me on the spot and they meant it. These people are animals.'

'What names?'

'Names? I didn't ask their names.'

'So what's this got to do with Liebl?'

'Liebl said he would deal with them if I did exactly what he told me. Today he telephoned and told me to tell your brother you were waiting for him.'

'What is this place in Potsdam?' George asked.

'It's mine,' Gunther answered.

His father had been a wealthy businessman. When his family came West the state had confiscated the house and it had been used by one of the ministries.

'The court gave it back to me last year. Liebl uses it sometimes.'

'What for?'

Gunther shrugged.

'Business.'

They were trundling over the Glienecker Brücke now and Valentin uncoiled the clothesline. He tied one end in a slip knot round Gunther's neck, examining his work with a critical eye, as if he was getting him dressed for a party. Gunther took it calmly, looking ahead as they came to the end of the bridge and pointing the way for George, as if there was no one beside him fiddling with his throat.

'What is that for?' George asked, unable to contain his curiosity.

'Our friend loves dogs so much,' Valentin said, 'I wanted him to feel what it was like to wear a collar. When we get there I'll have him on a leash.'

He pulled the line till it was tight around Gunther's neck.

'How does it feel?' he asked in a considerate tone, but instead of replying Gunther turned to look out of the window, ignoring him.

In a few minutes they were cruising slowly along a quiet street lined with high brick walls, the tops of swaying trees obscuring sight of the houses.

When they pulled up in the drive the house was dark, but in the circle of light cast by the headlamps they saw the two Dobermans standing patiently, one immediately in front of the car, another by the door.

'I'm going to let you out to tie up the dogs,' Valentin told Gunther carefully. 'Stay where I can see you. If you try anything I'll shoot you and I'll shoot the dogs, and then I'll go in there and shoot your canary.'

Gunther got out of the car with Valentin letting out the line through the window. He bent over and attached the leashes to the dogs' collars. Then he tied them to one of the posts which marked the line of the drive. Valentin and George got out of the car, and Valentin tugged gently on the line.

'You go first.'

Gunther tried the key in the lock, but it didn't open.

'It's bolted.'

He lifted the big brass knocker and banged on the door.

'It's Gunther,' he shouted. 'Open up.'

When they heard the bolts being drawn on the inside Valentin took up the slack on the clothesline and held it up with his left hand, tight round Gunther's neck. With his other hand he pointed the gun. George had taken his Beretta from the boot of the car. It was a twin of the Centurion Valentin carried, but he held it down by his side, leaving the theatre act to his cousin.

The door opened slowly. The man in front of them looked like a hulking shape in the darkness of the hall-way.

'Where are the others?' Valentin asked. 'Tell them to come here.'

'What?'

'You're the only one here?' Valentin said. 'I don't think so.'

318

'Call them,' Gunther said impatiently. He put his hand up, trying to ease the tension of the cord round his throat. 'Call them.'

The man in the doorway turned his head, shouted, and another shape appeared. Together they looked formidable and oddly flamboyant. They waited for a few seconds, but no one else came.

'Is that all?' Valentin asked.

The man nodded, and Valentin motioned them back.

'Walk in front of us,' he said.

'Do it,' Gunther told them, and they walked down the hallway in procession.

'Where is he?'

No answer, then Gunther cried out in a strangled voice as Valentin twisted and tugged at the rope round his neck.

'Show him. Show him.'

At the top of the stairs one of the men unlocked a door and they saw Joseph lying slumped on the bed. George's heart leapt. He pushed past Valentin, shoving the wrestlers out of the way.

'What have you done to him?'

'Relax,' one of the men said. 'Only sleeping pills.'

George knelt beside Joseph to feel his pulse, and Joseph opened his eyes slowly when he felt George's hands, a languid smile on his face. George slapped him lightly.

'Come on. Can you get up?'

'I was asleep,' Joseph said, staring as if George was an apparition from his dreams. 'How did you find me?'

'Later,' George told him.

Joseph shook his head and began climbing slowly off the bed. When he put his foot on the floor a bolt of fire shot through his leg and he swayed. George caught him and held him upright.

'What's the matter?'

'My leg. The fucking dog bit me.'

'He won't bother you again,' Valentin told him. 'The dog is dead.' He laughed. 'So let's get out of here.'

319

They left the room, George supporting Joseph with an arm around his shoulders. When they were out on the landing Valentin ushered Gunther and the two wrestlers in, then locked the door.

'It will take them a long time to get out of that door,' he said. He rapped on it to show how solid it was.

'There's a man downstairs,' Joseph said. 'He bandaged my leg.'

'There's no one downstairs,' George told him.

'He said the cellar. I want to say goodbye to him.'

Actually the experience seemed like a nightmare, and he wanted to see the old man again to make certain that he was real.

'This isn't a social occasion,' George said. 'We don't want to hang around here.'

'One minute.'

There was a door under the stairs. Valentin drew the bolts back and they went down into a basement which seemed to run the length of the house. It was carpeted and lit by a row of neon bulbs, the walls covered in white paint. A snooker table stood in one corner, three young Kurds gathered around it. They had dark skins and the beaky profiles which marked them out as having origins in the Middle East, but otherwise they looked like the sort of young people who could be seen in the streets of any Western capital on any day, each one with a cigarette in one hand and a cue in the other. At the foot of the stairs there was a sofa on which three women sat, dressed in black, headscarves drawn over their faces. There were another dozen or so people in the room, and when the door opened they crowded round the stairs, then drew away at the sight of the gun in Valentin's hand, like a flock of sheep huddling together. They were muttering and whispering, though, producing a buzzing sound, like a roomful of big lazy flies. Salim emerged from the crowd when he saw Joseph.

'What's happening, my friend?' he called out.

'Who are these people?' Valentin asked.

'We're waiting for our papers,' a boy in the corner of the room with a snooker cue in his hand called out in German.

'Oh. *Dokumente*,' Valentin muttered to George, losing interest.

Joseph limped across the floor to shake hands with Salim. As he approached the group melted away in front of him.

'I'm not going to hurt anybody,' he said to Salim.

Salim shrugged.

'They don't like men with guns. Anything can happen.'

'Let's get out of here,' Valentin said.

'Good luck,' Joseph told Salim.

The old man smiled, but he didn't reply. George tugged at Joseph and they climbed slowly back up the steps. At the top Joseph heard the click of the snooker balls, and looking round he saw that the refugees had lost interest and gone back to whatever they were doing, the buzzing sound of their voices rising. Only Salim was still standing at the bottom of the steps, and when he saw Joseph looking he raised his hand in farewell.

TWENTY-FIVE

Slumped in the back seat, Joseph was asleep before the car had travelled more than a hundred metres.

'That was too easy,' Valentin said. 'If he was serious we would still have been looking. I think he was playing with you.'

George hadn't thought about it, but as soon as Valentin said this he found himself agreeing. Sending a car for someone to keep a non-existent appointment was an old Stasi trick, and Liebl couldn't have known that Joseph would be dumb enough to fall for it. On the other hand, even if his brother had known the call was a fraud, the attempt would have been alarming enough. This was the sort of psychological manoeuvre in which the Stasi had specialised. The message was that his family could be reached anywhere at any time, and Liebl would have expected him to understand.

'What do we do now?' he asked Valentin.

George expected an answer. Without working it out consciously he also knew that when it came they would argue for the next couple of hours, and during that time the decision would be made. He couldn't put his finger on the moment when the two of them had begun to operate in this way, like a double act, but nowadays they were both conscious that they relied on each other. The strange thing, he thought, was that his real brother, the one lying asleep behind him, was a man he hardly knew and didn't understand, while his cousin had become, to all intents and purposes, as much of a brother as anyone could be.

'We should take him to Katya's apartment,' Valentin said, looking at Joseph in the mirror. 'He needs a doctor for that leg. She'll know what to do.'

'I don't want her involved in this,' George said automatically.

'So what would you do? Leave your brother at the door of a hospital? Or just dump him at the hotel? That's not wise. He should change hotels anyway. To be safe. And what about your father? What are you going to tell him? Some dog just came up in the street and nearly chewed his son's ass off?'

George shrugged.

'It's difficult. I don't want to tell her the whole story.' He paused, embarrassed. 'I don't know what she'll say.'

'I know what she'll say.' Valentin sounded amused. 'She already knows.'

'What are you talking about?'

'Why do you think I came to you with the painting that first time? I didn't know whether I could trust you. I talked to Katya about it. She said you might say no, but if you said yes you would never betray me.'

'Why didn't she tell me?'

George was thunderstruck. How was this possible?

'I don't know. I told her everything. She told me not to tell you. I don't know why. That you must ask her.'

At the apartment in Schöneberg they parked out in the street, woke Joseph up and walked him between them up the stairs. Katya answered the door.

'Ah. The boys,' she cried out gaily when she saw them.

She hugged and kissed George, but then she noticed Joseph's condition, slumped against the wall as if it was the only thing holding him upright, his trouser leg torn, the bloodstained bandage showing through it.

'What happened?'

'It's a long story,' George told her. 'Some people who were after me set a dog on him.'

She gave him a serious, direct look, and he returned it with the blank innocence he used with her when he was lying. She frowned.

'You can tell me later. We'll put him in your room. Take Serge out and put him in with Radka.'

323

When George went into the room the boy was asleep, lying on top of the covers. Beside him was a furry creature with bulging eyes, and a book whose cover showed a mechanical digger, its robot arm raised against a blue sky. Serge loved reading about machines, and passing building sites he would stand and stare at the tractors and cranes, gazing at the men in hard hats as if they were heroes on white horses. George smiled, thinking about it. His own dreams had been about rifles and men marching in shiny boots. He scooped Serge up in his arms, and the boy opened his eyes and smiled at him.

'*Vati,*' he murmured sleepily.

Disturbed by the movement the furry thing on the bed opened its eyes and made a farting sound. Serge giggled.

'*Er gefurzen.*'

George carried him along the corridor into the next room. Radka was lying propped up in bed, spectacles on her nose, reading an English book she had bought in a secondhand bookshop. When she looked up and saw them, she put the book down, took off her glasses and threw the duvet aside to make room for Serge.

'What's going on?'

'It's a long story. Joseph is going to sleep in there tonight.'

She made a face of surprise, and as he left the room she started getting out of bed.

In the sitting room, Joseph was lying half dressed on a sofa. Kofi had taken his torn trousers off and they lay on the floor in a dark puddle, topped by the coils of bloodstained bandages which Katya had unwrapped. She knelt alongside, surrounded by objects from her first aid kit, scissors, bandages, cotton wool and antiseptic powder, looking as calm and efficient as a nurse as she wiped Joseph's leg carefully with the antiseptic, cleaning the punctures gently. She was taking care not to hurt him, but he was, in any case, showing no reaction, lying back with his eyes closed, half asleep. Kofi stood alongside, his expression sober.

'How is he?'

Radka had come into the room, and she stood beside Kofi, peering over the back of the sofa at Joseph.

'He's okay,' Katya told her. 'It looks bad, but I don't think it's infected, and his father says he's had the tetanus vaccine recently.'

This was on the occasion of Joseph's solitary trip to West Africa a couple of years before, when he'd had every kind of inoculation to be had. Kofi had smiled broadly when he heard about his son's preparations, and Joseph, a little stung, had replied, 'I don't think your being born over there gives me some kind of immunity.'

When Katya was finished with him, Kofi and George helped Joseph up and walked him into the bedroom. Then they sat him down on the narrow bed, from which George had just taken Serge, and where he himself had slept as a child. Anticipating frequent visits, he had brought it from the old apartment near the Friedrichstrasse when they moved to Prague. They tugged his shirt and his jacket off, then, as he lay back, George covered him with the duvet. As he did so he had the curious feeling that he was handling his own body, the smooth ochre skin, the curling black hair, the stubborn stubble on the chin, more pronounced at the end of the day. He sat by the side of the bed watching, wondering about the emotion inside him. Joseph opened his eyes, then they fluttered shut.

'Good night,' he whispered. 'Thank you.'

George touched his brother on the shoulder, feeling as if a vibration passed between them at that moment.

'What happened?' Kofi asked.

His tone wasn't angry, but looking up George saw him frowning, his eyes fixed and intent. Under his gaze, George felt the urge to confess.

'It's my fault,' he muttered. 'It was me they wanted. I think the dog was an accident. It's just a madman who thinks I have something he wants. I was handling it, but I didn't think that anything like this would happen to him.'

Kofi rested his hand on George's shoulder.

'You didn't do this. I know how hard it is to stop things happening. You can explain later.'

He sat on the bed and waved George away.

'I'll stay with him. Get some rest.'

Outside the door Katya was waiting.

'Come.'

They went into her bedroom. It was a big, light room, so familiar as to give George a feeling of nostalgia as he settled down in the armchair. It was here that he pictured Katya when he was away, deliberately forgetting the other places where they had lived before. It was here that she seemed to have relaxed and arrived at a kind of peace with herself. The furnishings seemed to reflect her mood, a light-coloured oatmeal carpet, pale wallpaper with big patterns of flowers in gold. The room looked open and uncluttered, the big mirrors on the walk-in closet throwing back a bright sunny vista. On one of the walls there was a blown-up copy of the photograph of herself and Kofi. It had already been faded when the copy was made, and looking at the image, it struck George that it bore only a vague general resemblance to either of his parents. He had devoured this photograph with his eyes on innumerable occasions, but, since seeing his father, its significance seemed suddenly to have disappeared, and now it was merely a picture of two young people he hardly recognised. Opposite was a huge poster of Man Ray's photograph of Nancy Cunard. There were some other photos, of scenes which had a significance she had never explained to George. Krasnaya Ploschad, with the red sun rearing up behind the domes, a green ridge in Poland, the Charles Bridge in Prague.

'What happened?' Katya asked.

'Didn't Valentin tell you?'

'Are you jealous?'

They both knew he was, but he refused to dignify the question with an answer, so he stood and faced the wall, staring at the Man Ray photograph with its strange, translucent eyes. Katya once told him that his father had known this woman, and he made a mental note to ask Kofi whether this was true and what she had been like. Thinking of Kofi made him remember that for most of his life he had pictured him as a distant dream, floating between sleep and wakefulness, lost for ever. Occasionally he had wondered whether what his mother told him was entirely true. Now the man was sitting in the next room he didn't know what he felt or what to say to him. When they embraced he had tried to suppress his tears, uncertain whether Kofi would think it unmanly if he cried. Now he wondered what his father was angry about, what had happened to Joseph, and facing Katya he tried to guess whether she knew what Kofi was thinking.

He told her about Liebl and how the chain of events started when he went to Liebl for help in selling the first picture.

'I didn't tell you I knew about what you were doing,' Katya said, 'because at first it didn't matter. I only told him to show you the painting. I hoped you could help him. Afterwards when he told me he had a house full of treasure I suggested a way of dealing with it. Valentin is not a planner, and I knew that sooner or later you would do something crazy, once you'd had enough of kissing the ass of every tourist who came through the airport. He promised me that it would stop after you made some money, and I couldn't see how dangerous it would be. In my day no one would have been bothered about getting those pictures back. Why should they care? By the time I understood how things had changed the damage was done. I didn't want you to think I was interfering. I know how proud you are. Later, it was too late.' She paused. 'Also, I was excited about being in possession of the secret. No one knew except me. You know what that feels like.'

There was a peculiar expression on her face and George felt the back of his neck flush with heat. It had been more than a dozen years, he thought, and she hadn't forgotten or forgiven him. Even though she'd told him repeatedly that it didn't matter, and that she understood, the tension was still there.

He remembered the moment of discovery only too well. He had moved out of the apartment and he'd been squatting temporarily in a block in Prenzlauer Berg. He'd come back one afternoon and having let himself in, had the impression that the place was empty until he tried the door of her room and found it locked.

'Leave me alone,' she'd shouted back when he called out. Her voice sounded peculiar, strained and hysterical, and he persisted, fearing that there was something seriously wrong. She had taken his departure with equanimity. He had, after all, been away many times for varying periods, and she could understand him, at the age of nearly thirty not wanting to be tied to her apron strings. So that couldn't be the problem. He knocked and knocked and when she refused to come out, he settled down to wait. She appeared eventually, her face swollen and red as if she'd been crying for a long time. When he spoke to her she avoided his eyes. It was nearly another hour before she told him what had happened. Someone, a reliable person, she said, emphasising the words, had read her file. George's heart sank, because he knew that she had to be talking about the reports he had written about her. He had, of course, never given them anything which might damage her. There was nothing, in fact, apart from her boyfriends, who were all short-term and more or less harmless. Her experiences with men had put her off for good, she used to say.

'Let me explain,' he'd said.

'There's no need,' she had replied firmly.

Her friend had also read George's Stasi file. They had known about all his little tricks, dealing in army equipment and rations, trading in all kinds of goods with Russian soldiers, even a little pornography. He had only survived because of the errands he ran for the Stasi, and because his crimes were so petty, but that is exactly what he had been, a petty criminal and an equally petty informer.

'You were lucky,' she said bitterly. 'I expect that sooner or later they would have put you behind bars.'

She had never spoken of it even to Radka because she had been brought up to keep such secrets even from her closest relations. But George knew what she had been thinking, that his father Kofi would have had too much honour for such a career. No matter how many times they called him a black monkey, she had told George, he was a proud man.

'That was a long time ago, and he was born in a free country,' George had replied, forgetting for the moment that Kofi had actually been born in a colony.

There was a knock at the door and Radka opened it, looking, with an unreadable expression, at each of their faces in turn.

'Some coffee?'

Back in the other room Kofi was sitting opposite Valentin. Both of them looked up as George followed Katya in and he guessed that Valentin had been telling Kofi the whole story. The trouble was that Valentin, as George knew only too well, had no sense of shame about what they'd been doing, and if he felt he could trust someone he would have no compunction about boasting of how clever he'd been and how much money they'd been making. Of course, he'd stop short of talking about shooting the Georgians. He had that much sense.

'Valentin says the gangsters missed you and got Joseph,' Kofi said in English.

He was sitting back at his ease, one leg swung over the arm of the chair, and he smiled up at George as if he was talking about some childish prank.

Guessing that Valentin had told the story in that way, like one long joke, George felt a surge of irritation.

'Did you tell him about Konstantine?' he asked his cousin abruptly.

Valentin shook his head slowly.

329

'This is about more than Liebl,' he told Katya. 'He's playing games, trying to scare me. All he wants is money. If that was it we could work something out, but I think the people he's working with are different. They're real trouble. Georgians.' He hesitated, then took the plunge. 'We had to shoot some of them in Hamburg, defending ourselves. In Prague they killed one of our people. I think that they've been waiting for Liebl to do the business for them, and he's been waiting and watching to see whether he could get the pictures away from us without a fight. That's how he used to work, because in the old days you couldn't escape. He once told me that everything fell into his hands sooner or later. Now things have changed, and he's stepping up the pressure. Maybe they're all tired of waiting, and I have the feeling that if Liebl doesn't succeed soon, they'll be coming.'

Without a pause he told her the rest. As she listened her face grew pale and she sat down on the arm of Kofi's chair and took his hand in hers.

While George talked, Radka came in with a tray full of coffee cups and a percolator. Listening to his words, she stood there, forgetting to put the tray down, as immobile as a shop window dummy.

'This isn't just about pictures. They want to kill us, Mutti,' he said eventually, using the name for her he had grown up with. 'I don't think we can survive in Prague or Berlin. We have to get out of here, because it's only a matter of time now.'

This was the conclusion he'd come to. The logic was inescapable. He couldn't defend himself and his family indefinitely. In another country he might be able to drop out of sight. He might have a chance.

'Where would you go?' Katya asked. She raised her hand and began twirling one of her curls around her finger, a gesture he remembered from his childhood and which told him how worried she was.

'England maybe, I don't know. Or the USA. I have enough money. I don't have to stay.' He paused. 'I want you to come too. In England Kofi and Joseph will be there.'

He didn't look round at the old man. He didn't want to know what Kofi's reaction was, he thought. After all this time he couldn't back away.

'What about you?' Katya asked Valentin.

Valentin made a gesture of bewilderment.

'It doesn't matter. They don't frighten me.'

He still didn't understand, George thought. In George's mind his world seemed to have changed in a flash after Katya referred to the time when she'd found out the extent of his betrayal. 'I've had enough,' he wanted to shout in her face, but he knew also that his anger was for himself. It was as if, for all this time, he had been deceiving himself, pretending to be a man, when all the time he was still a child. Life has to change now, he thought, or he would die from being what he was.

'I think you're right,' Katya said. She looked at Valentin. 'Do what I tell you, *malcheek*. Don't go home. Go to a hotel. Five star. Enjoy yourself. Keep away from your women and no clubs. Stay out of sight till lunchtime and then call me.' She turned to George. 'And you, go to bed with your wife. I have to talk with Kofi. I think maybe we can fix this. But go. Leave us alone. I'll talk to you tomorrow.'

Both of them nodded obediently. When they'd left the room Katya sat down opposite Kofi and looked at him steadily.

'Would you like a drink?' she asked him. 'I have a lot to say.'

TWENTY-SIX

For most of the day Kofi and Katya had talked together. They were at ease with each other, of course, but they had both shied away from the conversation which Kofi had come all this way to have. Instead, they talked about their lives and about what they'd done since their last meeting. Sometimes it seemed like an impossible stretch of years, a desert reaching back to a horizon which was almost invisible. Sometimes it seemed as if the time had passed in the twinkling of an eye.

Telling Katya about his life, Kofi was astonished at how little he had achieved, and how quickly his energy had trickled away. He had gone back to Ghana, working for Makonnen in the Ministry of Tourism. Within a year he had been sent to London where he worked in the Mission, his occupation sitting behind a desk and shuffling papers. From time to time he had been despatched to various capitals, but after his marriage to Caroline he always had a good excuse for returning to what was now his home. Then, in what seemed like an incredibly short time, Osageyfo's reign was over. He had been dismissed and sent into exile, and Mak, Kofi heard, was in prison, awaiting judgement. The headlines in the newspaper were like an announcement which told Kofi that his own career in diplomacy was over. Without waiting to be recalled to Accra, he simply left his desk and went home. In the intervening years he had tried his hand at a number of things, working to make a living, busying himself with his journal, his horizons shrinking to the round of his daily routine and the walls behind which he lived. In the end there was not much to tell. He had existed, it seemed, somehow apart from all the events and people who mattered to him, a kind of spectator.

In comparison, Katya's exile had been an escape to a new life.

'There is so much to tell you,' she said.

Unable to stop himself, he yawned.

'I'm tired,' he said apologetically.

It was past midnight, and in normal circumstances he'd have been in bed by this time. He wanted, more than anything, to lie down.

'You can sleep in my bed,' Katya told him. 'I was thinking about that, and I can't remember us being in bed together.'

In the bedroom she pointed to the big photograph of Nancy Cunard.

'I bought that,' she said, 'because I remembered you talking of her.'

He nodded, smiling at her to show his appreciation of her memory, but the truth was that he didn't like to see the picture. It made him think of failure, wasted promise, blasted lives, his own and others. This woman in the photograph had been there when he first met Osageyfo.

He undressed sitting on the side of the bed, watching Katya doing the same thing in the middle of the room. She had left only a dim lamp burning in the corner, and she stripped without a hint of coyness. As she took off her trousers, standing on one leg and smiling broadly, it struck him that although they managed to conceive a child together, he had never seen her naked. He hadn't known what to expect, and he'd been prepared for her to be wasted and wrinkled beneath her clothes, but her figure was still recognisable, the waist dipping in, her legs still long and straight. She kept her bra on, because she told him later, her breasts were no longer beautiful. 'They feel fine,' he told her. Her arms were thinner, the skin sagging round her shoulders, but as she walked towards him she still had the appearance of an attractive woman. Kofi hadn't thought about sex during the entire day, but his penis rose as if summoned to arms. Katya looked down, smiling, and patted his stomach, which since the years she'd known him had ballooned into a moderate paunch. 'This is a new thing,' she said. 'The other I know very well.'

They lay face to face, arms and legs wrapped round each other.

'It's been years since I did this,' Kofi said.

'Do you want to?'

'Yes.'

It was as if he had never been away, but, better still, Katya seemed like a new woman, one he had never known, while at the same time she was the woman he had dreamt and wondered about for so many years. He slipped into her easily and they moved together slowly. After a time Kofi began to feel his former power return, his calm deserting him and a kind of delight rushing through him as he moved inside her. With a strength that surprised him he turned her on her back and rode into her, moaning with joy. At the end she held him in her arms, stroking his face.

'Not so bad for an old lady,' he told her.

'I love you,' she said.

Just before they went to sleep, she propped herself up on her elbow above him.

'I'm worried about George,' she said. 'His wife is beginning to despise him.'

It was shortly after this that George arrived, half carrying Joseph, Valentin shuffling behind them, grinning when he saw Kofi. Another hour had gone past before Katya dismissed them, ushering Valentin out of the apartment and sending George off to the bedroom where Radka was waiting. Now they sat in the kitchen drinking tea, the scent of the honey-coloured liquid tinged with lemon. He sniffed at his cup, dragging the fragrance into his lungs. Forty years ago, in the hostel where she visited him, they had drunk tea like this.

'You said that you knew how to fix it,' he said. 'How can you do that?'

He knew better than to ask about talking to the police or any other authorities. He had already gathered from Joseph's hints that George was no ordinary businessman, and from the moment he had got out of bed and seen Joseph slumped on the sofa he had known that it wasn't a matter for the authorities.

They were speaking in English. Katya spoke the language now more fluently than she had before, but with a different accent, a little buzz which gave her intonation an American sound. Kofi found it disorientating, as if this was an imposter who looked exactly like the woman he'd known.

'It's your friend Valery,' she said. 'I think he would help us. For myself I would not ask him. I think he might say no, but now you are here it's different.'

Kofi was astonished. He hadn't thought about Valery in years, not since Chernobyl, and since then he had forgotten.

'How can he help?' he asked. 'He must be an old man now.' He paused, remembering. 'He wasn't a Georgian, was he? He was Ukrainian. Did he get to be an engineer?'

'Yes. He went to the Institute of Oil and Chemicals, and then he went to Siberia.'

'So he wasn't at Chernobyl.'

'Chernobyl?' She laughed. 'No. He was never that kind of engineer. Anyway he was in Siberia.'

'How do you know all this?' Kofi asked. It was as if she was telling him about a life he should have known or been a part of. In all these years he hadn't thought of it like this. On the contrary he had imagined their separation as one in which Katya had been cut off. Now he felt that he was the one who had experienced the deprivation of exile.

'He came to see me,' she said calmly. 'He was here to see a government minister. I saw him on television, but I wasn't sure, then in the morning I got a telephone call. Valery

335

Kirichenko, they said. The funny thing was, although it was a surprise at the time I was expecting it.'

'He's important, then.'

He was trying to call up a picture of Valery, sitting over the stove with a book in his hand. Instead he remembered the sneer on Hussein's face as he looked at him, and his sceptical remarks: *Be careful of that one.*

'You remember Hussein?' he asked Katya.

She thought for a moment, then nodded.

'He died,' he told her.

Hussein had died twenty years before, in mysterious circumstances in prison in Uganda, his publications suppressed, his careful charting of economic disaster scattered.

'Valery is very important,' Katya said. 'He's a billionaire. I think he might be one of the richest men in the world. He owns property all over, even here in this city. Now he's buying newspapers and TV.'

Kofi whistled involuntarily.

'Incredible.'

Katya shrugged.

'Everything changed ten years ago. For some it was a death sentence. They breathed and they walked around but they were dead. For some every door opened.'

'So he's a billionaire,' Kofi said. 'But he knew us forty years ago. We shared a room. Rich men don't remember what happened before they were rich. Not just rich men, at my age I find it hard to remember names and faces from the past.'

A dozen years previously he had been scanning one of the black newspapers in the newsagents in Ladbroke Grove, when he saw a picture of Calvin in a group of dignitaries. He wasn't sure at first, but the caption underneath gave his name and said that he was his country's Minister of Culture. Kofi laughed about that all the way home, but when he telephoned the High Commission they wouldn't give him Calvin's whereabouts or pass on a message. Eventually he found out that Calvin would be at a fund-raising reception at the Kensington Town Hall. The entrance fee cost him more than he could afford, but he was there when Calvin was ushered across the room, his wife, a young woman dressed in a sari who looked like a fashion model, clinging to his arm. Kofi smiled, remembering Marina and the pumping buttocks of the Minister of Culture. Seizing his chance he got in front of Calvin and put out his hand. '*Dobri veeyecher*, Calvin,' he said. Calvin stared at him, puzzled for a moment, then he took the offered hand and shook it warmly. 'How are you, man?' he said. 'Nice to see you.' Then he side-stepped Kofi and continued on his way out of the room. At the door he paused suddenly, as if hearing a voice call his name. He looked back at Kofi, a puzzled frown creasing his forehead, and Kofi stared back smiling, certain now that Calvin would return and throw his arms round him. Instead the wife tugged at his arm and said something, and Calvin, returning to the present, nodded his head and hurried on out of the door. That was the last Kofi saw of him.

'Valery will remember you,' Katya said. 'You were the reason he came to see me.'

'Me?' Kofi was bewildered now.

'He was the one who started the trouble.' She hesitated. 'Well. It was my father, in fact. I only learnt this a few years ago. After you came to our apartment I knew he was very angry, but I didn't know how far he would go. He sent for Valery and interrogated him about you. He ordered him to find ways to separate us. But it was difficult.' She laughed. 'Subtlety was not possible for them. The boys who attacked you were Party members. Valery found them and told them what to do. He said my father was pleased and excited, and that he would have liked to have seen it.'

'I thought they must have stopped you coming to Paris,' Kofi said.

She smiled.

'I was nearly there. My father wouldn't have stopped

me. I pretended that I had come to my senses and was getting over you by throwing myself into my work. I was sitting every night in the apartment writing speeches, going to Komsomol meetings. This was my conversion, and he believed it because he wanted to. My mother was different, but she was more angry with him than with me. She would never tell him my secrets. I knew I was pregnant. That was my secret. I was going to tell you in Paris.'

We would never have gone back, he thought.

'It was Valery who did it. It was my fault. I wrote you a stupid note. *Abyssinia*. I should have known better. It was the stupidest thing I've ever done.'

'I've still got the note,' Kofi said.

'Valery saw it. He must have been searching your papers, but I never guessed that his English would be so good. I think in those days he hid his cleverness. He told my father about the note and what the word meant. After that, no Paris.'

She stopped and put her hand to her face, as if the enormity of the moment had suddenly struck her. Kofi leant forward and took her other hand, stroking it gently. She raised it to his cheek, her touch warm and dry, the way he remembered her hands on his skin.

'It would have been good,' Kofi said. Their eyes met. She blinked and a tear trembled on her lashes.

'I had to get away before my father knew about the baby. I didn't know what he would do. They could have sent me to an institution.' She snapped her fingers. 'Committed me and got rid of George. I couldn't risk it. I volunteered for the Virgin Lands. Valery helped me to get to Siberia. I told people in the Party I had been raped and they kept it from my father. He didn't find out till it was too late. Afterwards he helped me get a job here in Berlin, working on translations. It wasn't the sort of life I had intended, but it wasn't so bad.'

Kofi thought about Valery looking through his papers. It wouldn't have been difficult. With everything he must have known and guessed about their relationship it wouldn't have been hard to spot the child's riddle of Abyssinia. Perhaps there had been a touch of sadness when he asked whether Kofi was coming back, which he imagined, at the time, was about the prospect of not seeing him again. There was no doubt about it, Valery had ruined his life. But Kofi found it hard to summon up any anger. After all, his roommate had probably had no choice, faced with the direct commands of an official like Katya's father. He did what he had to do.

'So he survived.'

'My father thought he owed him something. The first step is always the hardest, but he got him into management in the oil industry in Siberia. That's where he wanted to go, and he never looked back. He was a senior manager during the time of Gorbachev. Then they made him a deputy minister for oil and gas. Then he became president of a state company before privatisation, and he stayed there afterwards. In two years he was a billionaire. Now the politicians and officials line up outside his office begging to see him.' She smiled and gestured. 'No one would have imagined it. Perhaps I was lucky.'

Lucky to be out of it. Lucky not to be one of those who rode the Party like captains on the bridge of a ship just before it sank below the waves.

'When I saw Valery, he said he had been full of shame for what he'd done. He liked you, but that was how we lived. This was brave of him to come and see me. He was ready for me to curse him and spit in his face. But I didn't blame him. Only a few years before there were men who could commit any crime if you didn't do what they ordered. He said that if there was anything he could do for either of us I should telephone at any time.' She put an engraved card in front of him. It had Valery's name on it, and a single phone number. 'I think you should call.'

There was something about her tone, almost challenging, as if she was testing him, finally handing over the responsibility for all these matters. Hearing it, he decided against asking her what to say. He hesitated for a few seconds, thinking about the time. In the Ukraine it would be nearly three in the morning. At last he made up his mind. The time would make no difference.

'Give me the phone.'

She got up and brought him a handset and he punched in the number quickly. The phone rang interminably, and he was about to put it down again when there was a click and a woman's voice answered in Russian.

'I want to speak to Valery Vasselievich,' Kofi said in English. 'This is Kofi Coker.'

There was another burst of talk which Kofi didn't understand.

'Kofi Coker,' he repeated patiently. 'Tell him Kofi Coker.'

There was a silence on the other end. Kofi looked over at Katya and shrugged. Perhaps the number wouldn't work. He sat there for several long minutes listening to nothing, and just as he became convinced that he'd been cut off, Valery's voice spoke into his ear.

'Kofi?'

'Yes, it's Kofi,' he answered, feeling nothing but relief.

'Kofi.' Valery's voice sounded amused. 'I thought you were dead. Last week I flew over Kalinin. They call it Tver now, and I thought of you.'

'That's good,' Kofi said. 'I thought they killed you at Chernobyl or somewhere. Now I hear you're alive and ruling the world.'

Valery chuckled.

'The world's too big.' There was a pause. Then: 'I suppose you're with Katya. How is she?'

'She's fine. So is my son. We want to see you.'

'That's not easy.'

'It's a matter of life and death. Katya says you're the only person we know who can help. It's about our son.'

'I'm in Kiev,' Valery said. 'Tomorrow I'm in Prague. I mean today. Later on. After that Alaska.'

'Today in Prague,' Kofi said.

'Okay. We'll meet in the afternoon, drink tea and contemplate the Vltava. I'll make the arrangements. Someone will pick you up.'

'Okay. I'll see you later.'

He was just about to put the phone down, when he heard Valery say his name quietly.

'Kofi?'

'Yes.'

'I'm glad you made it.'

TWENTY-SEVEN

Radka and George conversed in whispers so as not to wake Serge.

'Why didn't you tell me about this?' Radka asked. 'We could have been in danger, me and Serge. And your mother. Liebl was watching us.'

'What would you have done?'

She didn't reply and he already knew her answer. She would have taken the boy and left, he thought.

'So what shall we do now?' she whispered fiercely. 'Wait until they kill you?'

'No,' he said firmly. 'If my mother has no solutions, we leave soon. In England we'll be safe.'

'Until the next time Valentin comes along with some crazy idea.'

'There'll be no next time.'

He had a troubled and broken sleep, lying on the edge of the bed on the other side of Serge. In their own apartment the bed was large enough to accommodate them all comfortably, but here at Katya's he had to take the rough with the smooth. In the early hours of the morning he woke up and realised that he couldn't get back to sleep. He went into the kitchen, made himself some coffee and stood in the sitting room looking out at the sky. It had been a full moon, but in any case, here in Berlin, the moon and stars were hardly noticeable in a sky flushed pink and yellow with the city lights.

He heard a noise behind him and assumed that it was Katya. She used to come up behind him like this when he was a teenager and he got up in the night to stare out at the sky. 'Is there something you want to talk about?' she would ask in a soft voice.

When he turned round, however, it was Kofi who sat in the armchair, one leg dangling over the side like before, looking intently at him.

'Hello,' George greeted him. He raised his cup. 'You want some coffee? Tea?'

Kofi shook his head.

'Maybe,' he said, 'we can talk a little. I would like to know you better.'

George cast around in his mind for something to say. He had dreamt of this moment many times.

'This must be very strange for you,' he told Kofi.

'For you too.'

George nodded in acknowledgement.

'The strangest part of it,' Kofi said, 'is that you and Joseph look so much alike, but you are German and he is English.'

'If I call myself a German,' George said. 'Other people are likely to say – yes, but what are you really?' He laughed, then a question occurred to him. 'What are you?' He wanted to know the answer. As a boy he had wanted to be the same nationality as his father, and sometimes when someone asked where he came from he would say Ghana.

Kofi considered the question with care.

'I was once a Ghanaian. Now I have a British passport. As for what I am in here,' he tapped his heart, 'I don't know any more. You can say I'm like the singer, the artist formerly known as Prince. I am a man formerly known as a Ghanaian.'

George guessed he was expected to laugh.

'What did you think when you heard about me?'

Kofi studied George, turning the question over with even more care.

'I was very happy. If I'd known at the time I would have been very pleased. Not having been there while you grew up makes me very sad.'

343

'But you didn't know.'

'I wish that I had.'

'Are you glad to see her?'

Kofi smiled.

'I didn't think I would ever be so happy again.'

Hearing this George felt a peculiar little thrill inside him, and for a moment he couldn't think what else to say. In another minute, he thought, his mind would be full of questions.

'Tell me something about your life,' Kofi asked. 'Did you have a happy childhood?'

'That is not how I would describe it,' George replied. 'It wasn't her fault, but I felt alone, you know, most of the time. At school they used to think I was American, or that my father must be a Yank. That's not so good. Sometimes they expected me to be able to sing the blues, or play jazz like I had some genetic heritage. When they knew my mother was Russian they said *Schwarzer Russky*, when they weren't calling me nigger. It was easier when I went into the army.'

'You should have gone to university,' Kofi said. 'It would have opened windows.'

He had the strange feeling that George was more like him than Joseph, and already he felt a kind of sympathy between them that was absent in his conversations with his younger son.

'I should have,' George said, 'but I wouldn't have known what to study.' He grinned at Kofi, struck by a sudden thought. 'What made you go to study in Russia? All the people there were trying to get out.'

'In some ways I was just doing what I was told. It was strange, yes, but all these white man's countries were strange, although not in the same way. Part of it was that we couldn't take anything on trust, because everybody in the world lied to us about everything. They really did treat us like savage children who were only entitled to know what they thought was good for us. So everything was a kind of opposite. When the British and the Americans said freedom, they meant freedom for themselves, servitude for us. When they said the Russians were enslaved it was not hard to believe that it really meant freedom.'

'It didn't mean freedom.'

Kofi shrugged.

'I still don't know what it meant. For me going to a place where you weren't supposed to go was a kind of freedom, like getting out of prison.' He smiled at George. 'Why did white men go to Africa? Europe was our dark continent.'

George watched him, searching for signs of resemblance. The eyes, he thought, were very similar.

'When I was younger,' he said, 'I couldn't understand why you would come to a place where you didn't belong and have a child who didn't belong either.' He hurried on to prevent Kofi misunderstanding his intent. 'Now I can see all this belonging is bullshit. You can belong where you choose to belong.'

'What did your mother tell you about me?'

George grinned at him. 'She said you were a kind of hero.' It would have been better, he thought, if I had believed you were an ordinary person. All his life he had felt that his father would have done things he couldn't.

'I'm going to Prague today,' Kofi said.

'Prague?'

George wasn't sure that he'd heard right.

'I'm going to meet an old friend.' Kofi hesitated, uncertain how much to tell him, then he described how he'd met Valery, and how they used to share a room in Cheryomushki. George was astonished. He'd heard the name on the radio and read it in the newspapers, but it had never occurred to him that the man had any connection with his parents.

'You know that man?'

'Didn't your mother tell you about him?'

George shook his head, and Kofi guessed that Katya

hadn't told him, either, about the part his grandfather had played in their lives.

'He can help us,' he said.

Somehow the conversation calmed George's nerves, and soothed the restlessness which had kept him awake. Kofi was talking about Valery, but his attention kept wandering, and in a few minutes he felt himself dozing off. When he opened his eyes again, there was a grey light gleaming through the window and Kofi had disappeared.

He went to bed, sliding in beside Radka who shifted to make room for him without waking. He woke again a couple of hours later, and walking into the kitchen interrupted Kofi and Katya who were sitting at the table conversing intently in quiet voices.

'What's up?'

'Nothing really,' Katya said. 'We were talking about what to do in Prague.'

George shrugged. He had been too tired to argue during the night, in the face of Katya's firmness, but in the cold light of day he found himself unable to believe in the idea that his elderly parents could resolve matters at a stroke. He was on the verge of opening his mouth to say so, but, looking at Katya's determined expression he changed his mind. After all it would do no harm for Kofi to go to Prague and see his old friend, and it might keep them quiet while he worked out a way of getting out of the mess.

After breakfast, when the arrangements for his father's trip had been made, and Kofi was waiting to be picked up, George telephoned Liebl's office. The receptionist put him through at once.

'I was waiting to hear from you,' Liebl said. 'Congratulations.'

'You fat shit,' George said. 'Next time I'll come looking for you.'

'Don't get so excited,' Liebl wheezed. 'It's your brother's fault. You should tell him to be more careful. I didn't think

346

anyone would be fooled by that old trick. I was so surprised I didn't know what to do with him.'

'He's not accustomed to dealing with criminals,' George said.

Liebl chuckled appreciatively.

'I take it you're ready to talk business.'

'Yes,' George told him.

He had discussed this with Katya and Valentin and they'd agreed that he should open negotiations with Liebl. That would give them a couple of days in which Kofi's billionaire might step in. If that didn't work at least they'd have a breathing space in which to make new plans. In any case, whatever they decided they would have to contact Victor and talk with him.

'I'm not the only one involved,' George continued. 'This will take a few days.'

'I'll give you another day,' Liebl said. He paused. 'Don't worry about the Georgians. If you take me as a partner I'll take care of them.'

TWENTY-EIGHT

Kofi's flight to Prague took off from Tempelhof in the middle of the morning. After breakfast, Katya had taken a telephone call from a young woman who spoke German with a snooty Wessi accent, and who said all the arrangements had been made. A couple of hours later a young man wearing a dark suit and dark glasses picked him up in a limousine and drove him to the airport. Before that, George, Joseph and Radka had all insisted that someone should accompany him to Prague, but he had shrugged off their arguments.

'I've done more difficult things through most of my life,' Kofi told his sons firmly, 'and this will be hard enough without having to look after you as well,' he said with finality. 'Stay here, and don't go out. I'll telephone you when I get there.'

A fortnight ago he would never have spoken to his younger son with such an assumption of authority, but now Joseph's manner had changed towards him, and, as if in imitation of George, he treated his father with a new respect.

The flight was uneventful. At the airport outside Prague another young man, also dressed in a dark suit and dark glasses, picked him up in another limousine. The car and the chauffeur were so much like the other one that Kofi was tempted to look over his shoulder to check that he wasn't back at Tempelhof.

They came in through Holesovice, swung right out of the Letenské Tunnel, drove along the embankment. It was a bright day, and the sun danced on the river beside them. He thought of George walking here, a solitary figure. It had been the same in Berlin. Looking at the landscape his mind had kept returning to the idea of George's footsteps branded on the pavement, trying to imagine what his son had been feeling as he passed through the streets. A phrase from the Bible occurred to him as he did so. A certain man had two sons. The prodigal son, he remembered, had been the younger one. Did that make a difference? Would Joseph eventually reproach him for what he felt about George? He craned his neck to stare up at the trees in the park, feeling as if they were acquaintances he had not seen for many years. Katya had said she loved him, but he didn't know how to respond. His emotions seemed to have been frozen for so long that he couldn't work out what they meant. Perhaps they could stay together. He smiled, thinking of her presence while he slept.

Opposite the old town, they crossed over the bridge into Narodni, and drew up in front of a huge office building. Like most of the new buildings in the city, it seemed barely finished, as if the workmen had only just packed up their tools and hurried off round the corner when they saw the car approach.

In the lobby of the building there was a reception behind which an elegant young woman sat, a telephone to her ear. Next to her was another desk which housed two men in what seemed to be the regulation dark suits. Kofi was just about to walk across the marble floor to the reception when another elegant young woman intercepted him.

'I hope you had a smooth flight,' she said in English as she shook hands with him. Her accent had a strong American tinge. 'Mr Kirichenko is waiting for you.'

When they got off the lift she led the way to another door.

'May I bring you something? Coffee, tea, vodka?'

'Coffee,' Kofi told her.

He had expected to be tense or disturbed on the brink of this meeting, but what he felt was an intense pleasure at the thought of seeing Valery again, and the building, the decor, and the evidence of his old friend's success gave him an odd sense of reassurance as if he was part of this power to shape the world.

She turned the handle of the door and pushed it open. It was a huge room which ended in a glass wall that framed a panoramic view of the river, beyond it the castle and the wooded heights of Letna. Valery was sitting at a desk placed in a corner of the room, where the curtain had been drawn over a section of the glass, blotting out the view and providing the illusion of a dark cubbyhole. As his visitor came in he rose up out of the shadows and came towards him.

Kofi would have recognised him anywhere. He had changed, of course, but it was as if his features had simply become more clearly what they had been. He carried his head now with a tilt which made his chin stick out, and his body had grown thick, not fat but massive, like something carved out of a giant pine in the Siberian *taiga*, the world's largest forest. He still had all his hair, which seemed to spring from his head in a brush of grey wire, and he wore a loose white shirt draped over his trousers and on his feet, a pair of trainers, with the tongues flopping out. He saw Kofi looking and he gestured at his feet.

'I lost part of a toe in Siberia,' he said in English, 'and these are the only comfortable shoes I can find.'

He shook Kofi's hand, then hugged him. They sat down in a little group of armchairs which had been arranged in the middle of the room, facing the window.

'This is the strangest experience of my life,' Valery said. 'To find us here, like this, after so many years.' He looked intently at Kofi. 'I never thought I'd see you again.'

'I never thought I'd see you again either. Your English is better.'

Valery laughed.

'It was always better than you thought.'

His face fell as if the memory had sobered him.

'Katya told you what happened? I'm sorry.'

Somehow Kofi didn't want him to apologise or be humble.

'It was a long time ago. I didn't come for revenge or apologies. I understand. You did what you had to do.'

Valery looked him in the eyes for a few seconds, a hint of curiosity in his expression, as if he was trying to make out whether Kofi was telling him the truth. Eventually he sighed.

'That is true,' he said. 'But you are a great man, Kofi.'

'What about you?' Kofi asked. 'I thought you were going to be an engineer and serve the people. Instead of which I see you've wasted your time becoming a billionaire.'

Valery chuckled.

'This is an accident.' He waved his hand around the room. 'You should come to Siberia with me and see where I started out.'

'I expect you've got buildings like this in a lot of cities,' Kofi said. 'No one does all this by accident.'

'Oh no. The accident was Gorbachev and Yeltsin. The rest was my own work.'

'What happened?'

Valery looked away from Kofi, staring out at the river, then he began to talk, launching into his forty-year-old memories as if they were fresh and recent in his mind.

He had still been in his early twenties in 1960 when he set out from Yekaterinburg in Western Siberia for the oil fields which were just being discovered to the north.

'*Sverdlovsk*, they used to call it.' Valery laughed. Yakov Sverdlov, Kofi remembered, had been the official charged with overseeing the executions of the tsar and his family in Yekaterinburg. As a reward he had had a city named after him. 'No one wants to remember Sverdlov now. Boris Nikolayevich was born near there too, in Butka, and east of there Rasputin.' He laughed again. 'They produce tough guys up there. They grow up pickled in vodka. You can't kill them.'

351

All this was tame country in comparison to where he started.

'There were no roads. In winter fifty degrees below zero was normal. One of the ways we used to amuse ourselves was coming out of our hut and throwing a cup of hot coffee in the air. It never reached the ground. It didn't freeze, it evaporated into a kind of vapour. Look down on the snow and all you'd see was a little brown powder. At first we lived with the Khants. They were nomads, living off the reindeer and the fish they took out of the river. Nowadays I can't even look at reindeer meat. Sometimes I see all that stuff about reindeer at Christmas. It makes me laugh. They were vicious brutes. Go near them and they try to hook you with their horns. But in those days when you walked out in the country your feet sank in up to the ankles. Look back and you could see the oil welling up in your footsteps.'

But even though they could smell the oil on his clothes, when he went into Sverdlovsk to argue with the Ministry for permission to begin drilling test wells, it wasn't until a few years later that they started hauling the equipment through the swamp. Over the next decade it turned into a mess. Valery's engineering background had taught him a precise approach to development and construction, but this was no place for careful techniques. Even at the time he understood that the rush for Siberian oil would be as wasteful, and as extravagantly greedy as the gold rush in Alaska a hundred years before. They were taking a quarter of the Soviet Union's oil out of the district, but they were injecting the fields with water to push the top of the field out, and then moving on to new ones because it simply wasn't worth pumping the water out to get at the remaining oil. They were burning the natural gas which would later be worth more than the oil they were pumping. They were leaving timber, which could have built houses for the workers, to rot in the swamps, and all the time the workers who were taking unimaginable wealth out of the

352

ground inhabited a city of flimsy shacks in a giant clearing in the *taiga*.

'An entire quarter of Nizhnevartovsk was metal wagons in which they lived,' Valery said. He shook his head. 'You had to see it to believe it.'

He had learnt the trade from the bottom up. His major achievement, he told Kofi, had been nothing to do with engineering. It was his ability to keep the workers happy and increase production targets every year. To this end he racked his brain to create incentives, freeing gangs to rescue timber and build housing for the families, finding space to fly sick children into the regional capital at Tyumen, and even flying to Moscow to return with cans of film for private showings at the Komsomol centre in Nizhnevartovsk.

'When Gorbachev came in the eighties he was horrified,' Valery said, 'that there wasn't a single cinema anywhere in the region. He lectured to the Party in Tyumen. Then he went away and started banning vodka. Somehow he didn't notice that only two men in the entire country supported him – Ligachev and Solomentsev, and they were both mad. Then the oil prices dropped to nothing and everyone else went mad. This was the worst time.'

That was the first accident, he said, the one with Gorbachev's name on it. But by then Valery was a senior manager, liaising with the Party and the Ministry over restructuring the state enterprises. When privatisation came in '92 he was already president of a company which he took over without much difficulty, converting the five per cent of stock given to the managers into a staggering twenty per cent by dint of his ability to sweet talk his employees. That was the second accident, caused by Yeltsin, but this one had put his engine back on the rails.

'Up there the state used to be king,' he said, smiling at Kofi. 'Now it's the company.'

'I don't have a story,' Kofi told him.

The fact was that listening to Valery's tales of his progress embarrassed and depressed Kofi. When his own opportunities arrived he had failed to recognise them. In the mid-sixties, for instance, he had been approached by a group of his countrymen who belonged to the opposition to the government. Their intention, they said, was to start a journal, which would be circulated in the country and abroad, detailing Osageyfo's corrupt practices and the waste and incompetence he had fostered. From one of the most prosperous colonies on the continent, he had created an impossible burden of debt and a vacuum which sucked up millions. He had converted a proud nation into an international beggar.

When they had finished listing Osageyfo's crimes the group of young radicals said they wanted to encourage protest against him, and to support a possible coup. The more the opposition exposed what was going on the easier it would be to get rid of him. Kofi would be a valuable addition to the editorial board, because, they said, he was well known to have been a protégé of the President, but one who had rejected Communist propaganda and fled Russia in disgust. In spite of this he had been given a secure billet in Accra from which he might have joined in the looting, but instead he had retired to London, his removal signalling his distaste for his mentor's tactics and his support for those radicals who had been imprisoned.

This interpretation of his movements had startled Kofi. It was true that he had made his objections to certain practices clear. One day dropping into a hotel bar for a drink after work, he had run into a woman he knew slightly. She was English, a young woman who had been, on and off, in the country since independence, and who worked as a public relations expert for a firm which had its roots in South Africa. She doubled as a reporter, from time to time despatching to the English newspapers a series of articles passionately defending Osageyfo's government.

At the bar she passed him a magazine which he assumed featured one of her articles.

'Look at it,' she said insistently.

Inside was a brown envelope full of hundred dollar bills, and Kofi knew immediately what he was being asked. The woman's firm was bidding for an engineering project connected with the planned hydro-electric dam.

'You can talk to the big man,' she murmured, 'or to any one of those guys. We're not asking for any guarantees. Just put in a good word.'

He'd taken the envelope without comment. Later on he heard that the contract had been awarded to the woman's firm. In London he'd told this story to Caroline and a couple of others at a party, emphasising that he'd reported the bribe to his superiors without result. Somehow it had got around, and now these radicals were convinced he was one of them. Without thinking about it he turned down the offer to join them, pointing out that everything of which they accused Nkrumah was part and parcel of the region's politics. Opposition, he told them, was not the same as betrayal. Immediately afterwards he had the uneasy feeling that he had been wrong. It had truly been disillusion of a kind which had barred his return to Africa, and his refusal to join the opposition had been nothing to do with loyalty or his political beliefs. Instead he had shrunk from driving the final nail into the coffin of his youthful hopes. A year later, Nkrumah had been deposed. In retrospect he had been a coward, Kofi thought. In comparison, Valery had learnt to live in the world he had inherited, taking it by the scruff of the neck and refusing to sit on the sidelines sulking.

'We have a problem,' Kofi said abruptly.

Valery's eyes were suddenly sober and intent.

'If I can help.'

'It's my son,' Kofi told him.

'One moment,' Valery interrupted. He got up, walked over to his desk and pressed a button. 'We eat while we talk.'

Two women in aprons came in and set up a table. Then

they came back with a couple of trays and distributed the contents round the table.

'*Zakusky*,' Valery said jovially. 'It's too early for serious eating.'

These were Ukrainian snacks, Kofi remembered. Black and red caviar, *pyrizhky*, *beruny*, little stuffed dumplings, *holubtsi*, stuffed cabbage rolls, cottage cheese, sour cream, and a variety of breads, *pampushki*, *khrusty* and *medivnyk*. The centrepiece was a big cut-glass bowl of fruit.

'This is not a snack,' Kofi teased. 'It's more like a banquet. Your expectations are inflated now you're a great man.'

Valery shook his head.

'Oh, you don't know. I can't go out and walk around like you. If I want to go to a restaurant I'm followed by three bodyguards. My security has to clear the place. It's easier to have a cook and a kitchen.'

'I thought that was only bankers.'

Valery gestured.

'Any businessman.' He frowned. 'Here is the irony. In the days when minor officials were drawing up lists which would send men and women to their deaths, they could walk safely in the streets. Now, to be engaged in business you need a bodyguard. That is one of the benefits of economic liberalism. Equal opportunity violence.' Suddenly, he burst out laughing, pounding the table with his fist as he spewed gust after gust of explosive guffaws. 'In any case,' he shouted, 'I own three banks.'

While they ate, Kofi told him the whole story, the smuggled pictures, the killings in Hamburg, the beheading across the river in Smichov, leaving nothing out. Valery glanced up a few times, his eyebrows arching, but he said nothing, concentrating on his food and occasionally encouraging Kofi with a grunt when he paused to think or remember some detail. When Kofi told him what had happened to Joseph, he frowned and taking a pencil out of his pocket wrote the names, Liebl and Zviad Abuladze, on a piece of paper.

'When Valentin came to Katya,' Kofi said eventually, 'she should have stopped him.'

Valery shrugged.

'I don't know why. It was a good idea.'

'I don't want my children killed,' Kofi said.

'Don't worry about that,' Valery told him. 'I think I might be able to talk to these people.' He paused, reflecting. 'Do any of these things come from the Ukraine?'

'Perhaps,' Kofi said. 'I don't know.'

After the meal they toasted each other in Zubrowka.

'Have you been in Prague before?' Valery asked Kofi, who shook his head. 'Good. My chauffeur will take you round the city. When you come back I might have some news about this little business of yours. Then you can go back to Berlin.' He paused. He waved his hand. 'One thing. We're not in some quiet little country like England. This is like the Wild West. If I do what you want there may be some killing. Just understand that.'

TWENTY-NINE

Radka disappeared for most of the day, to the house of a friend where Serge would visit the park and play with the other children. The doctor arrived shortly after she had gone, examined Joseph and said there was no sign of serious infection, but gave him a course of antibiotics to make sure. Katya saw the doctor out, before leaving the apartment; shopping, she said, although George had the feeling that she was escaping and going somewhere to be alone.

Around lunchtime Joseph got up and limped into the kitchen, where he sat with George drinking coffee.

'Time for explanations I suppose,' George said.

Joseph nodded, without speaking, and George guessed that he wasn't certain what questions to ask.

'You must understand this,' he said. 'It's my fault. If you hadn't been with me this would not have happened, but I didn't mean any harm to come to you.'

For a moment Joseph thought that he hadn't wanted to know George's secrets because he'd felt that if he did he would have crossed some sort of line. Now it was too late.

'Tell me.'

'Okay, but this is between brothers.'

Joseph nodded again, and slowly George began, searching for the right words, with how Valentin had turned up.

'Okay. I was with Valentin. We were moving some things from Russia and selling them. Then there was some trouble and we decided to stop. We thought it was all over until that night in Prague when you came to Smichov.'

The blood-drenched head sitting on the bonnet of the car in the silent warehouse flashed through Joseph's mind, and in the same moment the image was replaced by the idea that had haunted him since then.

'Is it drugs?'

George sat up straight, his eyes narrowing in surprise.

'No, no. I have nothing to do with drugs. This is art. Paintings and sculpture. Not even stolen.' He shrugged, grinning. 'Not really stolen. But not legal, you know.'

Joseph felt a relief which was almost physical. He'd been prepared to hear that George was involved in some vicious and violent crime which it would be impossible to forgive. Instead he was only a smuggler or some kind of black market hustler. Joseph had heard about such things, and he knew that more than one respectable businessman in this part of the world had started from similarly dubious origins. At least his brother didn't go around chopping off people's heads.

'What's the problem?' he asked.

'The trouble didn't start until they tried to hijack us in Hamburg.'

Looking back, George could see how tangled everything had become since the incident with the Georgians. The decision to move to Prague and set up a legitimate business had seemed a perfect escape route, but after the Smichov murder Prague was finished for them. Now they were trying to figure out how to stay alive and what to do next. Liebl, he said, was a complication, but not the most dangerous one. The problem was his Georgian associates. If Liebl gave up hope of making a deal from which he could profit, there'd be nothing to stop him telling the Georgians all he knew and turning them loose.

'That's not how it seems to me,' Joseph said.

George laughed.

'Don't worry,' he said. 'I've talked with him. We're safe as long as they don't know where to find what they want.'

359

'How about Radka?' he asked. 'How does she feel?'
George gestured.

'Oh, she's okay. We have Serge you know.' He paused, his expression suddenly downcast. 'Things are difficult between us. I can tell you this as a brother. She's not so happy always. But this is different. She seems different.' He thought about it. 'When I had to go away she was angry. Last night was not good. Then Liebl called. I went crazy, like, oh my God.'

Within a few minutes everything seemed to have changed between himself and George. The last time they'd been together he'd found it next to impossible to speak openly. Now, all of a sudden, it was as if they could tell each other everything. For an hour or so, Joseph even forgot about Radka, and the problem of how he felt about her. In the afternoon they drove through the eastern districts of the city, George pointing out places where he'd worked or well-known landmarks with the cynical pride of a typical Berliner. Joseph kept looking in the mirror, wondering whether he could spot anyone following them.

'You won't see them if they don't want you to,' George said. He laughed. 'You never see the bullet that hits you.'

Katya got back to the apartment shortly before dark, then Radka and Serge, the boy tumbling, boisterous with shrieks of laughter, punctuated with tears. He was exhausted, Radka said, and rushed him off to the bath. Valentin arrived next. He had spent most of the day, he said, trying to grow a beard. The result was that he looked exactly the same, except that his chin was covered with a reddish stubble. Katya greeted him, then, refusing any company, went off to Tempelhof where she was to meet Kofi.

The men ate a takeaway Chinese meal of the sort you could get anywhere in the world. Radka went out to purchase it, after she put Serge to bed, but once she'd delivered the bags of food, she retired to her room where she lay on the bed watching TV. She had hardly said a

360

word to either her husband or his brother, going about her business with a polite abstracted air which made it clear that she had nothing to say.

'What I still can't make out,' Joseph said, halfway through the meal, 'is why they think this guy can do anything. What is he? Head of the mafia or something?'

'Mafia doesn't exist in Russia,' Valentin uttered. 'He's a businessman.'

'So what can he do? Those guys cut people's heads off. They're not going to stand around listening to lectures in business ethics. We don't even know who they are.'

'You have to imagine what it was like before,' Valentin said.

He spoke carefully, choosing his words, but he wanted to tell Joseph about this because it was part of the life which had made him what he was. Outside of Russia and the republics, no one seemed to understand or care how the nature of people like himself had been twisted, this way and that, by forces which were too powerful to withstand.

'Everything businessmen did,' he told Joseph, 'was a crime. There are guys who used to be *fartsovy*, selling jeans or anything else you wanted in the street. Now they are millionaires. But before private enterprise was permitted they were criminals. The thing was that when they created private enterprise anything was permitted. No one knew the difference. Some people became bankers by lending money. Sometimes to get their money back they had to make an example of those who would not pay.' He pointed a finger. 'Bang. Bang. You pay or you die. They made work for gangsters, and so business grew together with the trade of bodyguard and assassin. And in the republics it was worse because the Georgians and the Ukrainians and the Azerbaijanis wanted to keep their business for themselves. In the old days when Russians tried to do business in those places they sent people to negotiate and they never came back.'

Several of his comrades in the old regiment had become bodyguards or private security men, and several of them had died in a hail of bullets along the major thoroughfares in Moscow and St Petersburg. Two friends, Mikhail and Anastas, had found themselves shooting at each other in the street outside a restaurant near Pushkinskaya. Luckily neither had been killed. But this was how it was for a while. The gangsters worked for the businessmen and became businessmen themselves. The bankers laundered the money until the gangsters killed them and took over their banks and laundered their own money, until another businessman came along and became a more efficient gangster. The most successful existed at the centre of a spider's web of the most violent and effective hoodlums. A man as rich as Valery would have had to manage and control the most ruthless network of associates.

'Business in our country,' Valentin said, 'is about influencing people,' he pointed, 'upstairs and downstairs. Valery Vasselievich Kirichenko is more powerful than any general used to be.'

Kofi and Katya returned halfway through the evening. They were smiling and cheerful, as if his efforts had been successful.

'What a great way to travel,' Kofi said. 'No waiting. No baggage. Just on and off the plane. One minute you're in Prague, next minute you're in Berlin.'

The journey had taken about an hour, and at both ends he'd been whisked back and forth by car. The whole thing had taken less energy than a trip to the supermarket. Kofi's sons listened to the description without enthusiasm.

'So what happened with the man?' George asked.

Kofi took his time, running through his memory of the day. He had walked across the Charles Bridge, pausing in the middle to admire the statues which lined it. When he eventually got back to the office Valery was standing by the windows watching the sunlight fade on the river.

He had talked with a politician who was also director of a rival company. This was Abuladze's patron, and eventually Valery had spoken to the security man himself. He knew Liebl. He didn't control his actions, he said, but he could certainly clear up any little problem that had arisen. The men who had worked with Liebl in Hamburg were free-lance bandits, but they had many relatives and friends who would need to be satisfied. Clearing up the mess would be expensive. On the other hand, considering aside the value of the missing relics, a bargain was possible. In the end Valery had made a deal. They would return everything which remained in their possession, pictures, sculptures, jewellery. In exchange the Georgians would pay them three million US dollars.

'A small portion of what we have would be worth three million dollars in the West,' Valentin muttered.

'If you could stay alive for another week,' Katya said sharply. 'Take it and hope that they think the bargain is worth it.'

'We'll take it,' George said.

They could pick the time and the place, Kofi told them, but it had to be soon, otherwise any number of things could go wrong. The other thing was that they would have to make themselves scarce for a while, in England perhaps, or somewhere further afield, like Australia. After the exchange Valery would be unable to protect them, but in a year or two this would be ancient history among the feuds and assassinations which had taken place, and it would be forgotten. Either that or the Georgians who knew the story would be dead.

'We must talk,' Valentin told George, and they got up and went out of the room. In a second the front door slammed behind them.

They stood under the tree in the courtyard below the apartments. Behind the illuminated windows, George thought, there were people eating and drinking and making love and children going to bed, who had no life or death decisions to make, and for a moment he felt an intense envy of their peaceful lives.

'What do you think?' he asked Valentin.

'I don't know what to think,' Valentin said. 'I hate to be robbed like this. Most of the stuff doesn't even come from Georgia.'

'We'll be rich. A million each,' George told him. 'That's what we wanted. And I can't live like this any longer.'

Valentin shrugged.

'Okay. To keep you happy. Screwing that fat Liebl is good too.'

'What about Victor?'

'Victor would like this to end. The sooner it does the sooner he can go off to the USA and become a rich American.'

Back in the apartment George told Kofi they'd decided on making the exchange within two days. That would give them time to reconnoitre a likely spot and work out the best way to do it. They would pass on the details at the last possible moment. Immediately Kofi telephoned the number Valery had given him. The conversation was brief.

'No problem,' Kofi said to George when he put the phone down. 'As soon as he knows the time and place, he'll make the arrangements.'

'I think we'll go and find Victor tonight,' George replied.

In the bedroom, he packed a bag and kissed Serge, who was sleeping soundly. Radka watched him moving around the room without expression.

'We'll talk when I get back,' he told her, his tone apologetic. 'But I must go tonight.'

'Be careful,' Radka said.

George smiled at her.

'You know me. All this will be over in a couple of days.'

THIRTY

'Let's go out,' Radka said to Joseph.

She had drifted in and out of the room for most of the evening, without speaking, somehow communicating the sense that since she had no say in the events that were developing, she wished to ignore them altogether. Joseph had felt the same, like a spectator at the theatre. Later he had wanted to talk to Kofi alone, without Katya, and he was sure that his father had sensed this, but instead of staying with him in the sitting room the old man had announced that he was going to bed. Immediately, the couple had disappeared together without another comment, as if they'd been doing it all their lives. Joseph had sat alone watching television and trying to decide what to do, until the door opened and Radka appeared. Now, following her through the silent apartment he had the feeling that they were naughty children sneaking out after bedtime. As he closed the door behind them he clicked it shut with exaggerated care, hoping that no one could hear them leave.

Neither of them cared where they were going. It was close to midnight and although there were still lines of cars around them, the traffic flowed freely. Once around the Zoo station she skirted the Tiergarten, heading for the illuminated heap of metal and glass which was the restored Reichstag.

'I want to leave George,' Radka said.

Her words didn't surprise Joseph, but he heard them with a sudden surge of excitement. At the same time he felt the taste of guilt behind it.

'Have you told him?'

365

She glanced quickly at him and away again.

'Not directly. I don't think he wanted to listen. He was thinking about this other business.'

'What will you do?'

'I told you before,' she said. 'I want to come to England. I can get work there.'

'What about Serge?'

'He's a little boy. He'll like it, and he'll be safe.'

She made the long circuit around the Reichstag. To his left Joseph could see the dark strip of land where the Wall had been. George and Radka had been part of what happened there. Perhaps, he thought, their separation would leave her with an area of emotional wasteland through which he could never venture. Gazing out at the landscape, he tried to imagine what it would be like living with Radka, seeing her every day. Lena flashed through his mind. What would he tell her?

'Is this about us?'

His heart beat faster when he asked the question. She shook her head quickly, but she didn't reply, thinking about it.

'I think I would leave anyway. Before it's too late.'

She was wearing a short black dress under her leather jacket. There was a split in the side of the skirt and the ends flopped back to show her thighs moving as she worked the pedals. Beneath the garish reflection of the street lamps her pale flesh glowed.

'Everything about the world has changed since we met,' she said. 'And we have both changed with it. The problem is that we have changed in different directions. If he had not been a black man I would have left long ago. Sometimes I came close but I felt like a traitor.' She laughed. 'This is funny. I think that it is your fault, and Kofi. Before you came he needed me. For Serge we needed a kind of,' she hesitated, '*Überzeugung*, what is that?'

'Belief?'

Joseph wasn't sure, but she glanced at him, smiling.

366

'Something more, but belief is okay. We needed belief in ourselves. We gave that to each other. When you came he didn't need me for that. Valentin made him restless, but that was okay. When he found you he became a different man.'

'I'm sorry,' Joseph said.

'Don't be sorry.' She smiled at him. 'You opened the windows for me too. Now Serge has a grandfather and an uncle who are negroes. If I leave George I won't be separating him from people like himself.'

'Don't say negroes,' Joseph told her. 'That's the first thing to learn.'

She drove through the Brandenberg Gate, turned right in front of the warren of ugly flats and headed back towards Kreuzberg.

'How will Katya take it?'

Radka smiled.

'I don't know, but she knows about such things. I think she'll come to England. She won't let your father escape a second time.'

'It won't be easy,' Joseph said.

Radka laughed.

'It will be easier than this.'

The apartment was still silent. In the sitting room the television set flickered. Radka took her jacket off and went to check on Serge. She was back immediately. 'He's asleep,' she whispered. He started to put his arms round her, but she took his hand, turned round and led him across the corridor into George's room.

They sat on the floor, kissing again, their arms around each other, leaning back against the narrow bed which had belonged to her husband and in which her son had slept. It was over in a few minutes. Without saying a word, Radka got up, settled her skirt, kissed him on the cheek and went out, closing the door quietly behind her.

Joseph woke early and went to stand at the windows,

looking out into the street. He had told himself in the moment after he returned to consciousness that he would think about what was happening between himself and Radka. Instead he found himself reflecting dreamily about the sound of her voice, about the way her hair fell around her face, and about the touch of her fingers on his skin. Outside the window the glow of the city was fading and, without being aware that he was doing it, Joseph watched the colour coming back into the trees and the details emerging along the outlines of the street. He was so lost in his dreams that when he heard his father's voice behind him he spun around, startled, as if abruptly roused from sleep.

'I heard you last night,' Kofi said without preamble.

He had come into the room quietly, closing the door behind him, and now he was staring at Joseph sternly, a frown creasing his face.

'We went for a drive,' Joseph told him lamely.

'I know what you were doing,' Kofi cut in. 'This is your brother's wife. It's the worst thing you can do.'

'It just happened, Dad.' Joseph felt like a child again, pinned beneath Kofi's accusing gaze. As if disclaiming the role, he shrugged and turned away. 'I'm getting out of here today anyway.'

'That's not an answer,' Kofi said. He moved around so that he was looking into Joseph's face again. 'If this is just a quick fuck because you're both nervous and lonely, that's okay. Leave it alone, say nothing and forget it. If it's more than that, you should do something about it.'

Joseph felt a kind of despair. This was the sort of confrontation he had feared, if only because when it came to the moment of decision all he felt was confusion.

'What can I do, Dad?'

Kofi's look softened. When Joseph spoke he reminded him of the child he had been, and he remembered also how unpredictably his own desires had driven him. He moved away from Joseph and sat down.

'I don't know, son.' He chuckled involuntarily. 'That's life. First you fix the hole in the roof, and then you find dry rot in the floor. I don't know what to tell you, except that the most dangerous enemy you can have is a brother.'

After his conversation with Kofi, Joseph found it impossible to remain in the apartment, or to face Radka and Katya. He dressed quickly, pulling on the jeans and the sweater George had left as a replacement for his own. Then he left, walking purposefully towards the bustle of the Bundesallee, retracing the path along which Radka had driven a couple of days before.

The streets were beginning to take on the crowded, jostling appearance of rush hour, and Joseph felt safely anonymous. Walking through the hotel lobby he looked round furtively, going into the souvenir shop and out again to see whether he could spot anyone waiting for his arrival. It took a few minutes to be certain that no one was interested in his movements, but eventually he was satisfied.

Upstairs in his room he got into his own clothes and lay on the bed watching the news. He had seen this channel, he realised, in every hotel room in every country to which he'd travelled recently. Hearing the familiar American accents he felt as if he was being greeted by old friends, even though the round-up of financial news and the details of business transactions held as little interest for him as if they'd been in another language.

He must have drifted off, because he was dreaming about living in a strange house somewhere in London with Radka and Serge. The window at which he stood overlooked a huge garden where Serge was playing on a climbing frame. Suddenly the garden began filling up with oddly dressed people. They wore stovepipe hats, long jackets, stockings, and shoes with buckles on them. Guessing from the clothes that they belonged to some kind of cult, Joseph rushed down the stairs with the intention of bringing Serge into the safety of the house. Radka was by his side and

369

together they each grabbed one of the boy's hands. They had nearly got back to the house when a man, dressed like all the others, but carrying an automatic rifle, stepped from behind a bush and began to fire. Joseph, his hands outstretched, saw the bullets emerging from the end of the gun and threw himself in front of Radka and Serge, knowing, even as he did so, a moment of pure terror, because it was too late to save them from being hit. He screamed and woke up to the sound of gunfire. On the TV screen the camera was tracking slowly along a line of dead bodies. The telephone rang. It was Kofi.

He was ringing, he said, to see whether Joseph was okay. Joseph told him he was fine.

'Your brother was on the telephone today,' Kofi said.

'Where is he?'

'In Düsseldorf, I think, but I don't know exactly where. I can give you the number of his mobile.'

Joseph dialled the number and George answered on the third ring.

'I want to see you,' Joseph told him. 'We have to talk.'

'Sure.' George's accent was more pronounced on the telephone. 'After the business is over we talk.'

'No.' In the moments between sleep and waking Joseph's mind had settled on this. 'I want to go home. Talking to you is the only thing that's keeping me in this country. Besides, you don't know what will happen tomorrow. We must speak today. I don't want to put it off.'

A few days ago he would never have spoken to George with such decision, but something had changed. It wasn't merely that he wanted to talk about Radka. It was something to do with Kofi and how he felt about George. Watching his father with his brother he had the odd sense of never having existed for Kofi. Now it was as if George had gone to fight giants while he sat at home cowering among the women and children.

'This is impossible. There's too much happening.'

'If we don't talk,' Joseph told him, 'I'll go now, and I'm not coming back.'

'Okay, okay,' George said quickly. 'Not on the telephone. Come to Düsseldorf. When you know your flight, call me.'

He hung up immediately.

THIRTY-ONE

It was early evening by the time Joseph got out of the terminal at Düsseldorf. Following George's instructions he walked through the car rental hall and stood on the approach road which led to the car park. In a few minutes a car drew up and the door swung open.

'Get in,' George called out.

They drove into the city on a highway which looked like every other motorway, and for a moment Joseph had the strange feeling of not being quite sure which town he was approaching or in which part of the country it was situated.

'Now I know that we're brothers,' George said. 'This is like every other younger brother I've ever heard of, turning up at difficult times, always hanging around.' He didn't smile, and there was a curious edge to his manner which Joseph hadn't seen before.

The last streaks of sunlight had disappeared as they drove in from the airport and along the Königsallee the huge shop windows were illuminated, glittering with mannequins in self-conscious poses, but now that the stores and offices were closed the city centre seemed curiously empty, like an exhibition centre where someone had suddenly blown a whistle and sent everyone home for the night.

George parked near a bridge over the canal which ran down the middle of the avenue and they walked through the old town, the Aldstadt, heading for the river.

'It doesn't look very old,' Joseph said, looking around.

It looked like one of those towns where the industrial quarter had outlived its relationship with the docks and wharves, and subsequently been converted into a beehive

372

of curving cul-de-sacs, fountains, bars and restaurants. In a few minutes they had entered a wide pedestrian precinct, beyond which Joseph could see the lights reflected on water.

'You want to talk about Radka,' George said.

He didn't sound angry, but Joseph couldn't reply for a few seconds, suppressing the desire to ask how George had guessed.

'I telephoned and spoke to Kofi,' George continued. 'I wanted to know what you were after. Radka took the telephone. She said she was going to England with you.' He paused. There had been a hint of a tremor in his voice. 'I guess you've been fucking my wife.'

Now he was looking at Joseph with an angry, challenging air.

'It just happened.'

'Ach, yes,' George said. 'You stumbled and fell on top of her. What a terrible accident.'

'What do you want to do?' Joseph asked him.

George was silent for a while, his eyes intent on the sparkling surface of the water.

'My doppelgänger,' he said eventually. 'You lived my life, you wear my clothes, you sleep in my bed, and now my wife.'

'It wasn't like that,' Joseph told him. 'Something happened between us.'

'If you had been another man,' George replied, 'it would have been easier. But this is very confusing. If I had known you wanted to talk about Radka I would have said no. I don't want to think about it right now.'

'I want to come with you tomorrow,' Joseph told him.

As soon as he said it he knew that this was really why he had come.

'You want to come tomorrow,' George said slowly. He took his eyes off the river and looked round at Joseph. 'You really want to be me, don't you?'

'No.'

'It will be dangerous. You're right. We don't know what will happen.'

'That's why I want to come. Maybe I can help.'

George laughed. He seemed genuinely amused.

'That's stupid. How can you help?'

'I don't know.'

'So why?'

Joseph thought about it. He had acted on impulse in coming here. Now that he was facing George, his desire to be present when the exchange was made seemed whimsical and foolish. What he couldn't say was that somewhere in his mind he felt a powerful sense of guilt. It had nothing to do with Radka. Instead, it was somehow connected with the fact that his life, when compared to his brother's, had been so comfortable and free of risk. When the dog clamped its jaws round his leg in Gunther's shop, he had been afraid, just as he was on the way to Potsdam, and if it had been required, he thought, he might well have betrayed his brother in order to make his escape. That was only one episode in his life, but George had lived with such choices from the time of his earliest childhood.

There was no logic to it, Joseph knew, but if he returned to England without taking the chance to share his brother's danger they would never be equals, or even friends. Liz, his former wife, would have called it macho bullshit. This was the sort of instinct, she said in moments of anger, that his African father must have passed on to him, even though he had told her repeatedly about his stubborn resistance to everything Kofi tried to teach.

'I don't know,' he told George. 'Maybe because we're brothers, but we're not. If we're together at least one time when it's important, perhaps it will be real.'

George grinned.

'You want to get killed for me? You want a brother so badly?'

'No, not killed,' Joseph said, 'but if I got my leg chewed a little more I wouldn't mind.'

'It won't make up for you being an arsehole,' George told him.

They met Valentin and Victor in a pizza restaurant next to a sex video store off the Haroldstrasse. The Russians shook hands with Joseph.

'How's your leg?' Valentin asked, grinning at him as if remembering some comic episode.

'Okay. I'm coming with you tomorrow.'

Valentin raised his eyebrows and gave George a quizzical look.

'Yes,' George told him. 'He can help.'

Valentin translated for Victor, who replied with a burst of speech, which George interrupted.

'No. He's not coming for money. He doesn't want anything. He's my brother. That's all.'

Victor shrugged.

'Okay.'

After midnight they drove out of the city on the road to Neuss, then cut south off the highway to Mönchengladbach, towards Wegberg and Niederkrüchten. The road here led towards the Dutch border and it was a flat stretch on which the villages were few and far between, cutting straight through a vista of empty fields and scattered trees. The darkness enveloped them, seeming to close in round the lane of light cast by the headlamps. George pushed the car along the narrow road as if confident about where he was going. About an hour and a half out of Düsseldorf, he pulled up at a crossroads.

'We'll do it there,' he announced pointing. Following the line of the headlamps Joseph saw a stretch of unlit tarmac. 'It doesn't go anywhere. Even during the day there's no traffic.'

He drove slowly up the road. After a couple of kilometres he turned and came back. As he'd said, there was nothing there. At the crossroads he swung west again, following the road to the Dutch border. In a few minutes he stopped at another junction.

'You pick them up here,' he said to Valentin.

They inspected the site solemnly. There was nothing there except a signpost to Niederkrüchten.

'What happens here?' Joseph asked.

'It's simple,' George replied. 'We'll drive the trucks to that spot. They'll be waiting by that signpost. If there's more than three we don't do it. If they're there, and there's only three of them, and they have the money, Valentin will bring them up the road to where the trucks will be waiting. They give us the money and drive the trucks away.'

'That's a lot of ifs,' Joseph said. 'How will you know if they have the money, and how will they know that the trucks aren't empty?'

'Modern technology.' George held up his mobile phone.

Joseph couldn't think of any more questions, or rather he could think of so many that there didn't seem to be any point in beginning to ask because he sensed that George wouldn't have the answers that he wanted. Everything depended on Valery Vasselievich's word, and apart from Kofi's faith in him, they had no way of knowing how good that was.

'Here it is,' George said.

They sped through a village, illuminated by a sign which read SPAR. On the other side was a wide gate flanked by a guard hut, beside which two soldiers lounged. This was the entrance to the base. In another kilometre the high wire fence gave way to a thick line of trees. George slowed down and turned into a dirt road which was almost invisible until they were on it.

They bumped slowly along through the dark wood, the headlamps bouncing off the tree trunks. The two Russians gazed intently at the fence, and eventually Victor tapped George on the shoulder. Beyond the wire Joseph had a vague impression of the rounded humps of the hangars. Valentin and Victor got out, pushed the fence back and George drove through.

The hangar was like a big warehouse, which had been

emptied of goods in a giant clearance. It was lit by a strip of neon bulbs along the centre of the ceiling which threw a lane of light along the middle of the floor, leaving most of the place in shadow. Parked in one corner the two trucks looked small and insignificant, like toys which had been abandoned by some giant child.

'We wait here till the morning,' George said.

They would make the exchange, he explained, shortly after dawn, when there was enough light to see across the fields to the horizon but when it would be too early for a stream of traffic. Afterwards they would drive across the Dutch border to Roermond, in order to shake off anyone who might be following.

The night seemed interminable. The Russians settled down in the trucks and went to sleep. George lay back in the driver's seat of the car and closed his eyes. In the back seat Joseph fidgeted.

'Can I look inside the trucks?'

'Help yourself.'

He tossed a torch back at Joseph. Inside the truck it was like an Aladdin's cave. The paintings were stacked along the sides leaving only a narrow aisle, which was choked with statuettes and boxes packed with jewellery. Joseph lifted one of the paintings away from the stack. It looked like a wheatfield. In the torchlight the colours glowed. He looked at another couple of the paintings, receiving a confused impression of naturalistic landscapes, then suddenly a bold kaleidoscope of angular shapes in grey, black and red. He lowered the canvases back into the pile and climbed down, his head spinning. Suddenly, he sensed why this treasure had been worth so much to his brother and his friends, and why the Georgians had been so relentless in their pursuit of it.

'There's enough there to fill a museum,' he told George.

He had only caught a glimpse, and he had no claim on any of it, but something inside Joseph burnt at the thought of tamely surrendering the heap of beautiful objects. He thought of pirates burying their arms up to the elbows in gold and jewels. It wasn't hard to imagine men killing merely for the thrill of possessing such things.

'Suppose it goes wrong?' he asked.

'Nothing will go wrong. Go to sleep.'

'It must be hard,' Joseph said tentatively, 'to give all that up. It has to be worth millions.'

George twisted round and looked at him, frowning, as if the same thought troubled him.

'They'll kill us if we don't.'

Joseph had anticipated lying awake, turning and sliding on the slippery leather, but the next thing he heard was the sound of voices and the thud of the boot behind him closing. He opened his eyes and looked around. On the other side of the window Victor was loading a gun. He pulled the slide back, squinted into the chamber and along the barrel, then slapped the magazine in. George opened the door and peered at him.

'Wake up. It's time to go.'

Still half asleep, Joseph stumbled over to the truck behind George. Valentin pulled apart the hangar doors, got in the car and drove out. Joseph climbed awkwardly up into the passenger seat of the truck high above the ground. Next to him, in the other vehicle, Victor waved and gave the thumbs up sign. Joseph felt like saying he wasn't ready, that he needed another hour's sleep. Starting up, the engines puffed smoke, turning the air in the hangar blue.

'Aren't you going to close the doors?' he asked George, looking back as they drove over the tarmac towards the fence, and knowing, even as he said it, that this was a silly question.

'Why? We're not coming back.'

The woods, which on the previous night had seemed so dark and forbidding, now sparkled green, and above the grinding of the engine Joseph could hear snatches of birdsong. There was a slight mist hanging over the fields

378

in the distance, but on the horizon, the streaks of bright orange promised a sunny day.

From the high vantage point of the truck Joseph could see a long way over the fields. George had picked the spot and the time shrewdly. Apart from themselves there was hardly anything moving on the road. They stood little chance of being interrupted.

The sun was up by the time they arrived at the stretch of road where the trucks were to be parked. The convoy stopped. Valentin got out of the car to consult with George. They spoke in German, George pointing his finger emphatically. They shook hands, then Valentin got in the car and drove away.

'What did you tell him?'

'If he saw more than three or four of them, to keep driving.'

He led the way off the road. The ground sloped down here into the field. Victor sat on the wet grass, pulling his coat round him, and sighted the Kalashnikov at the trucks. George paid no attention, shaking his mobile phone open and dialling quickly. He held it up to his ear and muttered, then winked at Joseph.

'Valentin.'

They stood like this, waiting. Somewhere nearby Joseph could hear the chirping of birds, but when he looked around he couldn't see any in the trees or bushes.

'They're coming,' George said.

At the same time Joseph heard the sound of the car turning into the intersection, and seconds later it came into sight. George stepped out into the road and stood next to the trucks. The car pulled up in front of him and a fat man got out. Behind him a couple of men Joseph guessed were Georgians followed. They looked around, studying the scene and then staring hard at Victor and Joseph posed by the side of the road. They were tall men, dark-haired and dark-eyed, both of them wearing identical black leather jackets. They looked impassive, as indifferent to their surroundings as if they were sitting in a café.

The fat man stood immobile in the middle of the road, his face creased in a grin.

'Good morning, George,' he called out.

'Liebl,' George said. 'Why are you here?'

'This surprises you?' Liebl asked. He grimaced as if suddenly hit by a revelation. 'Ah. We were going to be partners and you thought I would know nothing until it was too late. It was very clever. You must be a genius to have found yourself a patron that Abuladze was afraid of. Someday you must tell me how you did it.'

His eyes glinted with curiosity.

'Neither of us stayed where we were when we lived behind the Wall,' George said.

Liebl nodded soberly.

'Yes. I have to admit that, but you are still not my equal.' He smiled at the change in George's expression. 'Don't be offended. I had an advantage. You see, I have other partners. There was more than one card to play.'

George found himself searching for a reply that might puncture Liebl's self-satisfaction. Then he shrugged. It didn't matter. He waved the Georgians towards the trucks and they climbed into each one in turn, taking their time. From the roadside Joseph could hear them clambering about, surveying the objects inside. Liebl stood at the back, peering in and muttering to them in monosyllables as they showed him what they discovered. Eventually they seemed satisfied.

'I'm impressed,' Liebl told George. Inside the slits of flesh his eyes glittered. 'As a friend, I can tell you this is robbery. Or it would be if this wasn't already stolen property.'

He laughed. Behind him one of the Georgians flipped open his mobile phone and spoke into it. Then they stood there in the road, each one by the door of a truck, waiting.

In a couple of minutes, there was the sound of an engine

and a BMW sped into sight. Beside him Joseph felt Victor tense and he heard the sound of metal snapping as he thumbed the safety catch. The BMW pulled up in the middle of the road, a few metres short of the trucks, and another man dressed in the trademark leather jacket got out and handed George a large briefcase. The money was in dollars, packed in stacks bound together with rubber bands. George didn't actually count them, but he fingered through the stacks, checking the denominations. It took a few minutes. Nobody moved. Eventually George looked up. 'Okay,' he said.

Without a word the Georgians climbed into the trucks and began backing them into the turn. Liebl got into the BMW, gave George an ironic wave, and the driver reversed quickly and sped away towards the intersection. George and Valentin watched them go, standing motionless in the road. As the vehicles disappeared they ran for the car.

'Let's go!' George shouted at Joseph. 'Come on.'

The car rocketed away from a standing start, its wheels spinning in the grit by the side of the road. Victor unslung the Kalashnikov and put it on the floor. George laughed.

'We're millionaires!'

Valentin was holding the briefcase and he shut it and passed it back to Victor, who opened it again and began thumbing through the money, counting the stacks. The mobile phone rang, a piercing warble. George took it out of his pocket and held it in his hand, looking at it thoughtfully.

'Your father?' Valentin said.

George nodded, his expression lightening, and he put it to his ear. A moment afterwards he slammed on the brakes. The car stopped, slewing round in a skid which took them across one side of the road to the other.

George shouted in German. Joseph didn't understand what he said, but he caught one word, 'raus'. He scrambled for the door handle.

'Get out!' George shouted. 'There's a bomb in the back.'

They ran for the side of the road and threw themselves down on the grass. Now that the engine had stopped there was no sound except the chirping of the birds. Nothing happened. Minutes passed. Victor muttered to Valentin in a low voice as if worried about being overheard. Joseph could feel damp seeping through his clothes. George put the phone to his ear, then shrugged and sat up.

'Someone said they'd planted a bomb in the back.'

'If they planted a bomb,' Valentin asked, 'why would they tell us?'

'He said it was a message from Valery Vasselievich. He said to get out of the car immediately.'

Victor stood up.

'Wait,' George said.

'If this is a trick,' Valentin said, 'they'll be coming in a minute.'

He took the Beretta out of his jacket and began loading it. Victor gestured, a mime of aiming a gun and pulling the trigger.

'He's left his gun in the car,' George told Joseph. 'Wait,' he called out.

Victor ignored him and started across the road. He moved cautiously at first, looking to right and left, ready to dash back, then getting to the open door of the car he turned to grin triumphantly at George before reaching in to pick up the Kalashnikov. The car blew up then, the explosion thudding in their ears, before they saw the whoosh of flame blooming into the sky. In a moment there was the thump of another explosion. The column of flame and smoke mounted like a finger pointing. Huddled in the ditch, Joseph felt George tugging at his arm and he sprang up and ran behind his brother, putting a distance between themselves and the fire.

Joseph's ears rang, so deafened by the explosion that he didn't hear the car driving down from the junction till it was close to them. Valentin swung round, pointing the gun at the driver, who got out and shouted.

'Come!' he waved. 'Kirichenko. Come.'

They walked slowly towards the big black limousine. The driver, neatly dressed in a dark suit, ignored Valentin's gun and waved them impatiently into the back seat. He spoke rapidly as he gained distance from the burning car, his manner busy and matter-of-fact, as if he was a taxi driver picking up an ordinary fare.

'He says he's been sent by Valery Vasselievich to pick us up. He says he telephoned you on the mobile.'

The driver grinned back at them and waved his mobile phone. At the same moment they heard the sound of a siren and a lone police car streaked past, hurrying to where they could still see the column of smoke pouring into the sky.

A few kilometres further on the limousine turned into a narrow lane masked by a row of hedges. Beyond it was a farmhouse. They skirted it and pulled up in a broad yard ringed by trees. The two trucks were parked there, alongside four cars, including the BMW. There was no sign of the drivers.

Valery Kirichenko was sitting on a straight wooden chair below one of the trees, his legs stretched out in front of him, the trainers on his feet sticking up like the shoes on a tired athlete. Their driver waved them towards him. He was talking on a mobile phone and when they approached he closed it and put it away.

'I just talked to your father,' he said. 'I told him you were safe. I was told about the bomb earlier, but I couldn't let you know before.'

'Why not?' George asked. He sounded angry. 'If we had known one of my friends would be alive. We could all have been killed.'

'It was a risk,' Valery said. 'I'm sorry about your friend, but if you had been warned, the man who told me would have been killed, and the deal would have been off. It was worth the risk.' He smiled. 'I came to see the paintings. That was worth it, too.'

'You're keeping them?'

'Of course.' He paused, looking them in the face and smiling. 'I'm negotiating with a man who wants some of those things. He wants them very badly. Maybe he'll start a museum in Tbilisi. But I'll give them to him. He'll put a muzzle on your Georgian friends, or get rid of them.'

'What will he give you?' George asked.

Valery chuckled.

'Control of a company I want. There will be many more of these things in my possession. In Kiev they'll build me a statue.' He gestured. 'Benefactor of the arts.'

'Is this why you helped us?'

The smile left Valery's face.

'No, it was because of your father. But this is the best way. If I had offered to buy them from you, maybe you would not have sold, and then too many problems. How could I put pressure on Kofi's son? Now the problem is mine, and they'll leave you in peace, but don't go to Georgia.' He laughed. 'Don't go to Moscow, either. Go somewhere quiet.'

'What about Liebl?'

'Go look in the car.' George hesitated, and Valery made a gesture of command. 'Go.'

The neat young man in the dark suit led the way to the BMW. The car made a quick beeping sound, and he threw open the boot with a flourish, like a headwaiter displaying a dish. Liebl was lying, stuffed in the boot, dark blood staining his clothes and body. He was dead, but he looked relaxed and peaceful, one hand curled beneath his head, a smile still curving his lips.

Valery hadn't changed his position, still sitting on the wooden chair with his feet up, Valentin and Joseph standing a few paces away, looking towards George with puzzled expressions.

'Tell your father,' Valery said, 'the debt is cancelled.' He laughed. 'Tell him to keep out of the forest.'

Valery's driver dropped them off round about lunchtime

in Düsseldorf. Valentin had left his car in the basement car park of a hotel off the Haroldstrasse, and they went through the hotel lobby. Joseph was moving automatically, simply following George. It was as if he was too tired and stressed to think for himself, and for the moment, he was relying on his brother to guide him back to calmer waters.

'Let's take a drink.'

They went into the bar. Joseph sat at the nearest table, then, looking around, realised that Valentin had disappeared.

'Where is he?'

'He's okay. He's gone to get the car. Later we'll take you to the airport.'

'To the airport?' Somehow the idea of making the trip alone alarmed him. 'Why don't we drive back?'

'I'm not coming back,' George said. He reached over and touched Joseph's arm. 'I was thinking about why I was angry with you. Maybe because of my son. You know I always feared that idea, that she would leave me and go to another man, maybe a white man.' He laughed. 'Around here, almost certainly a white man. Then my son would be calling him his father, or thinking about him in that way. He would forget me or hate me. I don't know. The idea frightened me all the time. Then I was thinking, you are my brother. Kofi is my father. Katya is my mother. If my son was with you, how could you be cruel to your own blood? No problem. Maybe Radka understands that. You know it is strange. All these years I've had dozens of women. Suddenly she goes for my brother. I think she wanted to get rid of me without changing anything except me. The funny thing is that I feel the same.'

Joseph knew what he was saying, but somehow he couldn't follow George's reasoning.

'You want to get rid of her?'

'No. I love her, but I want to be another person.' He paused and gestured, trying to get his feelings into words. 'Mr Kirichenko. I admire him.'

Joseph was startled.

'He used us to get his hands on those paintings. He doesn't even want to keep them. All he wants them for is to get an edge in some business deal. I don't believe all that stuff about our father. If we had got in his way he'd probably have wiped us out just as quickly as he did Liebl.'

'I don't think so,' George said. 'But that doesn't matter. What's important is that he shaped himself to live in a horrible time and to get the best result. Look at me.' He tapped himself on the chest. 'I lived most of my life in a kind of prison. Now I'm lucky to be alive and lucky to be free. The way I live with Radka is not how I want to live. She wants me to be the way I was. I'll never be that again, but I want to find out what I am. You must understand. This is a new world for me. I'm going to shape myself to live on top of it.'

'How are you going to do that?'

George smiled.

'I don't know, but everything has changed. Ten years ago Valery Kirichenko was a kind of civil servant, now he's a king. I can do that.'

'You've got as much money as you're ever likely to need already. You can live how you want.'

'That's not the point,' George said. 'The point is that I want more than I can ever have, and I'm going to get it.'

THIRTY-TWO

In Berlin it was raining. The rain had a curious effect on the shiny façade of the new Reichstag, making it flash and go dim in different sections at the same time. Joseph had booked into a hotel nearby, and, from his window, he could see the top of it through the spray.

'Would you like to come and live with me in London?' he asked Radka. He didn't look round.

When he got back to Katya's apartment George had already telephoned and spoken to each of the family. Kofi and Katya were curiously philosophical, he thought, about George's leaving Radka and going off to make his fortune, or whatever it was he intended to do.

'We'll see him in London,' Kofi said.

Later on when Katya had left the room Joseph asked Kofi the question that was burning in his mind.

'What about Radka?'

'What about her?'

'Radka and me.'

'She doesn't want you,' Kofi said. 'She's like George. She wants to be free.'

'That's what everyone wants.'

'It doesn't mean the same to everyone.' He hesitated. 'They grew up with the idea that it was possible to be a new kind of person, that the kind of society in which they lived would reshape their identity. It didn't happen, so they've either got to give up or reshape life in some other way. That's what they have to find out.'

'It doesn't make sense,' Joseph said. He had the feeling, somehow, that everything that had happened since he met George would have a point.

'Don't expect everything to make sense,' Kofi said.

Gazing out at the rain Joseph was thinking about his conversation with Kofi. On the way back from Düsseldorf he had been certain of what he felt and what he wanted to happen. Now the ground had shifted under his feet, without his knowing how or why. He hadn't spoken with Radka about what George had said to either of them. She seemed as calm and collected as Kofi and Katya had been, and she had turned up at his hotel that afternoon and gone to bed with him as if it was the most natural thing in the world, but the moment he asked her about coming to live with him a pang had shot through his heart, as if he knew in advance that she would refuse.

'Will that money buy me an apartment?'

She was sprawled across the bed, her chin resting in her hands, watching him.

'It will buy you whatever you want.'

George had packed a chunk of the money from the briefcase into a bag and given it to him, and he'd held it by his side during the flight, feeling thankful that he didn't have to pass through customs. He hadn't bothered to count, but there must have been close on half a million dollars there.

'I think I'll live by myself in London,' she said.

'Are you hoping he'll come back?' he asked. A spike of jealous anger went through him at the thought.

'I don't know,' she said. 'But that has nothing to do with it. I just want to know what it's like.'

She was using almost the same words as George had, and listening to her voice it struck Joseph that perhaps they were more alike than he had understood.

The night before he left Berlin they had dinner together, early enough for young Serge to join in. At the end of the meal Kofi held up his glass in a toast.

'Here's to another life.' He pointed his glass at his grandson. 'This is for Serge, African, Russian, Czech, German, soon to be Englishman Serge. A new life for a new man.'

388

Katya leant over and kissed Serge on the cheek. Joseph avoided looking at Radka. He hadn't given up hope of changing her mind, but he didn't want her to see it in his eyes.

Serge had been silent for most of the meal, waving his fork, digging it into the food on his plate, but not getting much into his mouth. Kofi kept telling him about the lions in the zoo at Regent's Park and about how they would go to see them. Katya translated when Kofi's German failed, and the boy listened, eyes wide with pleasure at the thought. As they drank the toast he lifted his glass hurriedly in imitation of the adults.

'Will *Vati* be in London?' he asked.

Katya looked at Radka, who shrugged at her, as if declaring the fact that she didn't know what to say.

'Of course he will be,' Katya said. 'There'll be nothing to stop him.' She glanced at Radka. 'He told you that he would be there soon, didn't he? And I will be there, and Kofi, and Joseph. All your family.'

Serge nodded, as if he had the answer he wanted.

Later on that night Kofi walked to the end of the road with Joseph.

'That man,' Joseph said. 'Valery Kirichenko. You said he was your friend.'

'Yes.'

'I'm beginning to wonder what you mean by that. George said he admired him, and I expect you'll say that too, but he seemed like a bit of a bastard to me. He told you he'd help us, but he treated it like a business deal and walked away with a profit. On top of that, we nearly got killed.'

'You're alive, aren't you?'

'Yes.'

'That's what I wanted.'

A few weeks ago, Joseph thought, he would have been irritated by his father's complacency. Now he was curious.

'What makes you think he's so great?'

'I don't think he's so great,' Kofi said. 'I know what he is. Back in Moscow when we were both boys, he arranged to get me beaten up. Then he found out that we were running off to Paris, and he told her father, so they expelled me. That's how we never saw each other again.'

'Was he in love with her?'

'Oh no.' Kofi seemed shocked. 'He would never have done those things for a reason like that. He did it because a high official told him to. That was his way of surviving, and it bought him the favours which started him in the oil business.'

'See, Dad,' Joseph said, 'that seems despicable to me. I don't care how hard things were.'

'Don't imagine that he took it lightly,' Kofi told him, his tone a sharp rebuke. 'You have no idea, and in any case if that hadn't happened forty years ago you might not be alive now.' He slapped himself on the forehead, laughing at what he'd said. 'If. If. If. Did he tell you anything about himself?'

'No.'

'You saw the shoes he was wearing? The work he got as a favour for betraying us nearly froze his feet off. There's a balance to everything.'

'Even so, Dad, how can you like him?'

'Let me tell you something. He told me a story about Father Christmas.'

'Yeah. Right.'

'Father Christmas,' Kofi said, ignoring the sarcasm of Joseph's tone. 'In Europe and the USA they have this Father Christmas flying across the sky behind his band of reindeer. Valery said that when he first went to Siberia the tribe he lived with had a legend about a spirit which flew across the sky just like that. But he wasn't a jolly old man. Instead he was an evil, malevolent creature who would come down and rummage around in your yard and if he found anything that annoyed him, or didn't find something he wanted, he would come into your house

390

and take the children, smash your belongings and make your life a misery. Those were the kinds of gods those people believed in. When they discovered oil in their country the Russians came, ransacked the land, destroyed their villages, and drove their young people away.'

'I get the point, Dad,' Joseph told him, 'there's no Santa Claus.'

'That's not my point,' Kofi said. 'My point is that there is a Santa Claus, but there's a secret to controlling him.' He paused, and Joseph thought that he was about to reveal the secret, but instead he made a gesture of dismissal. 'I don't care about Santa Claus. I was born on the African coast in a country which didn't exist. I travelled to places I could never have imagined. Now I have a family I never dreamt of. Who knows what will happen tomorrow? We don't control how the world works. I don't think anybody does. It's a kind of magic which does unexpected things, but we have to survive wherever we find ourselves, and whatever the magic does to us. All I can tell you is to stay alive, wait and hope.'

Looking at him, Joseph was struck by the energy with which Kofi said this.

'Well, all right,' he said. 'But at your age, Dad, what are you hoping for? What do you expect?'

'I don't know what to expect,' Kofi told him. 'But I'm not dead yet.'